THE SHIPBUILDERS

AN ANTHOLOGY OF SCOTTISH SHIPYARD LIFE

MARTIN BELLAMY

Birlinn

First published in 2001 by
Birlinn Ltd
West Newington House
10 West Newington Road
Edinburgh
EH9 1QS

www.birlinn.co.uk

see page 216

ISBN 1 84158 163 1

British Library Cataloguing-in-Publication Data
A catalogue record is available on request from the British Library

Design by Janene Reid

Printed and bound in Great Britain by Bath Press, Bath

CONTENTS

This book is dedicated to all shipbuilders – past, present and hopefully future.

(Jim Dunn)

INTRODUCTION

When I grew up on the Clyde in the 1970s shipbuilding was still a major industry. It might not have been as vibrant as it once was, but the river was still definitely alive with ships. We would stand outside our Helensburgh home at Hogmanay and listen to the ships' hooters sounding from across the water at Greenock and Port Glasgow. To my young ears the sound was mightily impressive.

After a launch, massive baulks of timber would be washed up on the shore at Craigendoran, and my friends and I would aim our skimming stones at them. As we fished from the pier we would watch the ships sail up and down the Clyde. Among them were newly built tankers, bulk carriers, warships and who knows what else. I didn't really know what they were then, but I knew they were exciting. What I wasn't to know was that these were the products of an industry going through its death throes.

When I began studying naval architecture in the early 1980s, my tutors assured me that although shipbuilding was going through a hard time the upturn must surely be just around the corner. I remember passing by the oil rigs being built at Scott Lithgow's. They had found a new market, and I assumed their future was bright. We visited yards such as Yarrow's and Ferguson's to study their modernisation programmes. Yes, shipbuilding had been through hard times, but the yards seemed to be preparing for the future.

Despite trying to get a start in a Scottish shipyard it was Harland and Wolff in Belfast that took me on. Sadly, that upturn around the corner just never seemed to happen. I witnessed incredible waste and inefficiency. I watched men who had been in the yard all their lives being told that they needn't come back the following week. It didn't take long before I realised that perhaps this hadn't been the wisest career choice I could have made.

It is now many years since I worked in a shipyard and I have long since gone on to other things, but despite that I will always remain in my heart a shipbuilder. I am immensely proud of the fact that I was involved in the industry, even if it was only in a very minor way. And anyone who has worked in shipbuilding will tell you the same. It touches you in some way. You may be able to leave shipbuilding but it will never leave you.

So what is it about shipbuilding that makes people feel this way?

Essentially it has a romance and it has a history.

A romance because of the great ships that were built. The *Queen Mary*, the *Lusitania*, HMS *Hood*, and countless other great ships, caught the imagination of

Opposite:
A ship being built at Harland and Wolff's Govan yard in 1955. The cranes from the many shipyards dominated the Clyde's skyline. (Glasgow Museums)

QUEEN ELIZABETH

the people. The ships were world class, and the workers who built them were world class too.

The history of shipbuilding is therefore not just a history of iron and steel, of tonnages and economics, but a history of men and women, of families, characters and communities.

The story goes back to the beginning of the nineteenth century. Steamships were the new thing. Henry Bell launched the first commercial steamship service in Europe in 1812, and from then on the Clyde didn't look back. Bigger, faster, more powerful steamships were soon to follow, and it wasn't long before the Clyde became known as the cradle of steam navigation.

Glasgow had the engineering skills to build the new steam engines and the entrepreneurial flair to sell them in great numbers. To begin with, the engines were put in wooden ships, but the wooden hulls proved to be too fragile for the ever increasing size of the steamships. Iron was soon seen as the answer, and there was iron ore, and the coal with which to extract the iron, in abundance on Glasgow's doorstep in Lanarkshire.

The Clyde was not really an ideal shipbuilding river. It was long, narrow, shallow and winding. The Glasgow merchants had had to deepen and straighten the river in order to get their ships upriver. But if big ships could get up the Clyde then big ships could also get down it, and in 1834 two engineers, David Tod and John MacGregor, realised the opportunities and established the first shipyard on the Clyde specifically to build large iron steamships.

Robert Napier followed suit in 1841. He had made a name for himself as the best marine engine builder in the country, and he wanted to capitalise on his success by building the iron hulls for the engines that he was producing rather than subcontracting the work. He was a stickler for craftsmanship. Everything he produced had to be of the highest possible quality, and it was in his yard that the term 'Clydebuilt' was born.

Napier's yard in Govan was to be the training ground for Scotland's shipbuilders. Many of his senior engineers and managers could see the incredible opportunities that shipbuilding presented and set up shipyards of their own. Some of the most famous names in shipbuilding, such as Fairfield, John Brown and Denny, can trace links back to Robert Napier. It is no wonder that Napier is regarded as the father of Clyde shipbuilding.

As the size of ships steadily grew, so the size of shipyards also had to grow. The upper Clyde was becoming very congested, so new yards were established farther downstream on greenfield sites at Fairfield, Linthouse, Scotstoun and Clydebank. These were too far from the centre of Glasgow for people to get to easily every day, so whole new towns and communities had to be built in order to house the workers for these new yards.

Nor was it only on the Clyde that new shipyards were being set up. Dundee, Leith and Aberdeen all had considerable shipbuilding traditions, and it was not long before iron shipbuilding yards began to replace the old wooden shipyards in these towns. However, it was the Clyde that was to remain Scotland's most important shipbuilding river. The relative ease of transporting iron from

Opposite top: The *Queen Elizabeth* in dry dock. The 'Queens' symbolised the romance and the pride that was felt in the Scottish shipbuilding industry. (Scottish Maritime Museum)

Opposite bottom: John Dick, a burner at Lithgow's Greenock shipyard, was just one of the thousands of skilled workers who made the term 'Clydebuilt' a byword for quality craftsmanship. (Glasgow University Archives)

Making propellers at the Stone Manganese works at Yoker. (Glasgow City Archives)

Opposite: HMS *Diana* and HMS *Decoy* under construction at Yarrow's in 1949. (Scottish Maritime Museum)

Lanarkshire to the shipyards was one of the main reasons. The large number of businesses that grew up on Clydeside to supply everything that the shipyards needed was another key factor. There were engine builders, pump makers, compass makers, rope makers, electrical suppliers, upholsterers, carpet weavers and sanitary ware manufacturers all within a stone's throw of the shipyards. In fact, the Clyde seemed to have such an advantage that in 1850 Alexander Stephen decided to move his shipyard from Dundee to Glasgow. Alfred Yarrow also moved his yard from London to Scotstoun in 1908 in order to capitalise on these benefits.

The new iron shipyards that were growing up on the banks of the Clyde were very different from the traditional wooden shipbuilding yards. Iron was a very different material to work with, and the new shipyards needed forges, heavy engineering workshops and massive cranes. The workers who were required were also very different. Iron needed a great deal of manual labour to cut and shape all the frames and plates that make up an iron hull. It was hard and dirty work, but the shipyards found a willing workforce in the large numbers of Irish people and Highlanders who came to Glasgow in search of work.

The yards were dreadful places to work. The hours were long, the conditions were abysmal, and the employers could be unreasonable. Work started at around

1845
H.M.S.
DIANA.

six in the morning and went on until about half past five in the evening, with two breaks of three-quarters of an hour for breakfast and lunch. The precise times varied from yard to yard so that the flow of the thousands of workers going to and from their work could be controlled, but the average working week for a shipbuilder during the nineteenth century was fifty-four hours. The number of hours was gradually reduced over the years, but even until the 1950s there were no such things as holiday pay or official tea breaks.

Every yard had a strict set of rules and regulations that its employees had to abide by. Many of the rules were there for the workers' safety, such as no smoking and no drinking on the job, and no oiling of moving machinery. Most of the rules, however, were there to safeguard the employers' profits – no leaving before the whistle, no false timekeeping, no pilfering and no leaving the yard other than through the main gates. Some of the rules, though, were downright absurd. You were not allowed more than seven minutes to go to the toilet. Any longer than that and you would be docked a quarter of an hour's pay.

Virtually all the shipyard workers were employed on a casual basis and could be fired at a moment's notice. This was in order that the yards could more easily adjust their workforce to match their constantly fluctuating order books. However, many unscrupulous bosses used this as a means of intimidating the workers, who were constantly under threat of dismissal for the slightest of reasons. These poor working conditions ultimately bred an extreme militancy among shipyard workers. Their revolutionary socialist and communist beliefs are legendary, and the notion of 'Red Clydeside' has added greatly to the romance that surrounds the industry.

Most of the jobs were carried out by squads of men. Essentially men were employed by their squad leader rather than by the yard itself. The squad leader was given the pay for the whole squad, and it was up to him to divide this up into wages for each member of the squad as he saw fit. Steelwork was paid on a piecework basis and good squads could make good money. They got to know by instinct how the other members in their squad operated and their work rate could be tremendous. The down side was that if a key member of the group could not work because of illness or injury the whole squad might not be able to work. The injured worker might get sick pay but his squad members would get nothing. If a new member then came into the squad it could mean that the work rate was severely disrupted until he had learned the particular rhythm of that squad.

Because of the casual nature of the work, it was common for the steelworkers, or 'black squads', to be laid off once a ship was launched. This meant that there were squads of men who would travel from yard to yard to work on ships at varying stages of completion. There were some men who stayed loyal to a particular yard, especially in the family-run yards like Denny's or Stephen's, but most identified more with their particular trade and their squad rather than with a particular shipbuilding firm. This meant that they resolutely defended the rights of their own trade at all costs, and it was this attitude that led to the numerous demarcation disputes that dogged the industry for so long.

The 'black squad' proudly pose beneath one of their creations. (North Ayrshire Museum)

Left:
Consulting a plan. This was a common scene in every shipyard. In fact, idling shipyard workers could easily wander for days with a plan under their arm without being questioned. (Imperial War Museum)

Shipbuilding grew at an incredible pace in Scotland. Within thirty years of the first iron shipyard being set up, Scotland was supplying nearly a quarter of all the world's ships. On the Clyde alone there were dozens of shipyards. By the beginning of the twentieth century a single shipyard could easily employ three or four thousand workers and the industry as a whole employed over a hundred thousand. If you add on another few hundred thousand or so who were employed in supplying and supporting the shipyards and their workers, it is not hard to understand how vital shipbuilding was to the Scottish economy. In fact, so many people and so much of the economy were bound up with shipbuilding that it essentially became a part of Scotland's national psyche.

Everyone knew about shipbuilding. When the big liners were launched, the whole nation shared in the pride. Shipbuilding even became part of the popular culture of Scotland. It featured in the music halls, in films and theatre, in novels, poetry and art.

When the depression took hold in the 1930s the plight of the shipbuilding industry came to symbolise the fate of the whole country. The unfinished hull of the *Queen Mary* stood on the stocks for over two years as a potent reminder of the hard times that everyone was going through.

The decline of Scotland's shipbuilding industry was almost as dramatic as its rise. In the mid-1950s the industry still supplied about a seventh of the world's ships. Within a decade or so, the number of yards had virtually halved and Scotland had lost its dominant position for good. There are now only a few yards left, and their output is just a fraction of a percentage of world production.

The story of Scotland's shipbuilding decline makes for sorry reading, with inept management, over-strong unions and dithering government intervention all playing their part. The human cost has been great. Tens of thousands of people were put out of work. In many cases the physical difficulties of unemployment were coupled with the emotional trauma of coming to terms with the loss of an industry that had been a way of life for so many people for so long. This was particularly true in the communities that had been established specifically because of the shipbuilding industry, such as Govan and Clydebank.

Although we are now in a new post-industrial Scotland, shipbuilding at the moment still has an important place in the national consciousness. Just look at the newspaper headlines when another yard is threatened with closure or listen to the memories of Billy Connolly, Jimmy Reid and Alex Ferguson. But it will not be long before people will start to wonder what all the fuss was about. The current generation growing up on the Clyde will have little idea of the world-beating feats of engineering and human endeavour that were played out on the river, and they will be very lucky indeed if they glimpse a newly built ship sailing down the river.

Opposite: When Upper Clyde Shipbuilders went into liquidation in 1971 there was huge public support in an effort to save the Scottish shipbuilding industry. (Glasgow Museums)

A NOTE ON THE SOURCES

This book is not intended as a comprehensive history of Scottish shipbuilding. Instead it is an attempt to give an impression of what it was like to work in the shipyards and to convey the thoughts, feelings and emotions of those who were

astms
ASSASSINATION
J.B.E

The launch of *Sea Launch Commander* at Kvaerner Govan in 1997. (Author's collection)

involved. Through a collection of first-hand accounts I have aimed to illustrate the various jobs that were done in the yards, the conditions that the workers had to endure, the way in which the shipbuilders lived and the perceptions that people had of the Scottish shipbuilding industry.

The book is very much about personal experiences, so virtually all the material I have included has been taken from the first-hand accounts of people who have either worked in, visited, or had family members in, the shipyards. Everything that is described was either written at the time or within the living memory of the author. No purely historical accounts have been included.

There are a good number of memoirs and biographies written by or about people who have worked in the shipyards, ranging from directors to labourers. There is also a rich seam of oral history that has been collected from shipyard workers over the years. Shipyard house journals are another great source of information as they not only contain official yard stories but many of them also have contributions from the workers. The outsider's view of the industry has been taken from newspaper accounts, travel books and reportage.

Some extracts from novels, short stories and poems have also been included. Nearly all the authors that I have chosen either worked in the shipyards or had close associations with them. Again, the events described are all within the living memory of the authors, and no historical novels have been used.

Most of the extracts naturally come from the Clyde, but I have also tried to include accounts from some of the other shipbuilding areas as well.

Because most of the extracts have been taken from longer works I have, in a handful of cases, omitted, inserted or altered a few words in order for the extract to make sense in isolation. There are also some slight factual inaccuracies in a number of the extracts, but as they are primarily personal impressions and memories it would seem churlish to correct the odd misperception or fickle memory. After all, I am using their words, not mine.

Most of the material has already been published in some way before, but I have also included selections from archival and oral history sources and unpublished manuscripts. A full bibliography is provided at the end for readers who may wish to consult the primary sources.

The photographs in the book have been taken from a variety of sources. Some shipyards had their own photographers, and it is their work that makes up the bulk of the illustrations. Most official photographs show little activity by workers, but occasionally there are some great pictures, especially from yards that published journals in which human interest was more important than construction details. These photographs have in the main come from Glasgow University Archives and the Scottish Maritime Museum in Irvine.

During the two World Wars the government commissioned photographers to take pictures of the shipyards for propaganda purposes. These are now in the collections of the Imperial War Museum. Most of these photographs show shipbuilders at their work, and although many are obviously posed I do not feel that this makes them any less interesting. Special mention should be made of the 1955 Glasgow Survey photographs held by Glasgow Museums. These were taken by keen amateur photographers as part of a project to record everyday life in Glasgow and inevitably many included pictures of the shipyards. I have also included a few photographs from my own collection.

No. 523

CHAPTER ONE

THE POWER AND THE PRIDE

Shipyards really are truly amazing places. The first impressions of entering a shipyard can stay with you for the rest of your life. The sights, the sounds and the smells can leave you dumbstruck. The scale of the huge cathedral-like workshops, towering cranes and massive ships can literally take your breath away. There is also a palpable sense of history when you go through a shipyard. You cannot escape the knowledge that this was once Scotland's greatest industry and produced some of the world's finest ships.

You can sense in the workers a pride that stretches back generations. It is a pride that has been earned at the expense of much sweat and blood, and more than a fair share of lives. Conditions in the yards were notoriously bad. Danger presented itself at every turn, and the very fact that the workers could overcome these dangers was an additional cause for pride in itself.

And it is not just the workers who feel the pride. Shipbuilding in many ways became a part of Scotland's national identity. In most industries work takes place behind closed doors, but the outdoor nature of much of shipbuilding and its sheer scale meant that the ships could be seen growing above the surrounding buildings. So the fortunes and the products of the industry were plain for all to see, and when the great liners and battleships were launched the whole nation shared in the pride.

Many artists, poets, novelists and songwriters have been inspired by this great sense of power and pride and the irony that things of such majesty were created by men working in such harsh conditions. Some maybe took a rather sentimental and romantic view of the industry and its workers, but no one can deny that their impressions were founded on genuine wonderment at and pride in the shipbuilding industry.

It is only by understanding the scale, the pride and the history of shipbuilding that we can begin to appreciate the passions and emotions that it can evoke. Even today, when the size of the industry should not really merit it, every twist and turn in the fate of the shipbuilding industry makes front-page news. There is certainly far more to the industry than mere economics or technology. There is a power, a romance and a destiny.

Previous page: Ships under construction at Harland and Wolff's during the First World War. (Imperial War Museum)

A MOST HONOURABLE AND DIGNIFIED BUSINESS

Our modern university may not impress you, the cathedral you may never see (for lack of a native to lead you to it); but our shipbuilding yards are a different matter. Before you are two days in the city you are aware of their existence; and if their importance is a matter beyond you, at least you must be impressed by our belief in it. We believe, every Glasgow man of us, that our shipbuilding is a thing to be talked of; and a most honourable and dignified business to have for the chief industry of a city.

From James Hamilton Muir's *Glasgow in 1901*.

A LUMP TO THE THROAT

George Blake remembers the impact that seeing the Lusitania *had on him as a small boy in Greenock.*

She came at length, however, looming gigantic as she stood out in the ship-channel opposite the Custom-house Quay, and with her there came to the boy a sudden sense of exaltation and glory.

Was it the size of her, that great cliff of upper-works bearing down upon him? Was it her majesty, the manifest fitness of her to rule the waves? I think that what brought the lump to the boy's throat was just her beauty, by which I mean her fitness in every way; for this was a vessel at once large and gracious, elegant and manifestly efficient. That men could fashion such a thing by their hands out of metal and wood was a happy realisation. Ships he had seen by the hundred thousand, but this was a ship in a million; and there came to him then as he saw her, glorious in the evening sunlight, the joy of the knowledge that this was what his own kindred could do, this was what the men of his own race, labouring on the banks of his own familiar River, were granted by Providence the privilege to create. In that moment he knew that he had witnessed a triumph of achievement such as no God of battles or panoplied monarch had ever brought about.

From George Blake's *Down to the Sea*, 1937.

TRIUMPHANT PARENTHOOD

There are some kinds of manual work in which men do not easily take pride – work for which there is nothing to show, or only some trivial or rubbishy thing. It is not so with the building of ships. When the riveter's heater-boy said, 'Whaer wid the *Loocitania* hae been if it hadna been for me heatin' the rivets?' he expressed a feeling that runs through the whole of a shipbuilding yard from the Manager down. It is a feeling that may have animated the journeyman mason who cut stones for the Campanile at Florence or the cathedral of Rheims. Each man or boy employed in building a liner or battleship feels himself to be a part-author of something organic, mighty, august, with a kind of personal life of its own and a career of high service, romance, and adventure before it. For him it comes to the birth on the day when it ceases to be an inert bulk of metal propped into position with hundreds of struts and dog-shores. At last the helpless rigid mass detaches itself quietly like an iceberg leaving the parent floe, and majesti-

Nº524

cally assumes its prerogative of riding its proper element, serene, assured, and dominant. For the builder of ships nothing can stale the thrill of that moment or deaden his triumphant sense of parenthood. Long after the ship has gone out into the world from her narrow, smoky birthplace on the Clyde he will follow her career in the newspapers, exult in her speed records, and hope and fear for her when disabled or overdue. The murder of the *Lusitania* drew thousands of men of all kinds from all parts of the country and Empire into the army. One hardly needs to be told that on Clydeside there were many set jaws and lowering brows when the news came in. Others had lost countrymen by the crime; the men in that shipbuilding yard had also lost a child.

From C. E. Montague's introduction to Muirhead Bone's collection of prints and drawings *The Western Front*, 1917.

THE YAIRDS

John F. Fergus, although a well-respected doctor, obviously felt the pride of Clyde shipbuilding as strongly as the riveter he is emulating in this poem.

I've wrocht amang them, man and boy, for mair nor fifty year,
I canna bear to quit them yet noo that I'm auld an' sere,
The Yairds is just the life o' me, the music's in my bluid
O' hammers striking strong an true on rivets loweing rid;
I'm auld, I ken, but, Goad be thank'd! I hivna lost my pride
In honest wark on bonny boats that's built upon the Clyde.

Frae Broomielaw to Kempoch Point I ken them every yin,
I kent them when I was a wean when I could hardly rin;
I kent them as a rivet boy, I kent them in my prime,
An' tho' there's been an unco wheen o' chainges in my time,
Yet still it's aye a bonny sicht to see them in their pride,
Wi' 'weys' laid doun an' some big boat a' ready for the tide.

It's graun' to see the boats grow up frae keel to upper strake,
An' ken it's a' guid honest wark an' no' an unce o' fake;
It's graun' to see the muckle frames staun' up like leafless trees,
To hear the clang o' plates an' see the rivet furnace bleeze,
To see the bonny boats tak' shape just like a leevin' thing,
Eh, man, but it's a bonny sicht an' fit to please a king.

I've helped to build a wheen o' them in mony a different yaird,
Frae barges up to battleships the Empire for to guaird,
An' eh, the names I could reca' o' men noo passed awa
Wha planned and built the boats lang syne, aye trig and strang and braw.
The men hae gane, but left ahint a legacy o' fame,
For honest wark an' bonny boats that gied the Clyde its name.

Opposite: Ship no. 524 (*War Envoy*) under construction at Harland and Wolff. Note the riveter poking out between the frames. (Imperial War Museum)

Tod an' McGregor, Napier tae, John Elder, an' the Scott's,
Wi' auld Wull Fyfe, awa doun bye, aye buildin' bonny yachts,
The 'Limited,' an' Simonses, the Tamson's at Clydebank
(That's noo John Broon's), an' Stephens whaur the puir *Daphne* sank,
An' Caird's, an' Connel's, Barclay Curle's, an' Russell, an' Dunlop,
An' Fairfield, Beardmore's, Tammy Seath's – I've wrocht in every shop.

Ye'll hear it said the 'Black Squad' drink an' break their time forbye,
Weel I jaloose we hae oor fauts – jist let the jaw gang by;
But this I'll say that, gin we drink an' break oor time as weel,
Wi' a' oor fauts, by Goad! we ken jist hoo to lay a keel,
An' build a boat that nane can beat in a' the warld beside,
The best o' wark, the bonniest boats aye come frae oot the Clyde.

John F. Fergus, 1924.

A PRIDE IN THE HEART

The life at Señors absorbed Philippa to the exclusion of all else. She loved the yard, and never passed through it without a stirring of pride in her heart. There was a feeling of red-hot pressure these days. Men were working against time, great gangs of them in blue and brown dungarees; brawny arms wielding hammers as though their lives depended on their skill and speed. The wall of an unfinished vessel loomed darkly above the gates. On the sides of that wall, and in the hollow chasm within it, an Inferno from which the application of certain tools sent spitting tongues of fire, men crawled and moved perilously, puny figures who by some miracle had conceived a giant whose great force, if they were not watchful, might suddenly destroy them.

From Dot Allan's novel *Deepening River*, 1932.

LIKE SOME FANTASTIC PACHYDERM

Behind him reared the tanker. The base of the ship at the bow was actually twenty feet from the ground, but she was 750 feet long and 70 feet deep, so that she looked like some fantastic pachyderm whose legs had folded under her. To know that there, lording it over the sandstone cliffs of Govan, this vessel was the work of men who had pieced it together from sheets of steel, was to see a certain glory in her monstrosity.

Frank's route now lay between the legs of an iron giraffe which was a crane, then into the Fabrication Hall. The Hall had the vastness of a cathedral, but was dedicated to noise, dirt and fumes. It was littered with embryo pieces of ship and the air was vibrant with the beat of the pneumatic hammer.

From Jimmy Miller's short story *Before the Time*, 1967.

CLYDESIDE SHIPYARDS

Gaunt and black against the sky,
Great lumps o' girder-cradled steel,
Staun starkly naked, loomin' high,
Wi' a still power that you can feel;
A kind o' loveliness forbye.

A ship is born in dirt an' din,
Racket o' rivets, flash o' flame,
Fae the welder's torch, a clatterin',
O' blacksmith's hammer, a fretted frame,
O' tall cranes swingin' oot an' in.

Carpenters cover the steel wi wid –
Some has a pattern-shiny face,
But maist, like us, is plainly guid –
An' electricians clutter the place,
Wi' wires in a mystic, tangled grid.

Ahint the mess is a clear design;
Lads wi' black faces work tae it,
An' joke an' laugh, or fight; an syne,
The job is done, the great hull's fit
Tae plunge in the watter, an' does it fine.

Aboard her folk we'll never ken,
Will sail tae pairts we'll never see;
Will they no' wonder noo an' then,
At the power that set the big ship free?
The skill an' sweat o' the Clyde-yaird men!

By 'The Red Poppy', in the *Linthouse News*, January 1961.

A welder at work at the Ailsa yard at Troon. (Scottish Maritime Museum)

BIGGER THAN THE PYRAMIDS

Tom McKendrick, a shipbuilder turned artist, takes much of his inspiration from the incredible scale of shipbuilding.

Think about it for a second. Think about things that were built just at the bottom of your road which were bigger than the pyramids, which were greater than the rest of the achievements – it was the greatest age when the biggest man-made moving objects in the planet were literally built where we are standing just now. Think about that for a second.

Tom McKendrick speaking on the video to accompany his exhibition *Iron* at the Collins Gallery, 1997.

A LEVIATHAN IN LABOUR

Darker yit on midnight's darkniss,
like the shaddy o a monster
stauns the night shape o the shipyerd,
beast o steel an stane an timber.

Droonin stars wae floods o fire,
broodin noo, noo breathin thunder,
earth's a-shudder wae its power
power tae meld an power tae sunder.

Iron-bodied, iley blidded,
black leviathan in labour,
waarm within its womb o girders
sleeps the beauty o a liner.

Fed fat wae the sweat o workers,
fodder fur its belly's abyss,
dragon o ma chilthood windae,
whit god's, whit divvel's beast is this?

From *A Clydeside Lad* by Bill Sutherland, 1990.

A BOY'S FIRST VISIT TO A SHIPYARD

Shortly the shipyards' region surrounded him with new wonder. His father decided to call at a firm ten miles out, and as it was still very early they sauntered about the vicinity till starting-time. The boy glued his eyes on great cranes rearing over housetops like figures in a monstrous ballet, and his spirit followed their rhythm while he fired shrill questions at his father, who answered in his detailed, laborious manner. Then at a minute to six they followed the last worker going through the wicket door of the immense gates, and his father craved an attendant commissionaire's permission to enter and interview various foremen. The personage let them pass and immediately the boy was stunned in an ocean of sound, then as soon, struck by a tragic stillness. A procession of begrimed, bareheaded workers, bearing two stretchers, wended towards the ambulance-house at the gate. The boy's father stopped; other men paused a moment, removing their caps, then hurried to their work. The procession passed, the man on the first stretcher gallantly smoking a cigarette, smiled at the boy, but the face of the body on the following stretcher was covered.

The father removed his cap, bowing his head; the boy copied him. 'My, there's been a man killed already! It's terrible. Terrible!' The boy looked up, asking: 'Do they not stop the works when a man's killed, da?' His father answered, 'No, the work goes on, son. The work goes on!' The shipyard ambulance appeared, the bodies were placed within, a nurse closed the door and the vehicle sped through the gates.

The boy forgot the dead man as they went on through the yard amid mammoth sights and sounds. He saw a warship near completion, the mere ribs of ships just begun, liners in the repair dock and the pathetic end of a worn vessel in the hands of the breakers. All men seemed midgets here, the riveters' catchboys everywhere in the skeleton ships, like imps, handing red-hot rivets from portable fires to the holder-on, and his small self had never felt so insignificant. Then in pride at being here, he strutted along cloaked in rare distinction. 'Ye can smell the sea here!' said his father, but he only smelled rust, iron and steel, machine-oil and the smoke and heat of furnaces.

From Edward Gaitens' short story *Growing Up*, 1936.

FIRST IMPRESSIONS

When W. G. Riddell moved from a rural upbringing to a job in the engineering works of a Clyde shipyard he experienced a feeling common to many who came to Glasgow in search of work in the yards.

It was a dismal wet day. The silent deserted engine-works looked indescribably grimy and mournful. I passed street after street of sooty tenement houses. At the end of a street, I saw the masts of ships and soon I was at the harbour. I had never seen a big steamer, and I was amazed at the size of the liners lying at the

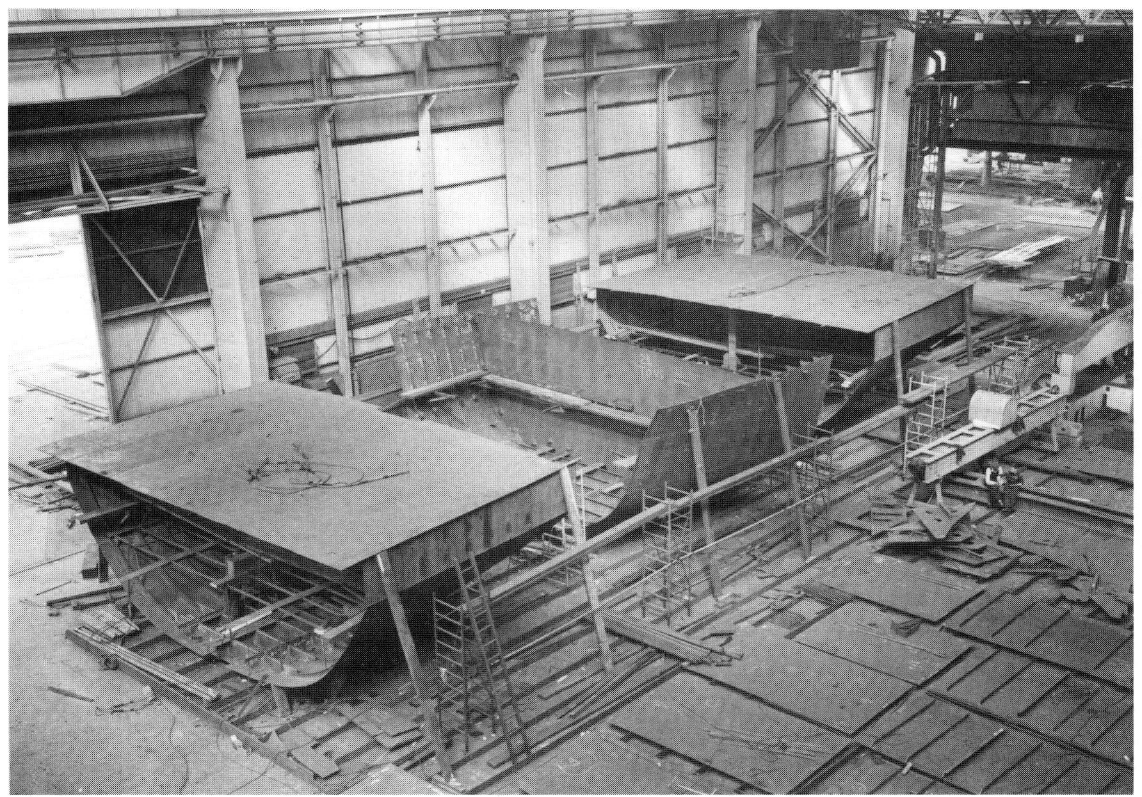

The fabrication shop at Fairfield's in the 1960s. (Scottish Maritime Museum)

quays. At that time a right of way ran for several miles along the river bank. The foot-path was bordered on one side by the hoardings which surrounded the shipyards. Looking through the spaces between the planks I could see great ships in every stage of construction. I forgot about the rain. I knew I had come to a wonderful place, for the Clyde was then, as now, one of the great sights of the world.

Next morning I started work. I was surprised that everything was so cold to the touch, and I found the noise bewildering. Mr Taylor, my foreman, was a small dyspeptic man with a pale face and a straggling red beard. He was said to be a great reader and an atheist. He taught me to face nuts on a little machine, and I continued to do this for several months. The work was easy but monotonous. For the first week or two I used to rise at half-past five, and while I dressed I boiled a kettle and made cocoa. I had been told that it was dangerous to work for three hours before breakfast without having something to eat, but I discovered that this was a fallacy so far as I was concerned, and I soon found that I could lie in bed till five minutes to six and dress in a minute, before I rushed

A ship under construction at Harland and Wolff's Govan yard in 1955. (Glasgow Museums)

out to join the trampling crowds in the badly lit streets. I shall never forget those unpleasant cold mornings. As we hurried along the wet shining pavements amidst the discordant din of steam-whistles and bells, I felt we were being called to attend the worship of some heathen god.

From W. G. Riddell's memoirs of 1932, *Adventures of an Obscure Victorian.*

THE CATHEDRAL

You step across the cobbles and the light-railway or crane tracks, through an entrance that can take half a dozen lorries or more, and you enter a building of cathedral size, dim, solemn and portentous. The impression that one has entered some profane cathedral grows as one walks down the wide aisles between the great black machines that dwarf the people working at them, as one looks at the bare brick walls and the high windows which have been darkened since the war by blue paint. When the welders tip back their masks or helmets they look like nuns or knights, and reveal that medieval aspect of modern industry which is confirmed by the sight of collective work.

Not individual people, but groups or gangs of people are important here; the individual is least, the group alone seems to have personality. And then, the sounds. There is no continuous racket of little machines. This diabolical religion is expressed in sounds more measured and portentous. There are great and sudden clangs, an intoned mutter runs between the greater noises, and there are bell-like, gong-like crashes which astound the ear and the mind. You feel you may be watching a rite devoted to the creation of the ship which belongs naturally – before anyone else – to these votaries who are building her. Human hands have touched every inch of that dour shell and given to their work an unconscious meaning.

From V. S. Pritchett's *Build the Ships* of 1946.

HELL

When I went into the shipyard at first I didnae like it. I was stuck in the bowels of the ship. I couldnae believe it; they were throwing red hot rivets to each other, it was dark and stinking because of the oil lamps they used. . . . I thought I was in Hell.

From Alan McKinlay's oral history of John Brown's shipyard between the World Wars, *Making Ships, Making Men*, 1991.

DANTE'S INFERNO

I had no idea what a shipyard was like; none of my family worked in a shipyard, but I was sent into a shipyard, to start my apprenticeship, and the blacksmith's shop was the first thing I looked in, because I had two pals worked in there, and I was convinced I was looking into Dante's Inferno. I was convinced I was looking into Hell: black with dirt, everything was covered in dirt, and all I could see was their teeth and their eyes, gloomy, you know. It was hellish.

The other thing that struck me was the sheer scale of the thing, the enormity of it. Walking down that three-quarters of mile down the front of the slipways, you were walking past ships as tall as tenement buildings, and as long as tenement buildings, you know: seven hundred, eight hundred feet long. I thought that was enormous. And the noise, the noise was absolutely deafening, absolutely deafening.

Pat, a foreman shipwright, speaking in *Made in Govan: An oral history of shipbuilding on the Upper Clyde 1930–1950*, 1991.

THE FIRST TIME

I remember the first time I stood in the yard with him and listened to the sounds of the Clyde. The thrum of generators, the groan and scrape of metal sheets, the sparks of the welders' torches crackling, and a hundred unknown noises clanking and crashing along the river. It had taken us ten minutes to walk the yard. We had passed in the shadow of the cranes, lowering over us like giant question marks, and down along the river to the dockside, where the huge launching chains, links thicker than a man's arm, lay coiled amid the flotsam cast up by the river on the flood tide. Jamie pointed out the landmarks: the dry dock; the paint shed; the prefab shed where the steel is cut into the shapes demanded by the owners; the tank assembly shed where the pieces become shapes you can recognise as parts of a ship. Inside the assembly area, great pulleys moved slowly down the length of the shed, with wide sheets of steel suspended beneath them, their advance declared by the steady pulse of a high-pitched alarm. I felt Lilliputian in this landscape.

From Fergal Keane's *A Stranger's Eye: A foreign correspondent's view of Britain*, 2000.

AMAZING!

Of all the impressions of working in a shipyard perhaps the most profound is the experience of walking underneath a ship on the stocks for the first time.

Brian had walked under her from stem to stern, gazing up with an appraising eye at the propeller and tail shaft, the huge rudder hanging down like a gigantic steel fin from the stern post, and the lovely curves of the boss plates. Yes, she was a beauty! Who would have thought that a tangle of rusty beams and plates flung together higgledy piggledy, a strip of shell here, a deck half covered there, gaping holes, beams and brackets jutting out at every conceivable angle, who would have thought that all that chaos had a design; that all the months of confused bawling and shouting, pulling, pushing, bending, cutting, hammering, all had the one objective, and that was this beautiful grey and red hull, with its lovely curves carrying the eye pleasantly from the keel to the rail on the top deck?

It was almost incredible that human hands, soft flesh, could cut and shape this steel monster that would carry twelve thousand tons and force its way through the heaviest seas. Brian climbed up on to the ways and examined the riveting and caulking where two plates joined. From here the ship's bottom was a massive steel ceiling. Imagine all this twisting and wrenching, pounded by

Inside the ribs of a ship in the 1920s. (Scottish Maritime Museum)

solid water for years and years, and yet at the end of it all each rivet, each joint, holding tight as it was now. All this created by weak, human hands that couldn't face a pin point without bursting. It was amazing! Incredible if you had just heard about it. But there it was.

From Edward Shiels' novel about Beardmore's Dalmuir yard, *Gael over Glasgow*, 1937.

A JOB WELL DONE

There was something about a shipyard. There was something about the characters who worked in a shipyard, something about their humour. Of course, there were lots of times when the work stopped – demarcation disputes and that sort of thing – which came from a sort of tribalism, I think, which should have been overcome. But basically I enjoyed all of those years. I never woke up in the morning thinking: 'Oh God, I've got to go and work in that place.'

The prefabrication shop at Lithgow's, with Yard no. 1150 (*Thorshammer*) under construction in 1963. (Glasgow University Archives)

Right:
Heavy engineering work at Alexander Stephen's yard. (Scottish Maritime Museum)

You always felt a certain pride when a ship left the yard, when you completed a job and you could see it coming down the Clyde, whether it was a tanker or a liner. You know? A job well done. That was us.

Robert Dickie, a joiner from John Brown's, speaking to Ian Johnston and Lewis Johnman in *Granta 61: The Sea*, 1998.

SYMBOL OF A NATION

For more than two years the Clyde had been like a tomb. Not a tomb newly made, but a tomb with a vast and inescapable skeleton brooding over its silence. For two years that gaunt framework had stood lifeless. It had sapped the vitality from a great town – aye, from a nation. Beneath its shadow men have crept about, battered and broken by enforced idleness.

These men – the finest, the most expert craftsmen in the world – had lived their lives in their work. Their joy as well as their livelihood lay in converting the vast masses of Nature's gifts into works of art, accurate to a two-thousandth part of an inch.

Workers in metal and wood, their brains and hands had become so well organised to work together that they could take the gigantic products of furnaces and rolling-mills and turn them into a thing of majesty and beauty. The highest talent of the sons of Tubal-cain, instructed of every artifice in brass and iron, was in their skill.

And yet, for two years and more, they had been shut out from the place of work and left idle in the street.

We think of prison as a place where men are shut in. It is worse than prison for men to be shut out of work.

And their wives – those heroic women of the tenement and the Guild – had seen their men depressed and nervous. They had long ago eaten up their little savings. They had struggled with untold splendour of sacrifice to pay the rent, to keep the husband and the children fed and clad; aye, and still more to keep up the spirit of their men. To them the sight of the closed gate and the horrid framework beyond had been a blight.

Better a thousand times that the great ship had never been begun than that it should have stood mocking us all these weary months, dangling hope before hungry eyes and dashing faith to the pit of despair.

On Wednesday, December 13, 1933, the Chancellor of the Exchequer spoke a few sentences in the House of Commons.

As I looked across the green carpet and the Treasury table, I saw him, cool, detached, matter-of-fact. His sentences were as precise as the sentences of a judge. I heard him sentence Clydebank to Life.

There was one thing I wanted at that moment – a microphone to send a broadcast message to the Clyde:

'Men of the Clyde, lift up your heads!'

And as I looked at him, juggling with the happiness of thousands, I saw behind him the long Dumbarton Road through Clydebank with four thousand men moving along towards Brown's Yard while the horn sang out the morning

A dramatic view of Lithgow's yard in 1961. (Glasgow University Archives)

welcome. I saw some whose pockets bulged with their 'pieces' and some who would march out at dinner-time with a new ring in their step. These were the men who, years later, would tell their children:

'I worked on the 534.'

Behind them I saw their homes, now so bare, gradually brighten with furniture and carpet and waxcloth, and children setting out for school, well fed and well clad. And I saw the wrinkles of care and anxiety smooth out from the faces of the mothers. And I saw the boys and youths eagerly awaiting the word 'Go!' to rush forward to begin the life that had so far been denied to them.

And beyond Clydebank I saw the glowing furnaces of Motherwell and Wishaw, the forges of Parkhead and the machine-shops and factories and wood-working yards of Glasgow. I saw the mines and the railways, the rolling-mills and the rivet factories full of energy and life. I saw engineers creating the giant turbines with 257,000 turbine blades.

I saw the anchors and the rudder, each weighing 140 tons. I saw the makers of glass preparing 2500 square feet of glass for side-windows and portholes. I saw the boiler-makers creating water-tube boilers of unprecedented accuracy with their 3000 feet of pipes. I saw gear casings weighing 200 tons and shaft brackets weighing 200 tons.

And I saw a shower of ten million rivets pouring down, each one to be fitted and welded with exact care. I saw weavers busy with carpets and linen; cabinet-makers and upholsterers, joiners, carpenters, plumbers, electricians – all the craftsmen whose skill and industry have made the Clyde pre-eminent among the famous rivers of the world.

When Mr Neville Chamberlain announced that work on the great Cunarder '534', was to be resumed, I felt that the Clyde, one of the most depressed of areas in Britain, would become active again. And it was so.

As the skeleton took on flesh and lived again, Scotland revived. We are a nation of craftsmen. The whole world acknowledges our skill with admiration. This great ship which had depressed us began now to vitalise us.

Think of it! The silence of years broke into the music of work. That grim, bare frame took on life and grew from hold to deck – four, seven, nine, eleven of them. Much of our depression had been mental. We had gone from bad to worse by thinking in terms of depression. Now, with '534' looming and growing, we began to throw off the chains of depression.

The '534' was our Statue of Liberty.

From David Kirkwood's memoirs, *My Life of Revolt*, 1935.

THE BUILDERS OF THE *QUEEN MARY*

Those workers of Clydebank. . . . It still seems impossible to understand them. The dramatic mind seeks continually to pin them down to type, and continually they elude characterisation. One could in the early stages of the ship's construction, when the interior of the hull seemed an iron foundry on the grand scale, discern the Clydeside artisan of the old tradition: the man of the Black Squad, with a terrific breadth of shoulder, a command of harsh language, a grim way of 'getting on with the job' and, no doubt, a noble capacity for glasses and pints. Yet that was a transient figure, perhaps a disappearing figure. A week later, and the army seemed to consist of halfin boys with such a passion for football in its sectarian aspects that, when they come at length to break up the *Queen Mary*, men will find chalked on the steel plates behind the elegant woods of the staterooms gross insults to the Pope and praise of players long forgotten. At yet another stage, the alleyways hummed to the anxious debates of pale electricians, lovingly technical and deeply learned in the incredible intricacies of the circuits. Or one would see the army dispersing in the evening – a fleet of buses at the gates to take many of them to far-distant housing schemes, their gardens and their wireless sets. One could surmise of most of them that they were strictly sober, decently educated men of the new dispensation: the frivolity of the youngsters limited to prowess as Sunday cyclists or to expertise in the dance-halls. The abiding impression was of youth: of a new, clean, efficient youth, defying sentimentalisation as the rough diamonds of yesterday's fiction.

These men who built the *Queen Mary* defied sentimentalising to the end. There was an end to the ship so far as the rank and file were concerned on the 24th of March, 1936, when she was canted out of the builders' fitting-out basin and taken down to the sea, never, in any reasonable calculation, to return to the place of her making. That was a much less spectacular business than most people had anticipated. The tugs got her out of the basin in no time, and she bumped the mud of the channel when a strong wind from the east caught her on a bend at Dalmuir, and she was lying off Greenock at two in the afternoon. She filled the channel on her way down-river, as a cathedral dominates a city, and one may imagine that a lot of emotion followed her in the forms of pride in a job well done and regret that a vigorous spring of employment had dried up. But it was essentially a job of work: and Clydeside got on with it. If one looked for the satiating meed of melodrama the workers of Clydebank certainly did not provide it on that crisp and sunshiny morning of March. One may remember a queer encounter with the naval architect of the building firm, under the gantries. He, who had his own heavy load of responsibility for that day's work to bear, was so very anxious that the broadcaster should be at his post in time to see the ship move out earlier than had been expected: so fast was

The plate bending rolls at Lithgow's. (Glasgow University Archives)

the tide running up the river that morning. Then the flash of humanity emerged when it was revealed that, in the background of the naval architect's mind, was a sick little boy at home, waiting eagerly to hear how the *Queen Mary* fared on her way to the sea.

That was a grand enough spectacle – an enormous mass being coaxed out of a box of water, as it were, into a rivulet. It was done with ease so apparent as to be preposterous. Tugs pulled at her stern and nuzzled into her sides. An antique winch ground at a wire hawse to assist her away from the quay. The foreman rigger used powerful words. We saw a sudden swirl of brown – creaming water under her stern – the first cut of the mighty propellers under power. Yet the workers of Clydebank let her go away from them forever with hardly a cheer. The hooters had called them from their jobs on other hulls to watch the pride of the yard go out. They appeared in their hundreds, swarming up the gantries and on to roofs. Again they seemed very young and insulated against melodrama by a pervading facetiousness. One cheer they did raise was half-hearted, semi-satirical; as if they must resist emotion. Or they were not aware of emotion at all. One will never know. In silence they let the *Queen Mary* go, and then they went back to their jobs.

From George Blake's *Down to the Sea*, 1937.

Fitting one of the propellers onto the QE2. (Scottish Maritime Museum)

THE PRIDE

It is now many years since there were liners being built on the Clyde but the resonance of the once great industry can still be felt today.

TOJO: What a day, eh? I've never seen so many people. That turn-out was incredible. And the racket. And folk kept coming up to me and shaking my hand, clapping me on the back. I felt like I'd won the World Cup.

ALAN: It just lets you see the support, how people feel about the whole thing. You see, you forget how important shipbuilding is to the idea of being Glaswegian. We just went straight into the yards from school because that's what you did. But to people out there, there's a pride in being part of that. Being associated with, I don't know, a symbol of excellence.
(*shrug*) Ach, maybe I've had too many.

WUMP: No, no Alan. You're alright, a wee bit poetic there but not wide of the mark.

From Frank Miller's play *Work-in*, 2001.

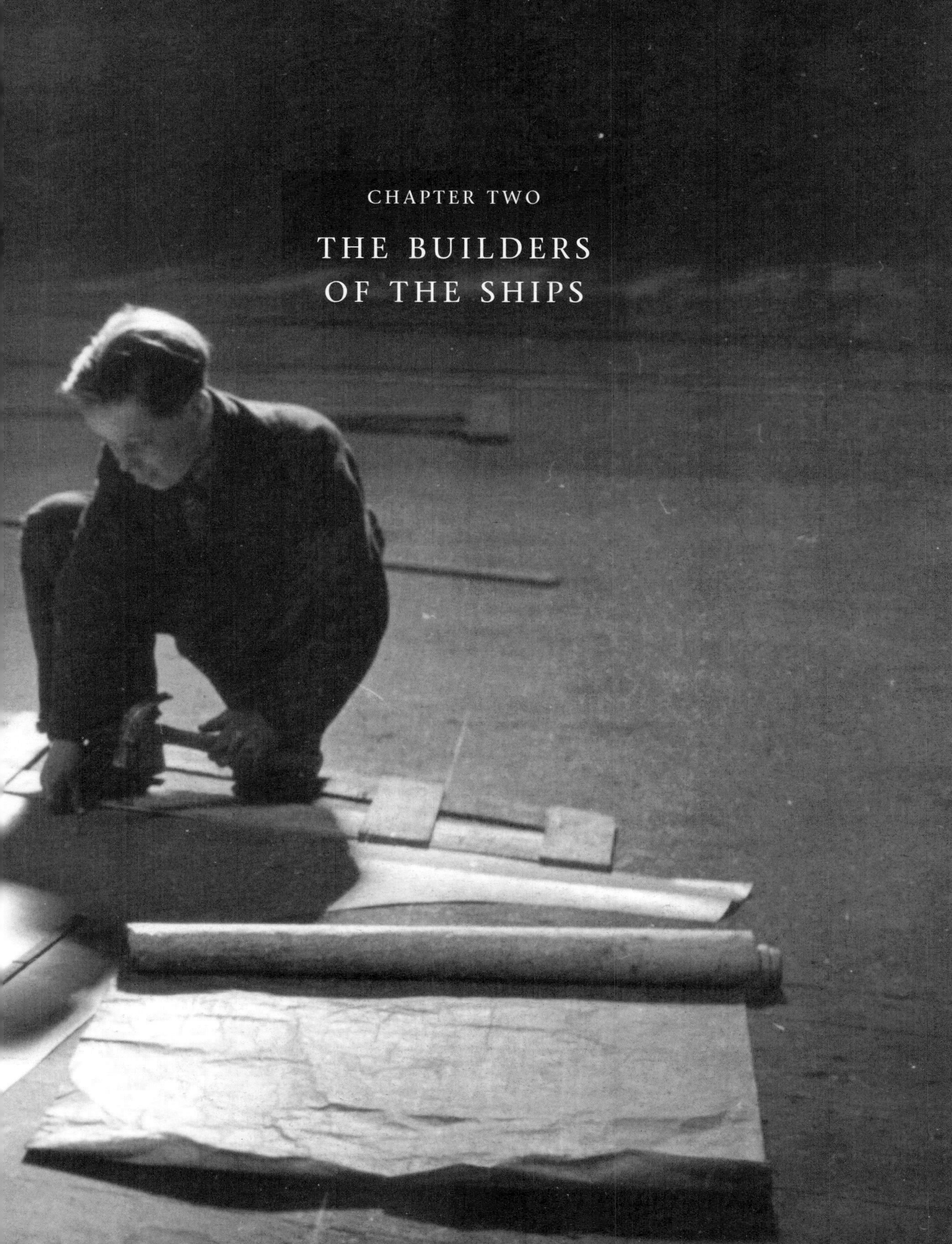

CHAPTER TWO

THE BUILDERS OF THE SHIPS

The building of a ship is a highly complex process requiring large numbers of workers with many different skills.

The kings of the shipyard workers used undoubtedly to be the riveters. They commanded great awe and respect for their physical strength and skill, and many a legend grew up about them in the yards. They also commanded by far the highest wages. After the Second World War welders gradually took over the riveters' mantle as the backbone of the shipyard workforce. They didn't quite command the same awe as the riveters, but with their spotted 'Casey Jones' caps and their notoriously militant bargaining power, they soon built up their own mystique. The riveters and welders, along with the burners, platers, caulkers and shipwrights, made up the so-called 'black squad', the men who battered and formed and joined the steel together to make the structure of a ship.

Once the steelwork was completed, the finishing trades moved in. In many ways a ship is like a floating hotel, and everything that is needed to power and service a hotel needs to be installed in a ship. To this end there are engineers to fit the machinery, plumbers to connect all the pipework, joiners to fit out the cabins, sheet-metal workers to make all the ducting and ventilation systems, electricians to wire everything up, and painters to make it all look good.

To become a tradesman an apprenticeship of usually five years had to be served. During this time the apprentice was assigned to a journeyman, who was meant to pass on the intricacies of his trade, but in truth most learning happened by accident. More often than not apprentices were simply used as cheap labour.

There was a strict hierarchy among the workers. At the top came the skilled tradesmen, followed by the semi-skilled tradesmen, the apprentices and, at the bottom of the heap, the labourers and helpers who did all the shifting, fetching and holding in support of the tradesmen. It was extremely difficult, if not impossible, to progress upwards in this hierarchy. In fact many a rivet 'boy' would remain that till he retired in his sixties. Getting a trade was seen as the key to a successful working life, so apprenticeships were highly sought after. Patronage and influence therefore played a great part in the selection of apprentices, and it was common for sons to follow their fathers into the yards.

As well as the men who worked on the ships, there were also a number of ancillary workers in the yards whose jobs as crane drivers, stagers, storemen, gate-keepers, cleaners, and so on, were needed to support the men actually building the ships.

Traditionally, the two jobs that women did in the yards were those of tracing plans to make blueprints and French-polishing furniture for the ships. During the two World Wars many more women were brought into the yards. Most of them did ancillary jobs but there were also a good few riveters, welders and engineers. With the return of peace, however, most of the women 'dilutees', as they were known, were forced to leave the yards again.

To keep the yards running smoothly there were a relatively small number of managers. The most senior was the Shipyard Manager, who ruled all the work of the yard. He was supported by a handful of senior managers who specialised in different aspects of the work in the ships and the workshops. Between the managers and the men

Previous page: The mould loft. Ships were drawn out in full size on the mould loft floor. Templates were made from the drawing to get the shapes for all the various pieces of steelwork on a ship. Photograph by Cecil Beaton, 1943. (Imperial War Museum)

The Polishing Shop at Stephen's yard in 1950. One of the few jobs that women did in the shipyards was French polishing. (Glasgow University Archives)

were the foremen. The foremen were really the key to good shipyard management. They transformed the managers' wishes and ideas into cold hard reality. However, as production techniques became ever more complex with the advent of prefabrication, the number of managers and middle-managers increased inexorably. To service this increasingly managerial structure, swarms of office workers were also needed. There were design and technical departments, wages and personnel departments, estimating departments, planning departments and production departments. All these were full to the brim with clerks, designers, draughtsmen, accountants, planners, typists and sundry other office personnel.

At the very top of this pyramid sat the directors and the yard owners, who were very much the public face of the shipyard, responsible for gaining orders, financing deals and dealing with shipyard politics. Whatever the job a person held in the yards, however, whether as a labourer or director, the pride in the industry was such that they all regarded themselves first and foremost as shipbuilders.

GROWING UP

Crossing by ferry to the opposite shore was the next brilliant event. Now the river was mad with sunshine, and against passing and anchored ships the water splintered like golden glass. Amidstream, his father pointed out famous shipyards. 'Yon's Fairfield's away back, and there's Harland & Wolff's. That's John Brown's where we're going next, and yonder's Beardmore's! Yon's the highest crane on the Clyde!' and the boy looked far through smiling space at the goliath moving with relentless deliberation at its task.

And once again they were at shipyard gates, hanging about till the dinner-hour, when his father rushed forward to intercept a little man in a dungaree suit, spectacles and a sailor's cap among the hundreds of men streaming out. While the interview proceeded the boy could not take his eyes from the man's ardent red nose, abnormally small, above his grey moustache. 'Weel, I'm no sure!' said the foreman, 'I'm no sure! I'm pretty full up the now. But see me here tomorrow at six! And is this yer wee laddie? Will ye be wantin' a job for him, too? Weel, bring 'im wi' ye! One o' my platers wants a boy. Ye'll be puttin' him to a trade later on?' and walking in a queer, staccato style, he left them without waiting reply.

'God be praised!' the boy's father exclaimed jubilantly. 'That means a start for me tomorrow! He wouldn't tell me to come if he hadn't a job for me! An' you'll get a job, too, son, wi' fifteen shillin's a week!' The boy couldn't believe it. Fifteen shillings a week! Fifteen shillings a week! Immediately he was rich and in imagination scattering money right and left, buying long-desired things for himself, presents for his mother, father and brothers, making fabulous plans. They walked along with more inspirited step. 'Ye'll have a pay-poke on Saturday the same as me!' said his father, and the boy set his cap a little rakishly, plunged his hands into his pockets manfully and looked at life with tremendous satisfaction! . . .

The boy was in a state of sheer bliss with all he had seen that day. No boy had seen the wonders he had witnessed, and all the long ride home he fought sleep, wishful to miss nothing. When he had gulped down his tea he rushed into the back-court to tell his tenement friends. They were rooting for any objects of interest housewives might have thrown into the communal midden, which was beginning to exude its summer stink. They rallied, a charmed, envious circle, while he narrated, a little Homer of the back-streets. He had seen a dead man and the highest crane on the Clyde! His da had knocked a man 'right oot' over a table! – by now his father's adversary had attained prodigious proportions – and he had got a job in the 'Yards' with 'big money'. Suddenly he broke off importantly with: 'Well, I'll have to be gettin' home now. I've got to be up gey early for my job, ye know!' and swaggered away.

There was unusual tranquillity in his home that evening. His mother was pleased because all her menfolk would be in jobs, and she and her man were almost friendly. The boy tried to read a book, but the print danced and he could think of nothing but his fine job with big money. He would give his mother every penny. Keep nothing for himself. He would be a good son to her. She would see! He stumbled to her where she sat smiling, knitting a sock. 'Ye won't let me sleep in tomorrow, will ye, maw?' he said. She tousled his hair. 'No, son. I'll call ye fine an' early.' His father shook his shoulder ruggedly. 'Ye're a fine standing-up man, sonny! Ye'll soon be as big as yer da!' He staggered through to the parlour bed, drunk with the sweet opiate of healthy fatigue, hearing his mother say: 'Puir wee soul! He's gey tire't!' and his father: 'Ay, he's had a long day for a wee laddie.' Immediately he fell asleep, thinking vividly of the morrow's job, smiling, with the cries of seagulls in his ears.

All night he dreamt of exalted shipmasts and tall cranes bowing, proudly lifting, swinging their loads, while wild birds circled around them in brilliant sunshine. And the gallant Clyde, pursuing its historic journey to the mountains and the sea, flowed through his dreams.

From Edward Gaitens' short story *Growing Up*, 1936.

IN THE BLOOD

These are men who build the hulls of all our ships, even in an age of partial prefabrication, using skills that have run in families, almost in the spirit of the old guilds, for generations now. The Clydeside worker is an independent, unceremonious sort of chap; but it is to the continued existence in the shipbuilding towns of the riverside – Govan, Clydebank, Renfrew, Dumbarton, Port-Glasgow, and Greenock – of a pool of skilled labour almost by inheritance that the Scottish industry owes much of its predominance. Shipbuilding is in the blood.

From George Blake's *Scottish Enterprise: Shipbuilding*, 1947.

RUNNING IN THE FAMILY

Some of these jobs run in families. You see white-haired father and middle-aged son marking off the plates; and if that son falls sick, father simply sends down the yard for his other son. It is a kind of royal command. No one disputes the father's right to send for him.

From V. S. Pritchett's *Build the Ships* of 1946.

FAMILY CONTACTS

Helen's dad, Bert, worked in the Fairfield shipyard, which was Upper Clyde Shipbuilders in 1968. He was a sheet ironworker to trade and at that time was in production control. He organised a lunchtime interview for me with the ironworks manager, Jim Paul, who gave me a start after telling me, 'You have to work hard in here, son.' Three of Bert's brothers also worked in the yard at that time, Jim, George, and Thomas.

From Jim Collins' unpublished memoirs.

RUNNING FOR BUNS

Apprenticeship was a strange sort of business. You're sort of taken into the care and taken the Mickey out of simultaneously. It's only when you look back that you realise that you were actually almost adopted by this guy who was your master. You know, sometimes you'd get silent men that maybe over a period of

Opposite top: John McLean, a shipwright in Lithgow's East Yard, using his brace and bit in 1958. (Glasgow University Archives)

Opposite bottom: An apprentice fitter. Photograph by Cecil Beaton. (Imperial War Museum)

six months you got two words out of, or else you would get real characters, or you'd get people who would share things with you and discuss things with you, but generally it was a kind of abusive situation. You spent more time making tea and running for buns and getting chalk and doing all the dogsbody jobs than you done actually learning.

Tom McKendrick speaking on the BBC Radio Scotland programme *Clydebuilt*, 1990.

THE ROOKIE

was a smart arse
apprentice
who gave the men lip

and didn't realise
it was his job
to be told
what to do,
no matter what

until

a self appointed
committee
persuaded him to
enter the boiler room
where they
pinned
him to the floor,
pulled down his trousers
and smeared his balls
with axle grease
and waste oil,
muttering
pleasantries about his manhood

the rookie
had
a lot to learn.

From Brian Whittingham's *Ergonomic Workstations and Spinning Teacans*, 1992.

A NEW APPRENTICE JOINER

Ther's moss an dock an grass in dibbits,
the odd trang daisy tae,
graun oot this grimy shipyerd waw
thit locks me in the day.

Ma Da an uncles spoke fur me;
they said nae lad wis finer;
sae here Ah staun on ma furst day,
a new apprentice jiner.

The roar o' rivets, screech of cranes,
the groan an grind o gear
hiv numbed ma brain
bit cannae numb ma fear.

An up ower ther ten thousan men
made smaw agen the hull,
swarm like dark bees aboot a hive
or ants upon thir hill.

Ma fear tells me thit in this place
a soul cid lose itsel –
oh God, if only Ah cid wake
an find Ah'd dreamt o Hell.

Fur nowt thit's weak or frail, Ah know,
cin flourish in this place
an wurdliss ma hert begs release –
or else fur iron grace.

Bit yit high up yon murky waw
Ah see a floor is bloomin,
a sign tae say thit folk can thole
this Hell an still stay human.

Ootside this store noo gruff big men
grin ower an dunt thir mate
is Ah staun here where Ah've been sent
tae get 'a guid, lang weight'.

From *A Clydeside Lad* by Bill Sutherland, *c.*1988

A FEW RIVETS

It's a funny place – tae ye get used tae it – is a Boatyerd. I wis gie fear't the first mornin'; but it's no near as bad as the Infirmary, an' I wis there twice. Ye think that a' the men are awfu' angry, an there's a guid lot o' swearin'; but nae winner, jist see the big boats they build. Ye'll tummle tae it yerself efter, a man in a pucker can pu' twice as hard as an easy-oasy canny-gaun cratur.

The timekeepers are a kin' o' concaity lot; collars and ties an their hair weel greased; they seem to be awfu' weel peyed, and, by jings, tae hear them talkin', they aither want tae frichten us wee anes, or they're tryin' tae be somebody. There's ane or twa nice fellas among them, but no mony; ye'll no be lang here tae ye get the hing o' that lot. Passin' the Doctor is no sic a terrible thing efter a'. Av coorse if ye heeded a' the men tell't ye, ye wid be mair like passin' awa'. I like best tae watch the Riveters workin'; espaicially in below the boat – long slow strokes tae stave it, then they chip it, below wi' wee hammers, an teekle-leekle tae feenish it.

I think I'll be a Riveter masel, they tell me there's guid money et it. I aince had a notion to be a Plater; but I askit oor squad's richt-hander whit a plater wis. Did he tell me? Maybe no. But efter yon, I widna' be a plater for onything.

They've a rare thing in oor yerd the noo, a kin' o' machine that ye licht like the gas it sen's sparks doon a'body's neck an' taks shaves aff the iron plates like yer mither taks scuffs aff the cheese. It's fine tae watch it, an' they say it's chaper than caulkers cuttin' wi' the haun. I can weel believe this, because for every biler that's swishin' it aff wi' the fizzin' licht, ye can see twa caulkers howkin' awa', an' even then no gettin' on as quick. Apprentice Platers dinna hae ony gumption. Ye see them humphin' bawrs, brackets, an' a hunner ither things that wid be a guid load for a wee powny; an' a' ower the yerd there's lots o' iron barries. Maybe they're like the chap we used tae sing aboot at schule they'll hae lost their hurl on the barra'.

Aye, we're gie important are the pitter-ins; when ye get fly for the tank an' the names o' things, ye're gie usefu' tae. Aye, we dae lots o' things: ye fu' the squad's can, fit' the hauder-on's pipe an sneak a wee chow, rin tae the store for a bunnet-fu' a quarter langer an' trail the hauder-on's tools efter him; fu' the lamps cairy chaur an get caunels for the tank jobs. Naw, ye never weary, there's aye somebody swearin' at ye. Its aither yer ain boy, yer hauder-on, yer squad, or the squad below ye. Ye're kin' o' feart et first, but ye sune get used tae it; an' forby there's naebody means the wan hauf o' whit they say et their work. Slip ower tae oor job in the efternin; I'll gie ye a spell; onyway I want ye tae hear oor hauder-on sweerin'. He's the best sweerer ever I heard, an I hae kept ma lugs open a' the time; a rale top-notcher is oor ane.

William Percy of Glasgow marking beams at Harland and Wolff. He had worked in the yard for 29 years. His father had worked for 48 years and his grandfather for 46 years in the same yard. (Imperial War Museum)

Thae men wi' the saft collars and gaun-tae-sea bunnets is under-gaffers; them wi' the wee peakit stiff stanin' up collars (ye ken the kind that cost tuppence at the laundry) they's Manager's an' Inspectors. Anes wi' blue dungaree jaickets an a guid pair o' troosers is Platers; the awfu' iley greasy chaps is Holeborers. A' they crabbit-lookin' men are riveters, only if they've got toarn waistcoats a' roosty et the shoothers, they're hauder-ons. Them wi' the guid workin' buits and dacent kin o' shirts are caulkers; but if yer no shair, look for a wee square box that he keeps his tools in. The anes that are aye in a hurry are piece-workers; them slippin' roon like as if the morn wid dae as weel as the day are time men; men wha as faur as I can see, no' o' much account in Shipbuildin'. Mebbe I'm wrang af coorse; but I'm no lang in the yerd yet. Ye widna' hae a Woodbine nip, hae ye?

From 'Catch-boy Joe's impressions' in the *Linthouse Works Magazine* of December 1921.

THE RIVET SQUAD

The riveter is a member of the 'black squad' – a gang of four who turn up to the job with the misleading nonchalance of a family of jugglers. They are the riveter, the holder-up, the heater, and a boy. A speechless quartet, or almost speechless:

A rivet squad at work on the deck of a ship at Harland and Wolff during the Second World War. We can see the rivet boy and the left-hand and right-hand riveters. The holder-on is underneath the deck. (Imperial War Museum)

A pneumatic riveter at work on a deck plate in 1955. Rivet guns began to replace the hand-riveting squads in the 1920s. (Glasgow Museums)

Right:
A caulker at work on the deck of a ship. Caulkers made the seams watertight after the riveters had joined the plates together. Photograph by Cecil Beaton. (Imperial War Museum)

'Where's that boy?' is about their only sentence. The 'black squad' can set up shop anywhere and begin performing their hot-chestnut act. You see one swung over the ship's side. He stands on his plank waiting with the pneumatic instrument in his gloved hands. On the other side of the plate, inside the ship, is the heater with his smoking brazier – a blue coke haze is always rising over a ship: he plucks a rivet out of the fire with his tongs, a 'boy' (nowadays it is often a girl in dungarees) catches the rivet in another pair of tongs and steps quickly with it to the holder-up, who puts it through the proper holes at the junction of the plates. As the pink nub of the rivet comes through, the pneumatic striker comes down on it, roaring out blows at the rate of about 700 hits a minute, and squeezes it flat.

One of the curiosities of the ship's side – it is also one of those accidental beauties of line which are sought by modern artists – is the white chalk mark which the rivet counter ticks across each rivet, showing how many the riveter has done in the shift. One sees half a dozen plates cross-hatched in this way by the errant human touch, and a list of figures like a darts score is totted up beside them. Paid by the hundred, the riveter is keeping his accounts. He will average up to thirty-seven in an hour.

From V. S. Pritchett's *Build the Ships* of 1946.

SPOTTED HATS

(Imperial War Museum)

The welders
wore spotted hats
of many different colours,
crude leather leggings
aprons
and soft leather mitts.

They lit their cigarettes
off glowing ends
of hot electrodes

and would only
consider maintenance
when their cables
started to smoulder and smoke.

And when they weren't bevvied
or smoking
joints on top of the legs of the rig

they would artistically
weld pipes
with bevelled preps
and tackle 'overhead'
with a sureness of skill

molten showers of sparks
potholing
leathered protection
as they twisted their rods
to the most acute angles.

They viewed
green glowing arcs
as low-hydrogen fumes
snaked their way
round spacemen like masks.

The slag on the weld
curled up
like the tail of a scorpion.

From Brian Whittingham's *Ergonomic Workstations and Spinning Teacans*, 1992.

THE FORGE

In the main forge there are thirty or forty blacksmiths. The shed is dark. Each man stands before his hooded fire, his face smoky and reddened by the flame and glistening with sweat. This is one of the muscular, skilful and genial trades. The sweat pours out, the beer has to pour in – even at the present price, which hits the blacksmith hard. The masters of the craft often run to fat. The sound of each trade in a ship has its special quality – the riveter's and caulker's fusillade, the plater's solemn clang, and the elephantine thumping of the forge. These steel hammers, that come down like tree trunks on the anvil, shake the earth and the building and thicken the air with a cloud of reverberations. One is surprised that the foundations of the world can stand up to such a tonnage of blows in the belly. There are craftsmen here who have been forty years at the job, and their fathers before them; cunning men who will temper steel till it reaches the right degree of blue as if they were magicians.

Watch one of the master smiths at work. He and three helpers and a boy are there, waiting for a shaft to heat. They do not speak. They stand relaxed, gazing at the fire, each forming his opinion of the right moment to draw the shaft out. Even the boy who sits on a perch behind the hood of the fire, and whose job it is to pull the lever back and forth and release the enormous stamping foot of the hydraulic hammer, has an alert eye on the smith. This is the boy's first job. Two months ago he was thirteen and at school. The smith, wide and fat in his apron, wipes his hands on a rag and picks up his tongs. The three men crouch and lift the shaft – which is about twenty feet long and the size of a half-grown tree

A burner at work on the deck of a destroyer at Yarrow's during the Second World War. (Imperial War Museum)

Right: Working with a steam hammer in the engineering workshop of a shipyard. (Glasgow Museums)

A welder at work on a prefabricated unit in the Ailsa yard at Troon. (Author's collection)

trunk – by a grip arranged like a double wheel so that they can turn the load. A wall of solid heat moves forward and leans flat against you, and down comes the earth-shaking hammer, squeezing an inch off the thickness of the shaft like toffee.

As the smith directs the turns, his helpers crouch like wrestlers. They grapple and strain with the end of the shaft, their watchful eyes missing none of the smith's movements. It is majestic, smooth. Now and then the smith sprinkles a little water, like a baptism on the shaft, and adds an element of devilry and magic.

From V. S. Pritchett's *Build the Ships* of 1946.

THE PLATERS' SHED

When the 'green' plates are brought by the railway from the steel works to the shipyard, they have been cut approximately to the right sizes. But many will have to be cut down, trimmed; many of them will have to be given the curve of the ship's bows or the stern. So they go to the platers' squad. The platers form one of the main trades of the industry; a foreman plater is a great man, a king with his own entourage. The size of the platers' squad varies from yard to yard, but it is common to find a squad of twenty or more platers' helpers working together and keeping the flow of plates going from the shop to the hull.

The platers whistle up to the girl in the little box of the crane which travels overhead quietly from one end of the vast shed to the other. It rolls slowly across the roof towards them. Down comes the chain; by instinct the men whistle – the

The plate shop at Fairfield's in the 1960s. (Scottish Maritime Museum)

girl cannot hear it in the rumble of the shed but she sees a hand go up as well. One finger for stop, two fingers for go. You see a man, with a pot of paint, laying the wooden template or pattern on the plate and marking the rivet holes. Once more the hook of the crane comes down and the plate is carried to the one-man punch, which grips the plate, rolls it along and punches the holes in, while the one man sits in his epileptic chair above the machine, pulling and releasing the lever. Or perhaps the plate goes to one of those long machines which drill four or five plates at a time, while a man watches the steel shavings corkscrew out of the hole – all he has to do is to water the drill and keep it cool. There will also be a countersinking machine which bevels the holes; and then the steel plate is picked up in its sling of chain and carried to the shearing machine, which will cut its edge like cardboard.

But perhaps a curved plate is wanted, with a kind of leaf curl in it. If this is so, it goes over to the furnace and there it is made red hot in the ovens. There are large wide ovens for the plates, and long narrow ones for the frame. There is silence near the furnace, except for the faint tick of burning coke, as the gang of plate or frame benders wait for the steel to be at the proper heat. They stand there, a gang of half a dozen men, waiting with their sledge-hammers – once in a while you will see a hefty-looking woman. The floor is an area of iron grating, and the men have fixed the cradle over which the plate is to be bent. This is a job of muscle, dexterity, incredible speed and skill. For they must strike while the iron is hot; they are racing the dying heat, and every blow must be in the right place so that the plate does not rise too much here or stiffen there. You were standing at the far end of the platers' shed when, suddenly, above the mutter and banging of the punches, you heard a noise like the crash of a gong, like the beating of a barbarian's bell. That was the sound of the plate being struck to its shape, steel on steel, when it was drawn from the furnace.

From V. S. Pritchett's *Build the Ships* of 1946.

THE MOST DANGEROUS JOB IN THE YARD

When I became an apprentice loftsman one of the first jobs I had was making templates for the frames of a ship. If you imagine a ship growing, that sort of wonderful almost feminine form with these girders growing up that the plates were attached to. On this floor here was where they actually bent these huge beams to make these frames. One of the jobs I had was coming down and working with these guys that used to work in this place. It was an amazing sight because at this end of this frame-bending floor, as they called it, was a huge furnace that they would slide in a massive girder. They would wait till it was

Frame bending – the job described by Tom McKendrick as the most dangerous in the yard. (Glasgow University Archives)

almost white hot and they would say, 'OK, wee man, do the biz,' and I'd come along with a template, and I would lay it down on this floor and I would draw this particular curve, maybe 30 foot long, for a frame, maybe in the after end. Then they would haul this God-almighty great gleaming bar, and into these holes here they would bang huge spikes and things called dogs. They would have a big hydraulic ram that would actually start to push this thing on to the wee thin fine chalk line that I had drawn. It was amazing to watch these guys because this thing was white hot, they were wielding hammers, and all over the place there were dogs, and they would skip and jump and kind of dance, and there was a kind of poetry to it all. The thing that was amazing about it was that this was the most dangerous job in the yard, because you had all this kind of debris about your feet and one slip, one fall onto this white-hot beam, and you were a goner.

Tom McKendrick speaking on the BBC Scotland EX:S programme *Iron*, 1997.

ON THE SLIPS

The shipyard itself suggests a medieval city, self-contained and animated by a large number of independent trades. You are struck by the number of people walking about, apparently at random, but going from one job to another. Everywhere you see little groups of men or girls, to all appearance detached from any contact with the rest, huddled round some special job. Those welders, older men than the general run, who are doing the upright welding and not the easy welding on the flat, are working on a collection of conning towers for submarines. Stuck down there, the conning towers look like enormous pepper pots. These two flour-whitened youths stirring that white powder and paste are mixing the insulating material that will go on the walls of destroyers; those others are loading up the asphalt that goes into the anti-aircraft armour. This group following the crane are taking what is called the 'coffin' plate to the new tanker. Those girls are going on to a launched ship with their paint pots.

You hear a whistle from somewhere in the belly of the ship, and the plate with its lace of holes at the edges is stopped in its descent and men seize it to bolt it into place. Those bolts have to come out when the riveter gets to work, and a woman has got a wrench on them. The riveter is a man who will work anywhere on a ship. He may be sitting with his legs dangling from a plank behind the mesh of scaffolding on the ship's side. He may be down in the darkness, that dead steel darkness of 'tween decks, which hangs in a ship when it is just a collection of rusted steel boxes stacked together, before the paint has lightened and civilised it. He may be working on the high, wide flight deck of an aircraft carrier, on the giddy projection of its gun emplacements, on its bridge that rises like a tin hotel on one side amidships. The wind can blow pretty well strong enough across the shelterless deck to blow a man down. The riveter, like the welder, may have to go down inside the oil tanks of a tanker, where he will work with his lamp and his fan in the fumes, and you wonder that there is room for the man and the noise together inside that cistern.

From V. S. Pritchett's *Build the Ships* of 1946.

INSIDE THE SHIP

The noise of building reaches a note and volume which are unimaginable. From the distance it sounds like a thick gale of wind in a forest; in the yard itself, as the riveters' sparks dribble down from the ship's side, you seem to have got into a hot corner of a gunman's skirmish. In the yard you could hear if you shouted. Here your shouts are knocked clean out. You have to dodge around a corner and hope one word in six will reach the ear that is leaned towards you. The roar comes from above, below and on either side of you – a pandemonium of clangings, rappings and sawn-off-gun work, with men making rival roars in an alley-way a yard wide, that at first causes terror as you grope through the darkness. Hundreds of men seem to be lying, kneeling, crouching, crawling about. Here is a group of men chipping the top of an air-tight oil hatch. Those stage-lighting flashes are the eternal welders, the boys. For the caulkers are at work, easing up the edges of the plates to the rivet heads, to make the ship watertight and sound. You step over their heads and legs. Once in a while a face which has gone beyond indignation and resignation into a world of its own looks up from the level of your knees. It is the face of some caulker coming up for air after twenty people in boots that are not light have stepped over him as he worked.

You look down into the body of the ship, through the smoke haze of the riveters' fires, and watch the men step about there like little demons in the galleries of Dante's hell. It is like looking down the side of a bombed-out house, each storey naked and revealed.

From V. S. Pritchett's *Build the Ships* of 1946.

WOMEN'S WORK

Shipbuilding! The very word rings like the clanking of innumerable hammers, and creates the mind vision of tall, gaunt shipsides, propped by scaffolding; of men like adventurous little pygmies clambering all over them hammering, riveting, hammering – clankety clank – unceasing, monotonous, deafening. A man's job, you are thinking.

And then you see a figure, clad in blouse, tiny close-fitting cap, and what seem to be breeches, clambering also. Comical figure for a man you think, and suddenly you see it is not a man but a woman, and further that she is painting. You admire her, you cannot help it, nor should you if you could. She is one of a legion of women who, amid all those who have so gallantly tackled the men's jobs have hit on the shipyards as their sphere – have invaded the 'heart of the fortress' from the toiling, sweating, pre-war man's point of view.

The tasks women are doing in and about the yards and marine engineering shops are innumerable. That fact tempted an engineer to say two years ago that by 1918 women would be able to build a battle ship from keel to aerials. Too optimistic a statement, maybe, but let us consider for a moment what they have actually done.

I have before me a carefully compiled record of the multifarious jobs being done, and well, by women in and about shipyards and marine engineering

shops. Before setting them down I will quote the words of an eminent Scottish shipyard expert: 'Strength and endurance alone prevent women from doing all the jobs. They are intelligent enough – more intelligent than many of the men; they work hard; they don't get "fed up" with doing the same job constantly. Give them a repetition job that makes good pay, and they will go on with it week after week – quite happily. But there are jobs they cannot do: heavy riveting; working up to their knees in water and mud repairing the keel of a ship, moving ships around the yard, and so on.'

On board women are fitting electrical apparatus for yard lighting, mains and telephones, and doing complex wiring work generally. Also they are chipping, scraping and painting (doing dredgers and steam hoppers externally and internally). In the yards they are hydraulic riveting, scraping and coating the bottoms of destroyers and submarines, driving cranes (some of 50 tons), French polishing, labouring (carrying 60lb weights singly), loading into wagons and barges, cleaning and painting chain cables.

In the workshops in or near the yards they make and repair the overalls and 'Fearnaught' clothing, make flags and sails, and do upholstery. Many had thought that wood-working machinery ran at too high a speed for women, but women are operating machines for wood planing and for making wooden boiler plugs.

The engineering shops find them working 6in. and 8in. slotting machines, horizontal and vertical drilling machines and turret and capstan lathes (non-repetition work in very many cases and the women setting up their own tools). One woman, said to be able to turn her hand to any job, operates a radial turret drilling machine with capstan head which performs six operations. Overhead cranes are driven by women, and one woman drives a travelling jib crane among the small lathes. They are generally employed on radial and sensitive drills and milling machines and turbine blades are made and assembled by them. Women are also acetylene welding, nut facing and acting as plumbers' assistants. In the foundries they are machine moulding, core making, grinding, packing and sorting.

The boiler shops find them work drilling, boring, turning, slotting, helping light platers, painting, assisting with rivet machines, pickling boiler tubes, and plugging them, and turning tube expander mandrils. They are fitting and filing pipe and valve flanges, filters and valves, and bending super heater tubes. They are constantly working in the rigging house on wire ropes of $1^1/_2$ inch and have done 2 inches. In the braziers' shops they are repairing lamps and soldering.

Of the more readily suitable jobs, such as tracing, store keeping, time clerking, scutching and spinning fibre in rope shops, looking after switchboards in generating stations, and lacquering, there are a great number.

All these are not jobs ideally suited to women. That the women are doing them, and on the whole well, is sufficient tribute to their fearless adventuring on any task open to them, to their inspiring industry and their great and whole-hearted championship of the cause of humanity – the Allied cause.

By a correspondent to the *Daily Chronicle* of 9 May 1918.

Opposite: A girl welder. During the World Wars many women went to work in the shipyards. Photograph by Cecil Beaton, 1943. (Imperial War Museum)

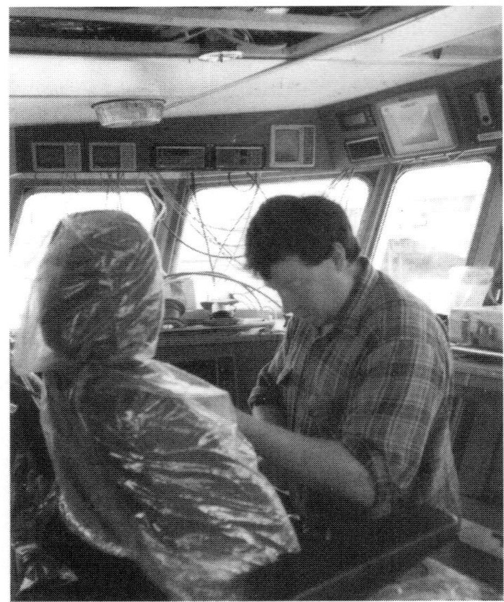

David Stephen wiring up the bridge on board the *Pleiades* at Buckie Shipyard. (Author's collection)

Right: Fitting out the QE2. Most of the pipework has been installed, some partitions have been erected and the electricians are starting to wire up the cabins. (Scottish Maritime Museum)

GETTING READY FOR SEA

There was plenty to interest him about the decks of the *Estramadura*. With a technician's contempt he looked at what the furnishers and decorators were doing to the saloons and cabins – dolling them up like boudoirs, and making, as an old foreman had once bitterly remarked, a whore's bedroom of a good ship. The South American taste was imposing on this one decorative ideas of unusual effulgence, and Leslie was glad to pass from these landlubberly excesses down to the engine-room where the real men in their dungarees were happy in their battle with the fretful complications of a huge power unit – a fractious beast in early youth but destined to lovely efficiency before it would pass out of their hands.

It was a joy for him to walk along the lighted alley-ways, to smell the fresh paint, to see this squad and that at their appointed tasks, all labouring according to a beautifully coherent plan to get the ship ready for the sea. Here were electricians, infallibly expert, testing circuits. On the promenade deck the caulkers were busy, so quick with chisel and mallet and tarred fibre that it was at once a delight and an education to watch them. There were more electrcians on the navigating bridge; a fractional error in their trials of the vessel's nerves might cost a thousand lives. At one point he came on a solitary man lost in the task of adjusting to a nicety the control-panel in the wireless cabin.

From George Blake's novel *The Shipbuilders*, 1935.

THE RED-LEADERS

MacKelvie had the toughest gang in the yard – the red-leaders. Theirs was the hardest, dirtiest and most uncertain job in the yard. It called for tough guys and tough guys it got. But MacKelvie had all the natural qualities of a leader and more than any other gaffer in the yard he held his men. And he did it without swearing and blustering – though he could swear to some holy tune when necessary. MacKelvie liked his mates. They were raw but they were genuine – when you got to know them. They weren't angels of course. Razor slashers, wife beaters, incestmongers, adulterers, drunkards, blackmailers, gangsters. . . . But a man, morally rotten, didn't work long with MacKelvie.

MacKelvie's leadership had been cemented by various acts. Once in the bottom of the dock, a leader, who had just started after a long spell of voluntary idleness and who had been living during this period on what the police described as the immoral earnings of his wife, flung down his brush and announced to MacKelvie that he'd had enough. In peculiarly offensive language he announced that his wife could go out to the streets again. MacKelvie promptly laid him out cold. Another man, who had overheard the conversation, emptied his pot of red lead over him.

Another time, when the time-keeper had cheated them out of a special rate, MacKelvie had scribbled a note and had it taken to Boreland. Boreland had sent for MacKelvie and had been so impressed by his fairness and candour that he

Painting the hull of a ship at Harland and Wolff. (Imperial War Museum)

immediately granted MacKelvie's demands, paid him some warm compliments, and then sent for Thomson, the head time-keeper, and severely censured him. The victory MacKelvie had won for his squad, though not a final one, had a permanent effect on MacKelvie's reputation.

Now, while Willie Donald worked with the dock labourers on the forward bollards getting *The Sunflower* properly centred, the red-leaders got into the flat punts and, with two to each side, commenced to wire-brush the plates. At every six feet the pumps stopped and allowed the men to finish till they came down to the rolling keel. MacKelvie himself did not work in the punts (except in some emergency) but directed operations from the dock-side. Not that there was much to direct on this routine job. After a walk round the dock-side he came back and joined the hats.

'There's the gangway, men.'

The craneman lowered the gangway. Simon Forbes, lanky and quick, was aboard even before it was made fast. Thomson, red and uncomfortable, turned towards the office, his eyes hard with hatred.

Thirty red-leaders clambered up the steps from the bottom of the dock. MacKelvie led the procession to the paint store.

Frank Pease had everything in readiness: a paint pot, a brush and a man-help for each man.

'I'd eight drums put down on the dock-side – that enough, Jock?'

'That should do.'

'Now get this, pal. I'm slipping across to The 'Aven come four. If you want anything you know where to get it.'

'That's all right.'

'Now come on, me lucky lads. What's that, O'Brien, you fornicating Fenian? They don't need red-leaders in the Green Isle! De Valera, strike me! Say, wot you doing 'ere if 'e's doin' so much for Ireland? Yes: well, you see the Dook of Montrose *is* a dook, see –'

The red-leaders exchanged cheery obscenities with the paint storeman. Had it been the football season there would have been some interesting asides on the relative merits of the Arsenal and the Rangers. But it was Saturday afternoon and the men were anxious to get out to the pub.

Their banter was short and sharp: having got their tools they trooped back to the bottom of the dock to paint the plates of *The Sunflower* with a coating of red-lead as far up as the boot top. In order to reach this height they were supplied with long poles, called man-helps, to the end of which they fixed their brushes. To swing a paint brush in ordinary paint is a tiresome job: to swing heavy red-lead over a rough surface is worse. But to swing a heavy brush on the end of a pole requires great effort and long practice. MacKelvie took a brush along with his men. He was no hat: at best he might be described as a leading hand. A leading hand has always to work with the tools.

From James Barke's novel *Major Operation*, 1936.

THE SHOP STEWARD CONVENOR

'People have very little idea of what a shop steward's job really is,' he says, 'Especially newspaper reporters. The newspapers always blame the shop stewards when there's a strike. But though the shop steward has a responsibity to point the way and lead the men as best he can, in the end the men decide.

'Strictly speaking my job is to hold meetings and pass on to the shop stewards any union or outside matters that have arisen, but there are a lot of personal things too – speaking to the management on this or that man's behalf, arranging more convenient timetables with the bus company, that kind of thing. And of course I have to carry messages both ways, men to management, management to men.

'I don't like a fight, though I'm prepared to have one if necessary. I believe in harmony, and that means I have to see both sides of a question. Otherwise it would be a waste of time. You can't judge a case on one side only.'

Patrick Burden quoted in the *Lithgow Journal*, Winter 1966/67.

THE LAST HORSE

Men and women were not the only workers in the shipyards. For a long time many of the yards also employed horses, which were used to transport material around the yard.

Darkie lingered on more for the sake of sentiment than anything else, an anachronism in a modern shipyard; but we were sorry to see him go.

'Horses could go where the lorries couldn't go, in the muddy places, the tight places. They were the cheapest form of short transport, and for that matter they still are. I'm very fond of horses and I believe that if the loads hadn't grown too heavy there would be horses in the shipyards yet.

'Until the first war', says Mr Pollock, 'they carried everything, heavy and light, even hauling loads to Glasgow if they were wanted there for fitting out. The steel for the yards came by rail to the station and was taken from there in one-horse loads, usually two plates of 2 tons each on a lorry weighing 30 cwt. A trace horse waited where the Plaza cinema now stands, ready to help with the gradient up to the East Yard. Rivets were distributed by horse from the station to the yards, as was all timber that was not floated in from the ponds.'

The big lifts – masts, parts of engines, rudder frames – were tackled by teams of horses, sometimes as many as twenty to a team: a single animal was harnessed to the lorry and the rest were arranged ahead of it in ranks of three, heaving on the traces.

All the horses had holidays, often more of them than men had in those days. They averaged two or three weeks a year out to grass; but the duration varied from beast to beast.

'The death rate was fairly high,' says Mr Pollock. 'The average working life of a horse in heavy work was five or six years only. In those days the price of a horse might be £10 average to £90 for a very good one, and you could feed them on good home-grown hay, good oats and good bran for 25s. a week. During the first war the price shot up to £200 for an ordinary working animal (think what that

Susie Loftus was in charge of the horse that moved the plates from the plater's shed to the berth at Harland and Wolff's yard during the First World War. Horses were a common feature of shipyards until the 1950s. (Imperial War Museum)

is in today's money), but it soon slipped back. Then there was a strange thing in the 1930s. A market grew up with the Continent in horse-meat for human consumption, slaughtered in this country and then exported, and when that happened any horse was worth £50 and that became the basic price. It still is, £50 to £60, so that's where you start from. A decent working horse today costs £80 to £150 and you'll be lucky to find one.'

The carters, he says, were in general very good men, able to stand up for themselves, often rough but good at their job. Those in the yard were a breed apart, trained to the work, different in their skills from the sugar carters in Greenock, or the wool carters. Many of them became tradesmen and foremen in the yards, and two became yard managers. The worst of them regarded their animals as so much flesh to be used. But most were fond of their horses and treated them well. A good carter and a good horse could work wonderfully well together.

'That last horse, Darkie, he was a bright one. He did a lot on his own, and he knew where to go for his morning roll and his afternoon cookie – a woman gave them to him every day, and they had to be in the right order. I paid £160 for him, and he worked in Lithgow's plumbers' shop for five years. Every year he went to Kilbarchan and pulled a 200-year-old fire engine in the annual procession. He was a quiet, innocent beast.'

For the last three of his years with Lithgow's, Darkie was the only horse in a yard where all the haulage was mechanised and tractors moved the loads which once would have brought out the 20-horse teams. Now he has gone – and not, we are pleased to say, to the Continent. Mr Pollock sold him to a dealer on condition that he would be re-sold as a work horse. He has settled in contentedly on a farm near Lenzie.

From the *Scott Lithgow Journal*, No. 4, 1970.

A SHIPYARD OFFICE

I was on my way to a shipbuilding office where I had once worked for several years. During my time there had been twelve clerks in it; they had now shrunk to six, and the six were on half-time and half-pay. Like the unemployed they were all sunburnt, since they spent half their days in enforced leisure. The office had always been a pleasant one to work in; for the cashier, an old gentleman now dead, had for fifty years or so resisted the importunities of travellers for newfangled devices such as adding-machines and filing systems, and had stuck to the methods he had found in operation when he entered the office as a junior clerk. When that could have been I have no idea, probably about 1860. We were all proud of him, and grateful for the way in which he left us to ourselves: I have never been in a little community where such an idyllic and quietistic atmosphere reigned. Something of it still remained when I paid my visit.

From *Scottish Journey* by Edwin Muir, 1935.

COUNTING OUT THE PAY

I used to count for the Caulking Department. Count the work the men did each day. If they worked overtime I would check them in, check them out and keep a record of their time and pay them according to the rates.

You got to your wee office, your time box, in the morning at quarter past seven. You had about a hundred and fifty men to check in with their badge numbers. You marked them in and docked them if they were late. You did the same in the afternoon. You went back to your office and marked them two strokes for morning and afternoon. When it came to overtime they'd completed, there was a wee space on the form where you would add up their premium hours, normal hours and overtime hours. It was quite a straightforward sort of job.

When you got on the boat, you'd ask the man what he'd done and he would show you. Then you had to take a note back to the office, make a copy, which the foreman signed. He would then give you a slip of paper and say: 'Give that man a penny an hour', which was a penny extra and quite a bit back then. Then

The sales and estimating department of Alexander Stephen's engineering works in 1968. (Scottish Maritime Museum)

Right:
In the drawing office. Photograph by Cecil Beaton, 1943. (Imperial War Museum)

we would calculate the pay and send it to the counting house where they would take off their tax, any savings, and make up his packet.

The packet then came to the time box. The wages clerk came in with the big box. The men were outside standing in numerical order. I was there to see that the men were getting the proper packets, and you took a note of the pay packets that were left. You countersigned. Then you were away home.

Willie Miller, timekeeper at John Brown's, speaking to Ian Johnston and Lewis Johnman in *Granta 61: The Sea*, 1998.

THE DRAWING OFFICE

After the dust, the cold wind and racket of the shipyard, the drawing office is quiet and warm. In the high, light room the air is almost aromatic with the smells of polished wood, pencil sharpenings, tracing paper and Indian ink. The gold-rimmed spectacles of the draughtsmen catch the light as their heads turn. The silence is studious: it is broken only by the discreet step of shoes on the linoleum or the soft swish of the tracing paper as clean hands roll it back and weight it down with the heavy, round rulers. The draughtsmen rarely look up when the stranger comes into a room, and you do not catch them nodding at each other as the men in the yard do, when you go out. Most of these men in the drawing offices come from the secondary schools; some of them get first-hand experience in the yard; the ones who will have executive jobs later on have probably gone to the university in the winter months, to get their B.Sc. in naval architecture, and work in the drawing office in the summer.

From V. S. Pritchett's *Build the Ships* of 1946

A FINE ART

My final year was spent in the Drawing Office among the soft-talking, paper-rustling, elite of the shipyard where I learned to fashion the ultimate and perfect 4H chisel-edge pencil, capable – if used – of making the very whisper of a line which had direction but no thickness. A line capable of transporting any female tracer to a distraction of delight and possibly an eye-specialist.

From Tom Gallacher's novel *Apprentice*, 1983.

LADY TRACERS

These are the demure damsels of tender age known as lady Tracers whose occupation (owing to the present exorbitant price of chocolates) mainly consists of deciphering technical constructional hieroglyphics and making facsimiles thereof with more or less success on specially prepared translucent fabric, by means of cunningly devised instruments periodically charged with diverse coloured opaque elements held in suspension in suitable liquid media, in the accomplishment of which (like all true Artists who see things in a particular light) they reproduce as 'they see', thus adding that piquant feminine touch which periodically prevents the draughtsman suffering from ennui.

From a satirical look at the yard's trades by an anonymous contributor to the *Linthouse Works Magazine* in March 1920.

THE SHIP MANAGER

Mr Andrew McLaughlin, at 47 years old, is the youngest of the firm's four senior ship managers. The fitting-out manager; the man who gets drawings of ships and translates them into teams of skilled men. The man who is the link between the white-collar workers and the blue.

The organisation of his day is deceptively simple. Start at 7:30 in the morning. Until 9 he is on the ship – at present the Swedish-America liner *Kungsholm* – looking at the work ('you never trust anyone'), meeting all his foremen at the side of the ship, detailing work and passing on worries developed during the night ('you can't stop thinking about a ship; it's with you all the time'). Then back up the outside iron stair-case to his office which overlooks both the *Kungsholm* and the berth for the Q4. There to pore over the drawings again, the ship divided into different sections, criss-crossed in different colours to show the stage it is at, the work that is being done. A general with his battle plans, calculating forces, deploying, strengthening, strategy – although in this context it is called planning – the essence of his work, which means his life. In the afternoon the same routine. The walk over the ship, missing very little; meeting the foremen; then back to the plans.

He was born, and has lived all his life, in Clydebank. He has two brothers also at John Brown's, although his father was a fireman in the town. For young Andrew there was never any doubt about where he was going, and at 17 he became an apprentice ship's draughtsman at Brown's. As with all such apprenticeships at that time, the management laid great emphasis on a truly rounded experience of all the work in the yard. So Andrew served time with the various trades – practical experience of the highest value, for at present he has directly under his chain of command electricians and plumbers, joiners and carpenters, sheet-metal workers and platers, welders and caulkers, and engineers.

From then on it was up and up, with the big break coming when he was promoted out of the drawing offices to the managerial side. Now the statutory bowler sits easily on his head, and as he walks confidently around the yard and over his ship, a man in control of his job and happy at it.

From David Rose's article 'Three Vital Members of the Body of a Firm called John Brown's' in *Scotland*, 1966.

A DIRECTOR'S JOB

In the various references I have recorded relating to the activities of my brother and myself, it might appear that I have given insufficient credit to Amos's share of our work. In the Burntisland venture he was, of course, my equal partner; he and I had increasingly risked all we possessed, and often indeed more. It was always a joint affair. We shared the risks, disappointments and failures; but we enjoyed the successes and rewards of our enterprise. We were not always in complete agreement on matters of policy, which, I think, was a good thing. Being five years junior in age, I may have been inclined to advocate taking greater risks in certain matters than Amos thought prudent. Perhaps the few years of disparity in age distinguished our viewpoints. It may be, he was right in imposing a measure of restraint on my virility at this time. Indeed, I am sure that whatever success we ultimately achieved during our Burntisland partnership was largely due to the fact that, in our respective outlooks, we often appeared to be opposites. Obviously, I was the adventurer, Amos the brake.

At the inception, we had mutually agreed our respective spheres of work in the day to day affairs of administration. Amos chose the path of looking after industrial and labour problems, for which he was well qualified through his activity in the Shipbuilding Employers' Federation which dealt, primarily, with all labour matters, and later through the Conference, others affecting the general welfare of the industry, commercial problems and their concern with Government departments. Through his clear vision and industry he became a tower of strength to the Federation. He knew his way through the Civil Service hierarchy, and he was able to influence many difficult and important industrial negotiations with Government committees and the trades unions to the benefit, not only of Burntisland, but of the British shipbuilding industry. He revelled in this aspect of his work. I was grateful that he had chosen this kind of activity because I had never been able to arouse much serious interest in wage and trade union negotiations. In matters of ship research, Amos was keenly interested in questions of hull design, analysis of data derived from experimental tank tests and propeller design and efficiency, all of which added to our store of technical 'know how' and brought some fame to our ship designs.

In our respective assignments it was agreed that I would undertake all questions of finance, ship designing, estimating, price tendering and development of our selling organisation. These divisions of responsibility worked out harmoniously, although it involved me in much travelling which, of course, was an essential adjunct of my job. While shipbuilding yards, here and there, were folding up, we had complete confidence in our determination to survive, whatever the future was for shipbuilding. If, on occasion, I felt that I was bearing the heaviest burden of our operations, I was satisfied that Amos was doing a worthwhile job of work. He had a flair for economics, which subject aroused little interest in me.

From Wilfred Ayre's memoirs, *A Shipbuilder's Yesterdays*, 1968.

CHAPTER THREE

DIRT AND DANGER

The yards were extremely dangerous places. The men had to work all year round in the open air with little or no protection from the elements. There was no safety gear to speak of. The workers simply wore everyday clothes and boots that they had to buy themselves. The only form of protective safety wear in the yards were the bowler hats of the bosses, which protected them from any stray rivets that might fall on them.

All sorts of injuries were common: falling off staging; getting caught in machinery; sparks in the eyes; being crushed under falling plates. To give an example of the number of accidents in just one yard in one year, the works ambulance report for Stephen's yard in 1921 gives the following statistics:

Total number of dressings 10,824; cases sent to Western Infirmary 103; cases sent to Eye Infirmary 64; accidents ending fatally 3; number of bandages used 30 gross (roughly 13 miles of bandage), plus 45lbs cotton wool, 40lbs lint and 30 gallons of Eusol.

As well as injuries, there were many other ailments that shipyard workers were prone to. Pneumatic riveters and caulkers suffered 'white finger' from the constant vibration of the drills; asbestos workers were so covered in asbestos that they were called 'white mice', and frequently they developed asbestosis, an inflammation of the lungs caused by inhalation of asbestos dust; fumes from oil, paint and welding caused other chest problems; and of course every worker suffered from industrial deafness. This was so common that an unofficial sign language was developed in the yards.

Sanitation was a chronic problem in the yards. As the official toilets were usually a long way from the work sites and use of them could risk the loss of a quarter of an hour's pay, it was no wonder that many chose not to use them. Despite all the dirt and grime that the workers had to endure, there was little provision for them to clean themselves. They went home smelly and dirty in their working clothes.

In most yards an accident fund was set up, funded by a levy on pay and usually also by the fines exacted for any breaches of yard regulations. If a worker could not work he was paid sick-pay from the accident fund, which amounted to a little over half pay. While this might provide a little succour to the injured man, it was no help to his squad. If a squad could not operate its members did not get paid, so an injury to one man could leave four or five men without a wage until a replacement could be found.

If a worker died, his widow might receive payment from the yard's benevolent fund. Not all yards had benevolent funds, however, and in these cases the widow would simply receive a whip-round from her husband's fellow workers. It was not until the Workman's Compensation Bill of 1898 that employers were liable to pay compensation, even if the accident had been a result of the shipyard's negligence.

Although injuries were feared by the men, they were so commonplace that they were almost accepted as an inevitable part of the job. The highly dangerous nature of the work also helped to build a common bond among the shipbuilders and increased their pride in being able to survive in such a harsh environment. In fact, the men were very resistant to new safety measures, such as hard hats and protective goggles, when they were introduced in the 1960s. They were hard men and felt that wearing safety gear was somehow a sign of weakness. This constant living in danger often found a release in humour, and many a joke was cracked in response to some awful calamity.

Previous page: On the deck of a new battle cruiser under construction at John Brown's during the First World War. Working high up on the exposed deck of a large ship could be very unpleasant in bad weather. (Imperial War Museum)

SHIPYARD SYMPHONY

The pneumatic drills beat shattering drum-like rolls on the steel plates; the rivet hammers beat like crazed woodpeckers; a plate slammed on the deck with a roar of protest: the gaunt holds reverberating in sympathy.

A rivet boy, whose rags were permeated with iron rust and powdered with a steel dust, toasted a rivet in his coke heater. Cornering a sound pocket behind the growing poop deck, he sang softly:

'I fear no a foe where'er I go
On the good ship Yakahickadoola.'

On the river, on her way to Princes Dock, *The City of Bengal* gave a throaty growl. A perky little tug yapped back.

From the sawmill at the head of number five berth, the saws shrieked and whined and moaned – *accelerando* – *rallentando*. But when was Bob Wyllie going to blow the whistle?

Opposite, in the platers' shed a wagon of steel plates was being unloaded. A hole-punching machine beat time. Perhaps the iron clerk was deaf. He lit a Woodbine and smiled sickly, ticking off a receive note. Music when soft voices die. . . .

The iron thunder was split with a shriek. The iron clerk dropped his cigarette and ran.

Christ! his leg was right through the rollers – above the knee. *Reverse the*

In the plate shop. Handling raw steel and working with heavy machinery were constant hazards in the shipyards. (Imperial War Museum)

bastard. Mary, Mother of God – that human blood could spurt like that!

'The horn'll blaw ony minute. Get the ambulance man afore he beats it.'

Fred Porter: storeman and first-aid man. He lived in Govan, across the river. You had to move some to be first in the queue for the ferry. He had washed his hands in naptha and locked up everything except the main door. The iron clerk crashed it open.

'What the hell – an accident? Jesus Christ – miss the bloody ferry another night.'

But his forefinger was rattling the receiver hook.

'Ambulance!'

Bob Wyllie raised his arm, pulled the hooter chain and nipped back into his box for safety. The flood gates were open: the stampede was on. Get in the way and be trampled to death.

Two plate-workers, carrying their dying mate to the store, were caught in the stream of liberated toilers.

'Gangway there!'

'Watch where the hell you're going!'

'Out o' the bloody road there!'

'What's the matter?'

'Oh, Christ . . .'

David Ramsey turned to look. He was knocked to the side, pummelled, pushed, shoved against the brick wall of the time office. In their blind desperate rush they didn't see him – didn't know.

The first wave of escaping workers had passed. The stream was becoming a trickle. David, overcoming the first spasm of nausea, staggered on. At the head of Dock Street he met the ambulance nosing its way determinedly forward. Workers stepped smartly aside to clear a passage. They turned anxious faces to each other. Has there been an accident? Must have been! Never heard! Not in our squad . . .

From James Barke's novel *The Land of the Leal*, 1939.

GLASGOW BRONCHITIS

I started in the yard in 1940, and I was struck with how old the men were, working in there. They were old men at forty. And the common thing: everyone seemed to spit. . . . Everyone had the Glasgow bronchitis: they all seemed to be bronchial. And once you went into the ships, it was easy to see why. There was no heating, they were cold, damp places. In the winter, the prevailing wind coming up the Clyde – the southwest wind – if you put your hand on the ship, your hand was liable to stick to it.

Pat, a foreman shipwright, speaking in *Made in Govan: An oral history of shipbuilding on the Upper Clyde 1930–1950*, 1991.

Opposite: Looking down through a partly constructed ship. One of the most common accidents was falling from staging or from unprotected deck edges. (Glasgow Museums)

WHEN WE BUILT THE BIG SHIPS

'Twas a Monday morn and the snaw was blawin'
o'er Yarrow's Yard in Scotstoun
when the lads did a dance thro' the big steel doors
in sartorial elegance wi' their woolly drawers
and umpteen pair o' socks on.

The weekend that had passed
got a verbal blast
that was high up on the agenda
Celts and Rangers both had won
and the Pubs had made a ton
noo the money was a' done
'Pss! Hey Jimmy, hiv ye seen the money lender?'

Then slow but sure came a familiar noise
as the steel breathed life, in rhythm wi' the boys
bolts were screwed and timber hewed
and engines put in position
gun turrets were marked
and welding rods sparked
'Naw . . . this boat's no' for fishin'!'

The giant cranes towered o'er the bleak shipyard
like massive grey flamingoes
letting oot their tongues, looking for food
as doon the oily sling goes
lifting loads here
an' laying them doon there
withoot even perspirin'
nae aches or pains
nae airms that were sair
for their diet wis strictly . . . iron.

And the cauld river blaws
excited the pace
of oor frozen fish-fingers
and blue tinted face
but oor bodies were conditioned
to beat the Big Freeze
by a can o' hot tea
an' a big 'piece' 'n' cheese
and Dumbarton Road has premises
tae gie us some mair cheer
a wee bet in the Bookies
or a big pint o' beer.

Opposite top:
The noise from pneumatic caulkers was incredible. Here A. McGavin is gouging a shell seam at Lithgow's without any ear protection.
(Glasgow University Archives)

Opposite bottom:
Working at a forge. Despite the extreme heat and danger the only protection this worker has is a sackcloth apron.
(Imperial War Museum)

Then in the afternoon we gave an encore
of oor efforts on the morn
workin' haun in haun taegether
for in spite o' the cauld weather
the Shipbuilding still goes on
for we're used tae this work
amongst damp an' cauld an' dirt
sometimes wi' heartbreak and pain
but we're all right Jack
the boilersuit's on oor back
but we've nae boilersuits on oor brain.

Ye see there's some high-up folks
that think that us blokes
represent the subservient knee
but they're never considerin'
that the goods we're deliverin'
sign freedom and seal dignity
as three thousand men
dae daily attend
tae the ship's every need
stage by stage
leavin' beds that are warm
for great deeds tae perform
fulfilling their Heritage.

Then the clock shouts 'half fowr'
and the day's work is o'er
it's hame tae a big warm meal
for we've done oor wee bit
in the name o This Land
tae satisfy the conscience
tae justify the man
and contentment's what we feel
and we started this morn
in cauld December's haun
when the snaw was blawin'
o'er Yarrow's Yard in Scotstoun.

From Alfred Forbes Smith's *A Parochial View of Glasgow*, 1997

THE COLD

Very cold in the yards, on the cold frosty mornings, and there was no heating at all, of course, in the yards, especially if you were working on the stocks. If the boat was in the wet basin, there was a chance of maybe steam in certain parts of it. It was maybe steaming up, you see. That's after it's been launched, of course. But in the actual process of building the boat from the keel, and the ribs, et cetera, and the insulation of the various cabins and departments and engining it, et cetera, it was very, very cold. You had to be well wrapped up, because you were exposed to the vagaries of the climate. There was no shelter at all, none whatsoever. Whether it rained or snowed you were there. Your tools were part of the job. You wiped the snow off. And it's been known for the spanner to stick to the hands. You had to be very cautious.

Colin, an engineer, speaking in *Made in Govan: An oral history of shipbuilding on the Upper Clyde 1930–1950*, 1991.

SNOW

A shipyard is not a pleasant place to work, especially in the winter. Before I began painting shipyard scenes there was many a day I hated going in to work. One evening while working late I was on the deck at the hatch guiding ventilation into the engine room. The engine room hatch is up level with the funnel and it had started to snow. There was only one way to signal the crane driver, which meant my outstretched arm had snow blowing right up it. I have seen us having to dig jobs out of the snow in the morning to rig them up for a crane lift and having to stand in the cold all day before getting a lift.

From Jim Collins' unpublished memoirs.

THE RUST

The dirt was the other thing. The theory at that time was, you got the plate from the mills, and there would be blue mill scale on them. Now that mill scale will come off eventually. It was a very expensive thing, in those days, it would have been very expensive, to chip that mill scale off, or to grind it off. So the theory was, you allowed the plate to weather. You simply fashioned the plate, rolled it, drilled it, riveted it, whatever, put it on the ship, and let it weather, until eventually the mill scale would fall off, and there would be a patina of rust on it. Then dimpled so you had a texture. And the theory was the paint would adhere to this. We know now it was rubbish, but that was the way it was. As a result, when you went in to the ship, if you were silly enough to take your hat off, and the riveters started riveting, then all this rust just fell on top of your head, you know. It was absolutely filthy.

Pat, a foreman shipwright, speaking in *Made in Govan: An oral history of shipbuilding on the Upper Clyde 1930–1950*, 1991.

WORKING CLOTHES

The situation was that you were not provided with protective clothing, unless you were a blacksmith: they might give you a brat or something like that. But the general run of the mill, the idea was you went to your work in rags. . . . I'd never been in a shipyard, but I quickly learned, when I was dressing myself for work, I would go round the family and ask brothers if they had any old jackets, any old trousers, to wear to the yard, the place was so filthy.

Pat, a foreman shipwright, speaking in *Made in Govan: An oral history of shipbuilding on the Upper Clyde 1930–1950*, 1991.

WALKING RAGBAGS

You couldnae get a dirtier job. . . You were black from head to foot: grime and sweat. Every riveter's shirt was torn – we walked about the shipyard like ragbags. There were no overalls, the only thing they gave you was a pair of gloves and you had to pay for them. Moleskin trousers were the favourite with riveters because they were hardwearing: they got so thick wi' oil they were like leather. . . You bought a pair of moleskins for your work, and they had to last you six months. When you took them off at night they could stand up themselves. Nobody ever washed moleskins; when a riveter came home he just dropped them off and put them into the press until the next morning. Moleskin trousers and a grey flannel shirt to soak up the sweat was the attire for the summertime. In the wintertime it was all sorts of gear – all sorts of old jackets and cardigans, all patches. We were like walking ragbags.

From Alan McKinlay's oral history of John Brown's shipyard between the World Wars, *Making Ships, Making Men*, 1991.

MOLESKIN TROUSERS

John stumbled in from the parlour, rubbing the sleep from his eyes, looking like a nigger-minstrel who has partially removed his burnt-cork complexion, his blond hair bedimmed with dirt and machine-oil. On returning from work at six a.m. he had thrown himself half-dressed and unwashed on the bed and had fallen into a profound sleep . . . then he stripped to the waist and began washing off the ingrained dirt and oil of two days and nights overtime at the shipyards. When he had finished he also stood posing admiring his muscles, filling the small mirror by the window with a fatuous smile of satisfaction. He was a plater's labourer. He helped the platers to place in position for the riveters the steel plates on the hulls of ships. He said that work fairly put the muscles on a man. . . . After his long spell of overtime, John said he felt as fresh as a daisy with only six hours' sleep. He looked at his moleskin trousers, stiff with rust, dirt and machine-oil, hanging like pipestems down his legs, and remarked that he had been three days in them without taking them off and what a fine pair they were.

From Edward Gaiten's novel *Dance of the Apprentices*, 1948.

RIVER DEBRIS

The floating carcass of the dog stank high to the cabins of the tower cranes. A pair of thigh boots tramped juicily in the sludge, stiffened and angled forward as Neilly plied his boat-hook. The dog was gaffed behind the neck, steered through the scaffolding uprights and pilings and made landfall at the end of the slipway.

Up on the skeletal structure of a ship, a squad of platers made great play of holding noses and screwing up faces. One wag roared down, 'Away to the store for some Aw dee Colong!'

Neilly ignored the remark. A final heave lugged the animal on to the bank. He laid the hook aside and grunted with satisfaction.

Neilly was proud that Burnhill Shipyard had the cleanest tidemark on the river. Even in the filthiest mood, the Clyde threw up nothing Neilly couldn't remove. Only a man of Neilly's sense of duty could have tackled its jetsam.

Neilly opened his toolbag and examined the contents like a golf champion. He selected a cleek, impaled the dog and dragged it along the shore to a small mountain of driftwood.

From a paraffin drum, Neilly withdrew a rod with a mop of waste attached. He emptied the oil on the wood, removed his elbow-length gloves, and put a match to the taper.

The flames lighted his silver-stubbled face. He bowed as if in deference to the animal. Neilly was a bachelor and had no relatives. Perhaps he felt that solitary creatures should preserve the decencies.

When the debris was well alight, Neilly collected his hooks and tongs and made his way across the shipyard. As he passed the building berths, men shouted greetings to him. 'Fine day, Neilly!' 'Any boadies, Neilly?'

He acknowledged them all, knowing their respect was deserved. Only for his work, the place might be reeking with the plague.

From Jimmy Miller's short story *Money for Dirt*, 1962.

A plumber at work in David Rowan's pipe shop. Even in the 1950s safety gear was almost non-existent. (Glasgow City Archives)

THE NOISE

It was all riveted. The shell was all riveted, the decks, bulkheads, they were all riveted. They talk about decibels. I don't think decibels were invented in these days, because you went on board the ship, and if you wanted to speak to your mate you had to put your mouth up against his ear and shout, because all these pneumatic riveters were working, and caulkers.

Willie, a plumber, speaking in *Made in Govan: An oral history of shipbuilding on the Upper Clyde 1930–1950*, 1991.

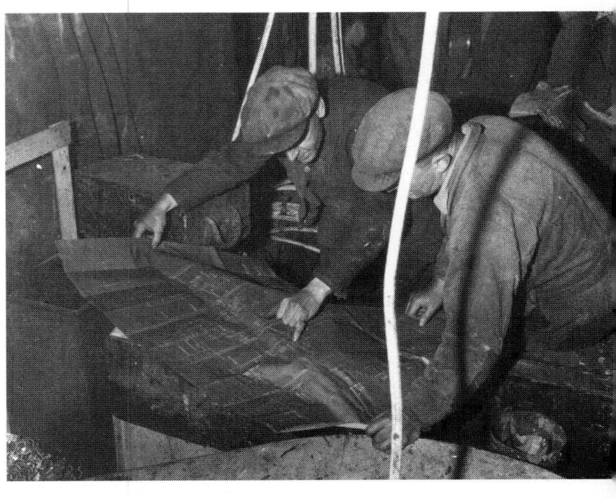

Consulting a blueprint on board a ship at Harland and Wolff. Much of the work on board ship was in small cramped spaces with poor lighting and hazards all around. (Imperial War Museum)

THE PLATER'S SHED

Clutha swung right and passed into the clanging shadows of the main platers' shed. Around him the big punching machines ranked like squatting mastodons, the thud of their beat tearing symmetrical rows of rivet-holes in steel plates, a constant crunch of power that was symbolic. The sack-aproned men who manoeuvred and manhandled the plates through the machines were as grim and grimy in outlook as acolytes in such a cavern had every right to be. They bawled curse and insult at each other with the inconsequence of men already half-deaf and half-daft from a hopeless defiance of din.

From Hugh Munro's novel *Who Told Clutha?*, 1958.

SILENCE

Brian sat on the tank top of the half-built *Kia Ora* holding a candle. It was a dull day outside with a thick fog rolling in from the river. Here, in the hold of the ship, the world had become a dark steel cavern. In the glimmer of the candle-light the black walls of the shell and bulkhead reared up through the shadows to the rosy glow from a rivet fire on the deck above. Now and again the red dusk up there would be splashed with the dancing light from a swinging, sparkling ruby scattering a shower of red stars down through the dark as a riveter grasped a red hot rivet in expert tongs and inserted it into a hole in the bulkhead plates. A bump from his heavy pneumatic hammer splashed sparks again as the rivet was bashed close up to the plate. Then the riveter braced himself for the kick of his hammer, the hanging plank on which he stood swinging out dangerously. Suddenly, from the other side of the bulkhead, came the roar of a pneumatic hammer battering the front of the rivet, while the man above Brian gritted his teeth and hung on to his dancing hammer which threatened to jump from his firm grip at every stroke. For every blow struck on the front of the rivet the hammer above Brian bounced and battered in return. As the soft metal of the hot rivet was crushed into the plate the hammers changed from a dull thudding to a high metallic clanging in a rain of blows tightening the plates together, the steel walls trembling under the terrific fusillade. The din stunned one's mind blank under the high pressure of sound. Then all at once silence.

It was these sudden silences Brian waited for. Not that there was a silence in the ordinary sense of the word. For from all parts of the ship came low bangings and clangings bumpings and crashings shouts whistles blowing and roars from a hundred rivet hammers. But after the terrific tattoo at one's ear ceased there was a comparative silence. So calm and peaceful it seemed to Brian. And the suddenness of it. A screaming nerve-wracking roar and then quick as light it ceased. Silence in the noise, a candle in the dark; just like a quiet pool at the edge of a waterfall.

From Edward Shiels' novel about Beardmore's Dalmuir yard, *Gael over Glasgow*, 1937.

SIGNALS

Finger tap on the wrist
asking for the time

flat horizontal hand
across throat,
a quarter past the hour

rotating finger points skywards
telling the craneman
to raise his straining load

cupped hand under left breast
showing far off figures
what they really are

forefinger and thumb pluck the air
asking for a chalk line

and head nods
to the right for

one more slight turn of
the angle bender,
extra inches on
the pyramid rolls,
a few more pounds of pressure on
the hydraulic press

in a galvanised shed
surrounded by
four walls of mayhem.

From Brian Whittingham's *Ergonomic Workstations and Spinning Teacans*, 1992.

SIGN LANGUAGE

He shortened his vision and grinned at a fellow apprentice who had been making such frantic endeavours to attract Brian's attention. Brian watched him put his hand to his chest, open the palm and gaze into it. Oh, what time was it! From where Brian stood on the top deck he could see over the roofs of Dalmuir to where the huge clock tower on the Singer factory reared high above the buildings. Five minutes to twelve! Turning to face the apprentice again, he drew his hand across his throat and held up five fingers. The apprentice waved a hand and hurried down a ladder.

From Edward Shiels' novel *Gael over Glasgow*, 1937.

I'VE SEEN A FEW DEAD IN MA TIME

Y' didna only have the riveters y' had the caulkers as well, which was the noisiest o' the lot. It was a pneumatic chisel, 2000 times a minute, and you're on the inside an' he's on the outside – you do'ny know he's comin' t' do it. Suddenly, yer brain goes blank, yer stone deaf wi the noise. Industrial deafness was a hazard. We'd got two deaths, they died from industrial deafness, it didna stop at the ear it went straight into the brain. No, there's a lot more in it than jist a ship. It's nice t' see them slidin' intae the water. I wish I'd a pound for every one I've seen. I remember the corvette, the *Hyderbad*, an' Lord and Lady Embray came t' the shipyard t' launch the ship. For the first time, there were Movietone news cameras there, and I was fascinated with it. Everything wis goin' fine; he christened it wi the champagne. Bang! She started t' move and suddenly she slipped right on her side. She took down stagin', air pipes an' cables an' a' thing. She hit the water alright but she took a bit o' a list. That's the head foreman's job; y' can imagine, he's shoutin' fer everybody t' get t' the other side o' the ship. Well, I don't know but that ship was a Jonah. A chap died in the tanks; we had a hell o' a job gettin' him out. We couldna get him out; we were in the bowels o' the ship. You'd give a rattle on the side o' the ship to let them know it was finishin' time – nobody carried watches in those days. Well, he didn't show up, and when we found him he was dead. We couldn't get him out so we sez to the managers, 'We'll hae t' tek off a shell plate t' get him out between the ribs.' 'Ye can't dee 'at!' We had to in the end cause there wis nae other way. He'd got jammed doon there be the propeller, an' the doctor came down wi a nurse an sez, 'You'll hae t' break his legs t' get him out.' We werna goin' t' dee 'at so we took off the plate. I've seen some bad accidents – there wis an engineer screamin' one day. We were liftin' a propeller to swing it in line wi the shaft an' the lugs that held the gear, one o' em broke an' swish, sliced off his leg. Oh yea, I've seen a few dead in ma time.

As a shipyard worker y' belonged to a race on yer own.

Walter Watt, a plater at Hall Russell's yard in Aberdeen, speaking in *Work Welfare and the Price of Fish: Life in Aberdeen 1925–1955*, 1995.

BINGY'S LEG

It was one of those days when the whole day was swamped with work.

Foster was going about like a wounded bear, The job was getting on top of him, but all the same he's inclined to let nobody live when he's in a hurry, and worse, he's not too safe.

I was cutting a lot of small stuff close by one of the big columns that hold up the roof. Foster was moving plates with the crane, but I thought I was well clear.

Foster took a short cut with one plate and brought it close up to the side of the shop where I was working. He had the plate slung on clips, just like pieces of angle bar. They're meant for raising plates about knee-high. The idea is that you balance the load with your hand as you walk with the crane.

The shadow of the plate crossed my goggles and Bingy roared:

'It's no right slung! Bobbie! Bobbie!'

I was wrenched from my kneeling position by Bingy, heard Foster swearing, then the wham of the plate as it hit the floor. I lifted my goggles and saw Bingy with his back to the column, his hands gripping its edges. One edge of the plate pinned his leg to the pillar.

Foster seized the plate and pulled it upright although it must have weighed four hundredweight. Bingy fell away from the column.

The place went silent and welders' flashes died all over the shop.

Bingy lay on the floor with my jacket under his head. We gave him a smoke and waited for the ambulance.

Foster sat on a box and wept and tears on that face was a sight that no man should see. He was moaning; 'It was clear, it was clear. Sully eejit – pulled the burner one way and shoved me the other.'

Bingy pulled on his cigarette. 'Was doing it a' for the best, Bobbie.' His hand was shaking so much that he had a job holding the fag. 'Ach,' he said, 'the best laid schemes – gang aft tae Paisley.'

From Jimmy Miller's short story *Bingy's Leg*, 1957.

I'VE SEEN A LOT OF PEOPLE KILLED

One of our mates got his head chopped right off. He came out of the mines, this fellow. He was kind of raw, you know. So he was over the side of the ship, fixing the rails, and that was the mast there, and the Carley floats. It was a quick release when everything happened. . . . So someone must have touched that and it come down and it chopped his head right off, and his head was in the Carley float. . . . He was running about the deck with no head on, that's the God's truth. Jimmy Russell, his name was, and the chap Doig who got his head out the raft, a year after that he was over on the West Yard testing a Rapier crane – he was a rigger – and the wire broke and it come down and it killed him. I've seen a lot of people killed. In fact it was one of the times when I was working in the smiddy. A chap came in. 'Alex, Alex!' 'What's the matter?' 'There's two men in the water.' So I ran down and the craneman had lowered the crane. They were carpenters. One of them hanging on to the hook. The other bloke was floating about in the water. I flung a rope in and pulled him out. . . . So we got the two of them out, and it was me and another chap that saved them. . . . You see, they were working on the dock side, you see, so they used to fix the wharf, you know, and they fell in. The wood was rotten, so they fell in. Aye, and another time I was going out and there was another one of these Rapier cranes. It fell over on its side, but by good luck there was a lot of pipes, and it fell at an angle. I went over and I pulled the chap out, but see if they pipes hadn't been there, he would have been flattened.

Alex, a blacksmith, speaking in *Made in Govan: An oral history of shipbuilding on the Upper Clyde 1930–1950*, 1991.

GAS

Bob Cunningham, the charge-hand caulker in a Scottish shipyard, looked down approvingly at Jock, one of his apprentices, who had just finished cutting out an opening in the deck of the ship.

'That's good stuff; propane seems to burn more smoothly than acetylene,' he said. 'Right, lad, you'd better get your gear packed up now. Don't leave your torch in this little compartment.'

He walked away as Jock straightened himself up, muttering.

'Och, it's after ten past five. I'll be late home if I have to coil up all my hose. Anyway, I'll be starting here again in the morning. I'll just leave it the way it is.'

He laid his torch on the deck inside the compartment and walked through the doorway to the gas cylinders outside. He was in a hurry, and didn't waste much time turning off the valves before he dashed towards the gangway.

First thing next morning Malcolm, a welder, came walking in through the same doorway with another man, a plater.

'This compartment smells fusty,' he said.

Aye, there's not much air in it with only that one door, but never heed – we shan't be in here long,' replied the other. 'Here's where we have to tack this cleat. Are you ready?'

'Right. Mind your eyes,' said Malcolm, as he bent over the cleat, preparing to strike his arc.

WHOOF!

The moment his rod touched the bulkhead a sheet of flame enveloped them both.

As they stumbled out of the compartment with burnt faces – and the plater's hands were burnt as well – they bumped into Jock.

'What happened?' he asked.

'I don't know,' replied Malcolm. 'The whole place seemed to go up in flames as soon as I made a spark.'

From the *Shipyard Spotlight*, May 1945.

THE JOURNEYMAN

Wurkin piecewurk in the funnel shoap,
buildin quick
but no quick enuff,
cursin an liftin an swerrin
cause it takes too long
tae wait oan the crane-man who
is lookin efter his mate
who stands him a few dinner time bevvies
at the *Seven Seas* public bar
an you know cause
that's wherr you get yir three pint chaser
fur yir ashet pie supper
that yi eat wi yir rusty fingers,
then yi fa oot wi the timekeeper
cause o the stupit time he pit oan the joab
an you kid oan the boey
who wiz daft enuff tae
let yi pit a brush handle
through the arms of his ovies
an you play
spin the hammer
like it wiz yir prize six-shooter
an you laugh when the boey tries it
an it nearly brekks his toes,
an yi go tae the burner
an patter him up
so he'll burn yir joab,
an yi momentarily watch
his torch ignitin
an you watch
the gas yi couldnae see
explodin
like a bomb,
an the cloud of rusty dust
an bodies hidin behind
guillotines an
flangers an
scrap-buckets an
yi squint thru the haze
at the guy that's no therr
cause he's been blown down the passage
wi a hole in his side
that he didnae huv
before yi pattered him up,

Opposite:
A busy scene on the deck of a ship at Harland and Wolff during the First World War. With so many tools, equipment, and braziers littering the deck, and with people all around, it was hardly surprising that accidents happened. (Imperial War Museum)

an yi stoat ower tae the first aider
who pits a dod o cotton-wool stuck oan
wi sellotape, ower yir eye,
an yi realise how lucky yi wur
an how lucky the burner wisnae,
then again,
he could huv been they guy
that fell in the furnace,
the first-aider wisnae much use tae him
neither he wiz.

From Brian Whittingham's collection of poems *Industrial Deafness*, 1990.

BLACKHEADS

Not all industrial injuries were quite so serious . . .

'These blackheids spile ma looks,' said John, facing the mirror, forgetting Norah and religion in concern about some blackheads which showed up vividly on his fair complexion. He took a watch-key from a drawer in the mirror and pressed some out of the bridge of his nose, frowning at the pain. 'It's the machine-oil that does it,' said Francie. 'It gets intae the pores.'

From Edward Gaiten's novel *Dance of the Apprentices*, 1948.

SANITATION

What you've got to remember is, the yard is three quarters of a mile long, and the idea of anyone in the middle of winter being absent from their work, whether they wanted to do it or not, but walking three quarters of a mile in order to go to a toilet. Now the other condition you had there, you'd men who were on piecework, and no way was the riveting squad going to stop while one of them went to the toilet, so the ship – their workplace – became the toilet. And the likes of the plumbers and the other people, if you're going into a corner, it had been used as a urinal for weeks.

There were no facilities for washing; no hot water. There was cold water, certainly, but no hot water. And no soap, not unless you went to the shipwrights and got black soap. No towels in sight, no toilet paper.

Pat, a foreman shipwright, speaking in *Made in Govan: An oral history of shipbuilding on the Upper Clyde 1930–1950*, 1991.

THE LAVVIES

When I was sixteen, a wee fair-haired boy, acne, I worked in the shipyards for a bloke called Sammy Boyd. And he was always trying to get rid of me – 'Oan ye go, son, awa' tae the lavvie,' I spent about five years in the lavvie. These lavvies were like something out of Dickens. The smell was horrendous. People had done obscene drawings on the wall and the years had gouged them into the wall so that even when the painters came and did them you could still see them. And I said to Sammy one day: 'These lavvies are disgusting, horrible places . . .' 'Luxury, son, luxury – ye should have seen them when I was a boy . . .'

According to him in those days there was no door on the cubicles for a start. Hence the popularity of the *Glasgow Herald*, which was – still is – a big paper. There were only half partitions between each lavvie so you could have a chat with the bloke next to you. No toilet seats as we know and love them: it was a bar, a wooden bar and you just hung on it like a budgie. And there were spikes sticking in the wall so that you couldn't lean back. The legs going dead, sitting like that. They didn't have bowls or anything like that. Just a long trough with constant running water . . . So that if the guy at the end did a wee jobbie it would come whooshing down. If the guy had had a curry the night before, everyone knew.

Apparently, the great game for apprentices was to bunch up a newspaper and light it and throw it in the trough so that it would float down ablaze – HELP! Big grown men leaping in the air with their pubic hair ablaze. But Sammy would say: 'They were hardy men in those days, son. They used to beat the flames oot wi' a *hammer*.'

From Billy Connolly's *Gullibles Travels*, 1982.

A CHANGE FOR THE BETTER

When women labour came in, there was an introduction of canteens, leisure rooms, improved toilets, and for the first time lockable toilets. Hitherto, the toilets were a metal trough where the men sat in a line with no privacy, no toilet paper, no running water. There was no means of cleaning yourself. But, as I say, with the arrival of women things did begin to improve.

They became pets. After all, they were the sisters or the daughters of work mates. They were respected. It was appreciated that they had a good improving influence in the shipyards, that when the girls got their rest room, we says, 'Well, can we not at least have toilets you can sit on properly?' When the girls got the facilities for washing and so on, we said, 'Well, at least can we not have a door on the toilet, and how about supplying some toilet paper?' you know. So we learnt from them.

Pat, a foreman shipwright, speaking in *Made in Govan: An oral history of shipbuilding on the Upper Clyde 1930–1950*, 1991.

MINOR IMPROVEMENTS

Yes, things were primitive. They were improving. There were cases, for example, where we put in wash basins and the men decided they didn't want them and they got broken within a very few weeks. I think this rather disheartened the management who were trying to improve conditions. One always had at the back of one's mind the problem of money, all these extra facilities could be very expensive, and we always seemed to be just a little bit short of money.

Sandy Stephen speaking on the BBC Radio Scotland programme *Clydebuilt*, 1990.

RATS!

There's a lot of rats, I mean, oh. There was one jumped at me one time! Aye! That's right. Right on there. It was in eating my piece in my pocket. There were nae

Two women workers take a drink of water from the water fountain. Sanitary conditions in the yards were terrible but when women came into the yards certain improvements had to be made. (Imperial War Museum)

canteen. My piece was cheese, and I took it out, and I seen it all nibbled, so what I done, I just cut the bit, the bad bit off, and roasted it, and ate it for my dinner.

Alex, a blacksmith, speaking in *Made in Govan: An oral history of shipbuilding on the Upper Clyde 1930–1950*, 1991.

MORE RATS

As a ship is constructed from the keel upwards, heavy equipment is installed on the relevant deck and secured before the deck above is laid. A large ship can take up to two years to build and a few months before the launch the pumps, which could have been delivered over a year previously have to be checked and started. One of the hazards in doing this can be rats, which are endemic to shipyards. As the boy on the job, it was my responsibility to clear each pump of any nesting rats before we started work on it. I only had one accident, when I foolishly put my hand down the exit pipe from a pump to clear away some straw without looking first or poking about with a crowbar. A nesting rat took a nip at my forefinger, which, although not serious, taught me to be careful in future. No one could understand why the rat population in this yard never went down, until it was discovered that their rat catcher was only killing the male animals; the females were left to breed, so that he would have a job for life.

One of the most incredible sights in a shipyard in those days occurred a few days before a ship was launched for its trials. It was completely evacuated of all personnel, every hatch was battened down, with only the openings through which the mooring ropes were secured left open. The ship was then fumigated, and all the rats rushed to the remaining exits and ran nose to tail down the ropes to the shore. Their numbers were quite amazing, especially if it was a large ship. Groups of workers stood at the shore end of the ropes with shovels and similar implements and tried to kill as many as they could. The shoreline was quickly littered with the corpses of the vermin, but it was only a fraction of those that had escaped the gas-filled ship.

From Nicholas Parsons' autobiography, *The Straight Man*, 1994.

A MAN IS DEAD

Big Fairy Feet and his mate seemed to fill most of the landing. Fairy Feet himself hesitated. Until this moment [Julia] had never looked closely at him but now she saw that either his face was different or her previous impressions had never been exact. It was not quite the mask of a monster. It was really only that of a tired and ageing big man. By comparison, the solemn, fresh-faced young constable with him was only a boy in uniform.

'Is this where Colin Haig lives?' Fairy Feet asked quietly.

'Ay.'

From habit she held the door half-open by its edge. Fairy Feet never took his washed-blue eyes off her. 'Are you Mrs Haig?'

'Ay.'

Suddenly something would not let her ask any questions. She just watched the big policeman with a queer, numb terror.

'Could we come in a minute?'

His civility paralysed her. She could not speak. She thought she inclined her head. She did not even remember walking the half dozen steps back into the kitchen. She only knew she was there waiting – and Fairy Feet, tremendous by size and implication, was there with her. She believed the young constable followed them but that did not register. She had a vague memory of Fairy Feet asking her if she was in the house alone. When she nodded she thought he glanced at his mate, but that was another thing she could not clearly remember. The one vivid thing was Fairy Feet's watchful gaze as he said, 'I'm sorry to bring you bad news, Mrs Haig, but there's been a bit of an accident.'

'Oh, no!'

She was sure it was someone else whispered the exclamation. Her brain was engaged with the picture of Colin going out that morning and putting his head back round the door to shout, 'And mind, Maw – have my suit laid out for I'll be in a hurry tonight. And if my shirt's no' well ironed I'll be lookin' for other digs.'

'Good enough,' she had cried, 'the sooner the better. Just you see how long a strange landlady would put up wi' you and your wants.'

And now. . . .

'Is it bad?' she heard herself ask.

'Never you worry about that,' Fairy Feet said illogically but kindly. 'Just you sit down a minute.'

'Is it bad,' she repeated, anguish resisting his gentle effort to seat her in the big chair.

His eyes were stolidly calm. 'I doubt it is, Mrs Haig.'

'My God! My boy!'

Power drained then from her limbs and she was sitting in the chair. She did not see the frown across Fairy Feet's face. But after an age she became aware of his stooped solicitude. She had to force herself to understand his words. 'This is an elderly chap, Mrs Haig. Is your man's name not Colin?'

'Collie!'

'Is he a rigger?'

And then, remarkably, her brain was very clear. She saw the young policeman hovering with Mrs Wilson in the background. Fairy Feet was pressing a glass of water into her hand.

'Where have they taken him?' she asked harshly.

'The Southern General.'

Without another word she rose and plucked her coat from its hook. Mrs Wilson said, 'I'll come with you, Mrs Haig; we'll get a car at the foot of the street.'

'You're sure you'll be all right?' Fairy Feet asked.

'Will anybody have told my boy?'

'Where does your son work?'

'He's a plater in Burnford's,' Mrs Wilson said.

'We'll get word to him.'

Dry-eyed, Julia looked at Fairy Feet. He was watching her with the cool, steady sympathy of experience. 'I'll be all right,' she said firmly. And then added with a calmness that won his silent admiration. 'And thank you – you've done all you could. . . .'

From Hugh Munro's novel *The Clydesiders*, 1961.

A CHAOTIC NIGHTMARE OF STEEL

From where Brian stood, on a staging hanging from the casing, the engine room looked as if it had received a high explosive bomb all to itself. Huge castings which seemed to have broken off half way, reared up from floor plates. Inside these he caught glimpses of bright polished shafts, pieces of brass, couplings, and bolts, lit up by the occasional gleam from a candle. Now and again a bare arm would pass over a light holding a spanner or a hammer. Then a man's legs, which hung grotesquely from a man-hole, began wriggling and twisting till the man's body emerged and he sat on his heels on the flooring plates, gazing at the small bracket in his hand, scratching his head and muttering in disgust at the unfortunate limitations of matter. Immediately below Brian was a clear drop to the engine room floor thirty feet below, where three workmen squatted over a job. A small candle burned in the centre of the group and from Brian's angle it looked for all the world like an illicit card party. A rivet fire filled the place with a blue film of smoke. A tangled maze of steel ladders and gratings, some completed, others leaping up from the floor to stop in mid air, or to hang from platforms, sprawled all round the walls of the engine room. Pipes, all sorts and sizes, rose, fell, crossed, turned, twisted in every possible shape and angle in a chaotic nightmare of steel. It might have been some imbecile giant's game of snakes and ladders for all the order or purpose one could see in it. An insulating squad had begun operations on the pipes, clothing them in white, fluffy asbestos. It seemed that for every piece they put on a pipe they scattered six pieces below, giving machinery and men the appearance of suffering a blizzard.

From Edward Shiels' novel *Gael over Glasgow*, 1937.

ASBESTOSIS

During my period 'at the tools' (1940–1964), I was constantly in an asbestos environment. To be on a ship being outfitted, i.e. nearing completion, meant that all outfit workers were exposed to asbestos fibres and filament for the whole of the working day, for the whole of the working week.

The laggers, who actually worked with the various asbestos materials were subcontractors working to very tight schedules and who were totally unconcerned with good housekeeping, safe working practice or consideration for other workers in their vicinity. If the weather was dry, their asbestos cement (monkey dung) was mixed on the dockside and slung aboard in buckets. If it was wet, the asbestos mix was made up on board ship in between the deck spaces, engine-room flats and gantries.

To work in engine rooms and boiler rooms meant that you were brushing against the laggers and their work – often I came home off the ship at the end of a shift white as a baker, totally covered in asbestos detritus which had rubbed off or fallen on me as I worked as a shipwright (a clean trade).

As the ship neared completion and prepared for ship trials, it was my job to arrange for engine and boiler rooms to be cleared of all rubbish and scaffolding prior to Admiralty and Lloyds inspection.

When scaffolders began to remove the scaffold planks they cleared them by turning them on their edge and passing them through the hatches to the upper decks for removal ashore. When they turned the 30/40 planks on to their edges all the loose asbestos particles and fragments floated down to the bottom of the ship like a snowstorm. It was impossible to escape the mess which was accepted as the norm for shipyard working conditions.

From 1940 till I left to join training in the 1960s, we were never warned or instructed about the dangers of asbestos inhalation; we were never issued with protective clothing or masks or restrained from working adjacent to the laggers. By the late 1960s or early 70s, shipyard workers were becoming aware of the hazards of asbestos and that it had an incubation period of 20 to 25 years before emerging as a malignant incurable cancer. Having left that environment around 1959 I thought I had escaped infection until 33 years later I went to bed a robustly well man in Christmas week 1991 and woke crippled with mesothelioma.

Pat McCrystal, speaking in *Clyde Shipbuilding: A collection of source material*, 1995.

Mixing asbestos insulation. Huge amounts of asbestos were used in the shipyards before its dangers were known. Photograph by Cecil Beaton. (Imperial War Museum)

THE AMBULANCE MAN

A camaraderie existed in the yard between the workers that I and most other ex-workers have never met since, although the actual working conditions were sometimes barbaric and welfare provisions were non-existent. On reflection, the accident rate was well below that of most modern establishments – ironically the fact that few safety precautions existed seemed to make everyone more aware for their own safety and consequently accidents were few and far between. The ambulance man was a strict disciplinarian called John Sim. John was a grand old chap. He was chief storekeeper. So the procedure when one injured oneself was to make one's way or be carried to the store to contact John who would then proceed to the first aid room with you. The kettle would be boiled and John would wash the wound and apply iodine in copious amounts without warning. Some said that if you fainted, John would give you a drink of iodine as this was his panacea.

From Thomas MacLean's memories of his life in the Ardrossan shipyards, published in Catriona Levy's *Ardrossan Shipyards: Struggle for survival 1825–1983*, 1984.

Opposite left: Erecting a prefabricated unit. With such huge pieces of steelwork being moved around the yards it was inevitable that accidents sometimes occurred. (Glasgow Museums)

Opposite right: Although shipyards are now much more safety conscious, and workers wear safety gear, accidents can still happen. Here an angle grinder is at work high up on staging at Macduff Shipyard. (Author's collection)

HARD TO CHANGE

'Gravity is the enemy in shipbuilding,' he says. 'People fall and things fall, nearly always as a result of carelessness. Somehow we have to persuade people to take a safe attitude to their work. It is easier said than done. Safety is always uphill work in a traditional industry like shipbuilding where men are set in their ways. If we feel strongly enough about it some of it will rub off, some people will respond; but it takes time.

'For example, it is hard to persuade people to use their safety gear properly; and the older the industry is and the longer people are in it, the harder it is to change them. A lot of persuasion is needed even in an obvious matter like goggles. For three years now there has been a law that says men in certain jobs must wear safety goggles; but although most men do have the sense to protect themselves we have cases where they don't. There is still a need for education.

'There is even more need where safety helmets are concerned, because there is no law about them and there are circumstances when they can be difficult or uncomfortable to wear. On top of that, some people seem to have got themselves mixed up in their minds with the old gaffer's bowler hat, and won't wear them for that reason. Yet anyone who stops to think about it knows perfectly well that helmets prevent injuries and save lives. It is our job to make everyone think.

'We have set up regular meetings of management and of employees where we discuss accidents, equipment, working methods, anything that has a bearing on the job. There is always a first time, and when it happens there is no sense in keeping it to yourself. One reason why sharing information is important is that many accidents are not caused by one big mistake. They arise out of several trivial little things that add up and become a disaster. It is very important to exchange experiences about accidents like that. That way you develop a nose for the small things that matter.'

Shipbuilding, he says, does not stand high in the safety league. There is room

for improvement. It is his ambition to have the Scott Lithgow yards recognised as the safest in the country. If he can persuade the rest of us that safety is a personal problem there is no reason why he should not realise it. All we have to do is think safe.

J. P. K. Garthwaite, Safety Officer for Scott Lithgow's, quoted in the *Scott Lithgow House Magazine* of Summer 1977.

SWALLOWING PRIDE

There was no helmets worn at all, other than maybe a hard hat, such as all the managers and the foremen used to wear bowlers, and there's no doubt they must have protected them in some way. But the headgear for a worker in these days was just simply a cap – you only wore a cap, you never wore a hard hat of any kind. Coming into modern times, there's very few men'll wear hard hats at their work. I know myself in my own experience, for a long time I wouldnae wear one either, until I felt, being a foreman and also being on the Safety First Committee that I felt more committed to wearing a hat, with the result that I just sort of swallowed my pride and I wore a hat.

Bobby Aitchison, foreman shipwright at Henry Robb's shipyard at Leith speaking in 1984, on a tape held at the School of Scottish Studies.

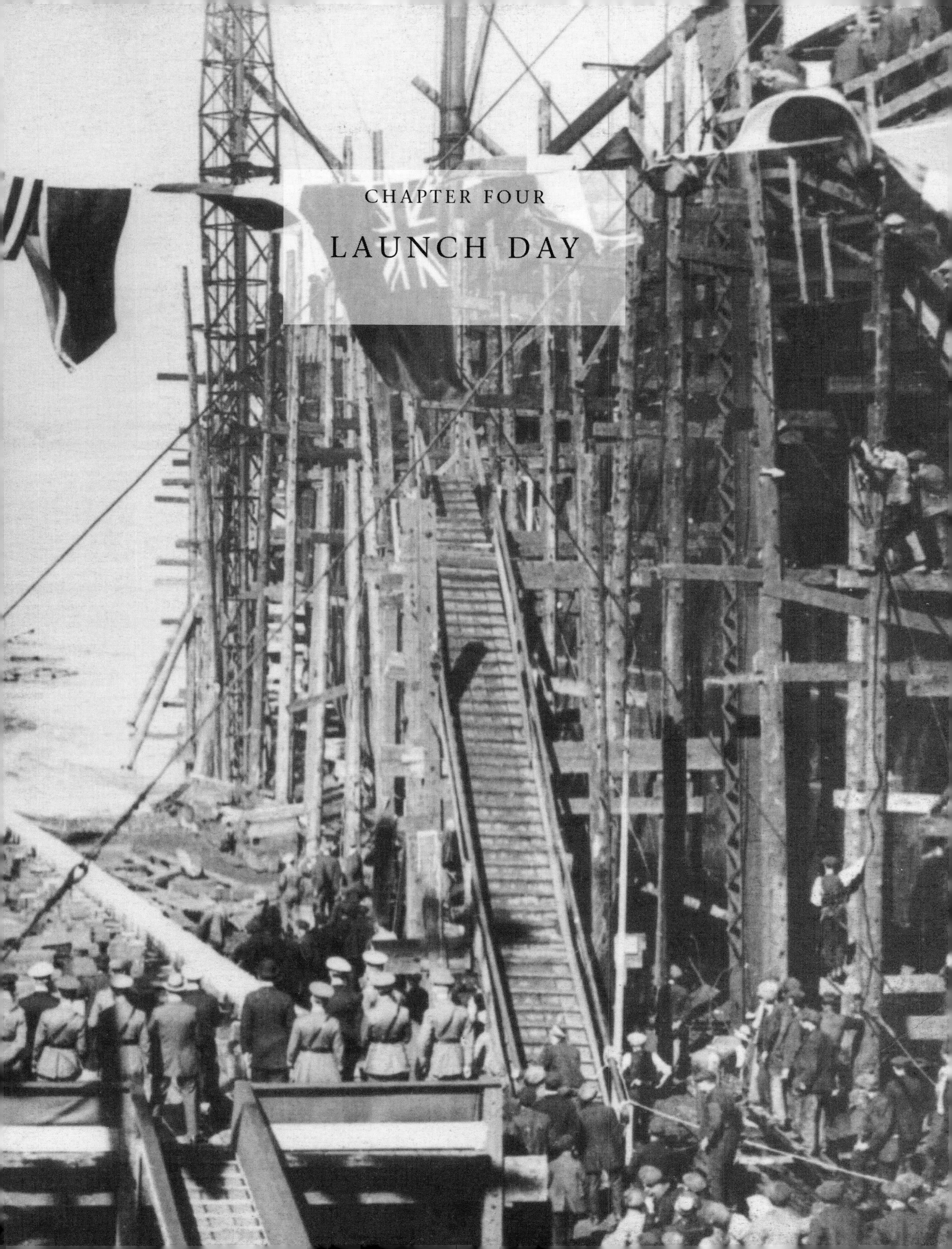

CHAPTER FOUR

LAUNCH DAY

The launch of a ship is the single most exciting thing to happen in a shipyard.

In other industries there is little ceremony or ritual involved in the completion of the end product. Cars simply roll off the production line and consumer goods are packed away quietly into boxes for delivery. In shipbuilding, however, the sheer scale of the endeavour imbues the whole process with a certain kind of mystique. Only in shipbuilding does all work stop and everyone gathers round to see the product leave the factory.

To the men who sail and build them, ships are like living creatures, and the launch of a ship is treated as a birth and a christening all in one and is given the respect that such an occasion deserves. Here is a massive structure weighing thousands of tons, the largest moving thing made by humankind, released from the cradle of its birth to slide into the element for which it was designed. Depending on the type of ship, it may travel faster on the slipways than it will ever travel again.

Some launches were quiet affairs, but generally the shipyard would make it a great occasion. The shipowners and local dignitaries were invited to the event, the ship was decorated with flags, pipe bands played, and the wife or daughter of the shipowner, or perhaps even a member of royalty, would smash a bottle of champagne over the bows. After the ceremony a lavish feast was laid on for the launch party and the shipbuilders did everything possible to make an impression. Not only was the launch dramatic in itself, it was also an important economic milestone for the builder, who received a substantial part of the contract price after a successful launch. It also gave the shipbuilder an opportunity to impress the shipowner in the hope that further contracts might come as a result.

A launch was also an important occasion for the local population who would gather to watch the event. School children were often allowed out of their classrooms to see the spectacle. Just before the launch the workers would down their tools and gather around the slipways, many joining their families who had come into the yard, to watch in awe as the product of their sweat and labour took to the water for the first time.

Not all launches were successful. Sometimes disaster struck. The worst launch accident occurred when the Daphne *was launched from Alexander Stephen's shipyard at Govan in 1883. The ship overturned when it hit the water and 124 men were killed. Until this time the launch of a ship was an inexact process governed more by rule of thumb than exact science. As a result of the* Daphne *disaster, new regulations were brought in regarding the stability calculations that had to be carried out, and from then on only essential personnel were allowed on board for the launch.*

However, even successful launches were not always happy occasions. The casual nature of shipyard employment meant that for riveters, welders, platers and other members of the 'black squad' the launch of a ship could be the end of their work. Unless they could find work elsewhere, the launch of a ship could signal unemployment for many men or, if there were no more orders on the books, even the closure of the shipyard itself.

Previous page: A ship being launched by King George V at the Greenock and Grangemouth Dockyard in 1917. It was very unusual for a man to launch a ship, but obviously the propaganda potential of the king launching a ship was too great to miss. (Imperial War Museum)

I NAME THIS SHIP . . .

Julie Greig was the happiest and proudest young woman in the city of Glasgow. She had never looked more glamorous and she knew it. Always an outstandingly beautiful woman, she had spared neither the time nor the expense in order to make herself even more beautiful, more desirable, than she had ever looked before. She walked between Sir John Blair and Adam Glober at the head of a small procession making its way along the narrow road lined on either side by hundreds of smiling workmen, their wives or girlfriends and many clamorous children. Straight ahead was the shining grey ship it was going to be her duty to name. She and Sir John exchanged smiles when the shrill whistles of the workmen fell on her ears above the babble of women's admiring voices and the thumping of martial music.

The procession had reached the red-carpeted stairway of the launching platform as Nan handed the binoculars to her husband. He focused them on Julie Greig. Under his breath he said to Nan, 'I wouldn't mind a walk with her on a dark night.' Nan dug her elbow into his ribs.

'You'd be lucky to get the chance, I'm afraid,' she teased. 'That girl wouldn't look the road you walk on. Never mind, she's got good taste, I admit that. I certainly like that white hat she's wearing.'

Andy grinned, continuing to stare through the binoculars.

'I'll buy you one the same on Saturday.'

He swept the binoculars over some of the other members of the launching party. Sir John, in dark grey, was a distinguished figure, and Glober, smart as usual in his customary dark blue, was actually smiling. Miracles would never cease. The other members of the procession were not without their glitter. Senior Naval, Army and Air Force officers with their colourful bars and shining swords. Fashionable men and equally fashionable women. Finally, two men in their robes of office – the Lord Provost of Glasgow and the clergyman who was to ask for God's blessing on the ship.

Satisfied that he had seen more than his fair share of the colourful procession, Andy returned the binoculars to Nan. She smiled acknowledgement and instantly raised them to her eyes. Julie, guided by Sir John, had now mounted the stairs and was being presented with a bouquet of flowers by the firm's youngest apprentice, a fair-haired youth, immaculate in a white boiler suit.

Julie graciously accepted the bouquet. Her thanks made the boy blush, but this was nothing to the embarrassment he suffered when, in answer to requests from the photographers, Julie planted a cool kiss on his flushed cheeks. The apprentice stumbled away and Julie allowed herself to be led by Sir John to a small table at the front of the platform and directly beneath the towering bow of the ship.

Her eyes settled on the bottle of champagne, decorated with silk ribbons, that was fixed to the highly polished mechanism. Sir John opened a carved wooden box on the table and withdrew a slender mallet. He handed it to Julie and as her fingers closed around the shaft she felt the ridged edges of the carved wood pressing against her skin.

The *Baron Kilmarnock* is ready to be launched at the Caledon shipyard in Dundee in 1953. (North Ayrshire Museum)

Right:
The launch party assembles, for the launch of the *Baron Kilmarnock* including representatives of the ship's owners, the Hogarth Shipping Company. (North Ayrshire Museum)

'Remember,' Sir John emphasised, 'you strike the push button with this immediately after you name and bless the ship.'

Julie returned his warm smile.

'I understand perfectly, Sir John. My lines are on the very tip of my tongue. I'm all ready to go.'

'Good . . . Oh, by the way, I think Mr Glober would like a word with you. Go ahead, my dear . . . we still have a few minutes to spare.'

The sloping platform was now crowded to capacity and Julie was forced to apologise on several occasions as she edged her way through the throng of guests to where the managing director was standing beside the safety rail. He gripped her arm too firmly for her liking, but she showed no sign of her discomfort as he started to explain the intricacies of launching a ship into a narrow river. Very soon the technicalities were boring her, for there was a great deal of activity going on around the platform. Anyway, she thought, Alan would tell her all she wanted to know at Lady Blair's reception party at Blair House in the evening. . . .

The band stopped playing abruptly and almost immediately the noise of the crowd surrounding the platform dropped to a subdued murmur. When Julie looked down she saw the bands-men drawn up in a circle, their instruments held as if awaiting a fresh signal to begin. She noticed Slaven nervously clenching and unclenching his long, thin hands while talking to two men, who, like himself, wore dusty bowler hats.

Out of the corner of an eye she saw a flash of movement and looked up as a gull swooped and wheeled in the warm air, then went into a graceful glide which took it across the bows of the destroyer. It was then she noticed that the man standing on the forecastle deck had changed his red flag for a white one. It was now fluttering gently in response to a quiet breeze drifting up the river. Glober, too, had seen the signal. . . .

At a nod from Sir John the minister stepped forward to a microphone which had suddenly and mysteriously appeared at Julie's left elbow. When the crowd spotted the black-robed figure the muted babble of conversation ceased. The overwhelming silence was electric in its intensity and in the hush Julie heard a sharp creak from a plank as Glober moved position in order to signal to someone on the ground. As his hand dropped there was a fanfare from the trumpets, followed by a long slow drum roll. The crowd appeared to sway and shuffle as the men bared their heads and stood to attention for the playing of the National Anthem.

As soon as the music ceased the minister was praying, offering up the ship and her future crew to God. . . .

The amen was a ragged muttering from the throng of spectators. A moment later six apprentice shipwrights appeared and formed a semicircle below where Glober stood on the platform. Their faces shone with sweat and their mouths hung open, gasping for breath, but in the gleam in their eyes and the triumphant manner in which they each held aloft a slender piece of metal there was an attitude of naked excitement. The crowd seemed to sense this, too, and there was a sudden, sharp gasp – the tremor from a thousand throats that rose

Mrs J. M. MacLeod, wife of one of the Hogarth directors, prepares to launch the *Baron Kilmarnock*. (North Ayrshire Museum)

up and seemed to urge the swift completion of the act they had gathered to witness. Glober's eyes glared more fiercely than before as he counted the metal daggers. Sir John watched him carefully. He saw the managing director tense his body, then turn. His lips were pursed, but the nod of his head indicated clearly that all was ready for the launch. Without a word Sir John lifted the mallet and handed it to Julie. . . .

'I name this ship *Saturn* and may God bless and protect all who sail in her.'

The mallet seemed to fill the lenses of the binoculars: Nan was unable to suppress a gasp as the wooden head swung down, dead on target. Julie felt the wood strike home, releasing the catch holding the locking device. She saw the knife-edged bow rearing above her, towering into the sky and the decorated bottle, held firm in its clamp, spring towards the stem. She jerked her head involuntarily as the bottle shattered and slivers of glass and bubbling liquid cascaded in a furious burst of foam against the shining grey hull. As the champagne trickled away the ringing of a bell sounded somewhere, far in the distance. For several seconds nothing appeared to happen. The crowd were still, watching, waiting, and on the platform Julie could hear the breathing of the guests as they stood in silence, not daring to move a muscle; as if, somehow, all were enmeshed in the spell cast down by the aura of the ship.

The supporting cradle started to creak; the timbers protesting, groaning and grumbling as their charge began to tremble with the first faint signs of life. Slowly, the *Saturn* inched away towards the waiting waters of the Clyde, a slippery journey that became more ominous as the water frothed and appeared to boil in the path of the speeding stern. On the ground the crowd were unable to restrain their feelings any longer. A wave of cheering erupted from eager throats and the outburst grew in intensity, each burst of cheering following more loudly and more quickly than before as the band joined the tumult with 'Rule, Britannia'. The tug-boats were the next to join in, the shrill piping calls of their whistles piercing the air, a symbol of effervescent joy in contrast to the sombre wailing of the sirens, as the Clyde saluted the birth of her latest creation.

From Alexander Highlands' novel *The Dark Horizon*, 1971.

A SHIP IS BORN

Now, underneath the ship, under that low black mine-like ceiling with its corridors of pit props, where the ground is littered with wood chips and where you are glad of a bowler hat to take the crack of a beam you did not see, the men are preparing for the launching. Two more rows of blocks have been built on either side of the row that held the centre keel, and on these blocks are the launching ways. They are really a wide pair of wooden, scenic-railway tracks on

The launch of the *Cerdic Ferry* at the Ailsa yard in Troon in 1961. Rather than swinging the bottle from a rope a more sophisticated mechanism was used. The bottle was released after hitting a button with a gavel. This system was common in many Scottish yards. (Scottish Maritime Museum)

Proud workers at Ardrossan pose underneath their ship before a launch in 1946. (North Ayrshire Museum) which another pair of tracks, called sliding ways, are resting. Thick yellow grease is melted and poured between them. At the fore-end and after-end of this track are the launching triggers.

Their mechanism is very much like that of the trigger of a gun, and when it is released – that is to say, when the men have knocked away the props – that small finger of wood comes down, and out slides the ship on its journey. At the side of the launching ways you will notice heavy coils of rusty chain, a pile of it looking like guts; they have not been dropped there by accident. They are used to brake the ship when she goes off into the water. Remember she has no engine in her. She is light and free. The naval architects have had to calculate the strength of the tide, the ship's weight and speed, the angle of the launch in regard to the width of the river; and when they have made this calculation they know how much chain she must drag, like the brake of a balloon, to check her at the right point in the river. Otherwise she might hit the opposite bank. She moves out slowly, momentously, to the plunge, and in the water glittering against her wide hull a mess of debris has gathered round about. This is not the rubbish of the river, but the blocks of the sliding ways which she has taken down with her, which are held together by wire and will presently be fished inshore again. A ship has been born and looking as plain, blind and unhopeful as any new-born thing. Those blocks are a sort of afterbirth. The tugs, like midwives, come along and take her down to the marine engineering works to get her boilers and her first feed of oil.

From V. S. Pritchett's *Build the Ships*, 1946.

Opposite: The *Baron Kilmarnock* on its way down the slipways. (North Ayrshire Museum)

The *Baron Kilmarnock* takes to the water for the first time. (North Ayrshire Museum)

Launch of the *Ville de Papeete* at the Ailsa shipyard at Ayr in 1929. (Scottish Maritime Museum)

THE CHRISTENING

There was a man
And all his life
He'd worked in a shipyard;
And he had a baby,
And it was going to be christened;
And for a week
He couldn't sleep nights,
Because he was worried
For fear the minister
Would hurt the baby
When he hit it with the bottle.

An anonymous poem from the *Linthouse Works Magazine* of July 1929.

GOVAN LAUNCHINGS

It was in keeping with that inspiring maritime prospect from our windows on Partickhill that most of our nearby friends and neighbours were in some way occupied with the building of the ships or the construction of engines for them, and when the launching of a new vessel was in prospect we could always learn of it in time to gather for the stirring sight. The great shipyards at Govan and Linthouse lay plainly under our eyes, and we could see the construction of a ship from a gaunt skeleton on the stocks to the magnificence of a fully plated liner standing beflagged and erect on the river's bank to await her formal baptism. A launching at the Govan shipyards could best be seen from the pasture-fields at the western end of Laurelbank, and it was there the children of the district assembled to enjoy the spectacle. There was no appearance of haste in the ceremonial. Let the day be fair, we were there to see the peopling of the decorated platform erected at the bows or the gradual encroachment of the shipyard crowds on nearby points of vantage. How the great new ship with her canopy of gay flags seemed solidly immoveable, highly perched over there on the river's bank . . . and how long the waiting before high water came. Then would come the shrilling of steam whistles from the tugs in the river and the engine-shops on its banks to give us word of her release. Movement, impatiently looked for, was painfully slow until the ship herself took charge and gathered way to back majestically into the river, brimming its banks with the foam of her displacement.

But even on Clydeside not all ship launchings go smoothly and according to plan. I remember returning from school on a summer afternoon in early July of 1883 and seeing my mother's serving-maid rushing frantically down the Crow Road towards the river, shrieking wild cries and from time to time throwing her apron over her head to veil her grief, in the way Highland people do. I learned later that the newly built *Daphne*, in which her father was employed, on being launched at Linthouse, had overturned in the river and that many workmen – our Mirren's father among them – were believed drowned.

From David Bone's autobiography, *Landfall at Sunset*, 1955.

APPALLING CATASTROPHE ON THE CLYDE

An accident of unparalleled magnitude in the annals of shipbuilding on the Clyde happened on the river today, when a steamer which was launched by Messrs Stephen & Sons capsized with a large number of workmen on board. There is a great diversity of opinion as to the number of men who were on board and the number that have been saved and drowned.

The information vouchsafed regarding the catastrophe by Mr Scott, manager for Messrs Stephen & Sons, Linthouse, is that a small vessel, the *Daphne*, of 500 tons, built for the Glasgow and Londonderry Steam Packet Company was being launched at half past eleven o'clock today from the firm's yard at Linthouse, when it listed over on its side, and all on board were plunged into the water. The firm's representatives compute the number drowned at between thirty and forty men, while workmen who were on board and others who saw the vessel leave the ways say over a hundred men must have been carried down with the ship. Sadly enough, it happened that more than the usual number of workmen were on board at the launch, as the quickest possible completion of the vessel was desired. Most of these men were engaged in the interior part of the vessel, and they could not free themselves so easily as those who were on deck.

It is thought by employees of the yard that about 200 men were on the steamer when she left the ways. Before she had slid far down the slip it was observed that she was somehow top-heavy. As she cleared the ways she quickly fell over on the port side, and as the tide was full she was, with the exception of the point of the bow, completely submerged.

Many men swam ashore, and two tugs that lay on each side of the slip gave every possible assistance to the strugglers in the water. Small boats were quickly put out from the yard, and they did a great deal of useful service in saving life. Ropes, too, were thrown to the almost spent swimmers as they reached the pier skirting the yard.

Those rescued were attended to with the greatest alertness, some taken home and others sent to the Infirmary.

From the *Evening Times*, Tuesday 3 July 1883.

A SIDEWAYS LAUNCH

On the banks of the Forth and Clyde Canal at Kirkintilloch the shipyard of J. & J. Hay were famous for building small steam coasters called puffers. Because of the restriction of the canal their ships were launched side on. This made for a very dramatic spectacle.

Kirkintilloch experienced all the thrills of the launch on Wednesday afternoon last, when the single-screw coasting steamer *Tuscan*, built by Messrs J. Hay and Sons at their Kirkintilloch yard, was launched on the waters of the Forth and Clyde Canal. This was the second launch in a period of almost two years.

A start was made at the vessel in July of this year, and, in order to have it completed for launching on the day fixed, it was found necessary for the yard employees to work overtime almost every evening during the past few weeks.

A trim, sturdy coaster, she was the cynosure of thousands of eyes on Wednesday, for the fact that she was to be launched that day was known to almost everyone in the town. The launching was timed to take place at 2.15, but by 2 o'clock the various vantage points were literally black with spectators. The old wooden bridge would not have been able to stand the weight of the crowds which lined its sturdy successor.

Among the crowds were children of one of the schools, who had been given leave of absence under one of the teachers to see the launch, which was the first most of them had ever seen. The younger school children climbed onto the higher stretches of the opposite embankment, where a first-class view was afforded.

In the presence of officials of the firm of Messrs J. Hay & Sons, the supports were knocked out from beneath the steamer, and, to the accompaniment of a terrific roar from the spectatorate, the ship was launched broadside on. She took the water gracefully, a great flood of water swamping the canal walk for a distance of about 50 yards. In several instances wet feet were the reward of those who ventured too near.

From the *Kirkintilloch Herald*, 28 November 1934.

LAUNCHING THE *QUEEN MARY*

They launched the *Queen Mary* in a downpour of rain on the 26th of September, 1934, and the story of that daring exploit is safe and full in the records. There were memorable passages in King George's speech. The little hesitations of Queen Mary and the whispered promptings of Sir Thomas Bell, local managing director of the building firm, are now part of an oral legend. There were yards of ermine and gold braid, and a long roster of resounding titles, behind the rain-flooded glass of the launching dais. A bottle smashed high up on the precipice that was the port bow of the ship – a curiously feeble sound in the rain-filled space of the yard. Heavy hammers thumped on blocks of wood. One seems to remember the thin pipe of a whistle, probably blown by some bowler-hatted gaffer in the echoing chambers beneath the hull. One eye, matching the bow of the ship against a distant chimney, saw a gap of emptiness suddenly created between these fixed objects. Thirty thousand tons of steel, painted white, were moving, nay, plunging towards the water. Chains whipped and lashed like snakes. There was a spurt of flame, dowsed in clouds of oily smoke, over the greased ways. She seemed to move at terrific speed. She was surely rushing to disaster. The army of spectators was silent. Then it liberated itself in a roar. For there was the *Queen Mary*, no longer a number in the books, riding high and light in the narrow river, and the tugs bearing down on her with the purposefulness of terriers after a rat. The rain had suddenly, miraculously stopped. Had we really seen a man, high on the uttermost bow of the ship, waving his cloth cap like a madman? Anyhow, the ship was launched, securely water-borne. That was that part of the job done.

But the inwardness of the job, so elegantly withheld from the men in the silk hats and the fancy uniforms? That nerve-wracked man in the bowler hat under the hull, the whistle bitten into by his teeth? The yard manager on a little, separate platform of his own, and on him the intolerable fear that she might stick on the ways, or rush to destruction, or topple over on the open mouths of

The launch of a puffer at Hay's yard in Kirkintilloch. (Auld Kirk Museum, Kirkintilloch)

the mob of spectators? The inwardness seemed to be perceived by him who was then the Prince of Wales, now Duke of Windsor. The royal procession and the marshalling of it were stately, but then one saw a young man, fascinated by the spectacle of a huge ship ready for the launching, twisting his head and shoulders, and his body from the waist, to peer up at the frowning, formidable bows of the thing of which the launching was but an entry in the royal diary. The common humanity glowed there for a moment.

Another little thing. The broadcasting of this launching ceremony was a business of great moment since millions in all parts of the world would surely be listening, and the exact timing of the thing became therefore a matter of anxious concern. British royalty goes about its ceremonial affairs with an exact regard for the time factor, but while officials knew the probable order of events beforehand, there were in this case some awkward imponderables to be considered. No man could tell to a minute when the tide in the river would serve; and on such a day of rain the programme might be curtailed in the interests of an invalid monarch. (In the event, the omission of one small bit of ritual did throw the schedule out by an awkward minute and a quarter.) But the private problem of the broadcasters was to know when – and exactly when, to the quarter-minute – the royal procession would reach the gates of the shipyard. It was solved thus. The route from the city had been laid down; a royal car moves at a given pace on these ceremonial occasions. So a private car made an experimental journey at that stately rate of speed, establishing the fact that, from a certain post office on the way to the yard gates, the journey must occupy exactly nine and a half – or was it fourteen and a quarter? – minutes. Thus, if the postmistress could call a certain secret number precisely as the King's car passed her door, the rest would follow. And so it came to pass. Unseen by him who described his approach, a short, familiar figure in the uniform of an Admiral appeared above the heads of the crowd precisely as had been said it would.

That, however, was a trivial enough matter of staffwork behind the scenes. Something else, a much grander and more dramatic thing, happened in the open yard, and only a few had eyes to grasp its lovely significance. As has been told, the shipbuilder's yard manager stood apart that day on a little platform of his own to watch the great ship take the water. It was a delightfully characteristic figure he cut there – a sturdy man of Clydeside in the traditional bowler hat and familiar bow tie – but there were some to know what a burden was upon him in that moment. This was his essential, ineluctable responsibility – this hurtling of thirty thousand tons of metal into a canal that was in breadth less than half the ship's length. He was, in reality, the central figure on the stage. Yet the cameras of the Press did not turn that way. There were so many thundering titles, so much gold braid, within the dais. The yard manager stood alone and, alone, faced his trial.

The ship was launched. The tugboats took her in charge. Down from the dais streamed the party of notables, heading for cake and wine, the bloodhounds of the Press hot on the trail. Still the yard manager stood on his little platform watching his ship. It was as if he could not yet resign his responsibility to the pilots and the berthing foreman of riggers. But at last he turned away and stood down; and as he did so, a tiny group of shipyard workers, standing there to do some little job of their own, took off their tweed caps and cheered him. It was not a loud cheer, the bellow of a throng. It sounded a little feeble in the emptiness where the ship had been. It was a private affair – a few workers who knew their job saluting a worker of whose job they knew the significance. But to one watcher of the odd little scene it seemed the biggest thing of the day.

From George Blake's *Down to the Sea*, 1937.

UNDERNEATH THE *QUEEN MARY*

I can remember the day I was in the team that was underneath the ship for the launch. It was very grey and dark, and the rain was pelting down and even then there were thousands of people gathered and we were given the shout. Then the royal couple arrived, King George and Queen Mary – we had a good view of them from where we were. I remember that we had another six blocks to take out, and we were to the minute. But we had tally plates – they told you if the ship was moving – and one was on the move. The ship had moved about half an inch with all that weight on it so we gave the word that it was getting quite dangerous, so the speech was hurried up a wee bit, so that the King could get his hand on the lever and let it go. In fact, we didn't have time to knock down the last half a dozen blocks because we had to run for it through a wee passage and out.

From Alan McKinlay's oral history of John Brown's shipyard between the World Wars, *Making Ships, Making Men*, 1991.

A RARE HONOUR

An honour, very rare in the annals of British Shipbuilding, has come the way of Mrs McCaig, a French polisher at a Renfrew shipyard. She was asked to launch a small warship at the place where she has worked for more than half a century. It was at Lobnitz's yard that this took place. A suggestion was made that the workers should be allowed to nominate a woman to perform the launch. The management readily agreed – as a tribute to the workers on the job.

Then a meeting of the yard committee and representatives of the unions was held. The names of those present were put in a hat and the winner of the ballot was given the privilege of nominating the launcher. Mrs McCaig was his choice.

The temporary platform in front of the ship's bows presented an unusual sight; instead of being occupied by shipowners and their friends, it was crowded with shop stewards and yard committee members.

At first Mrs McCaig was just a little embarrassed at the enthusiasm of her fellow workers who cheered her to the echo, but then she pressed the trigger confidently and another British warship was going down the ways, well and truly launched.

As Mrs McCaig is the oldest woman employee of the firm the honour was well deserved.

From the *Shipyard Spotlight*, December 1942.

A BEAUTY OUT OF HELL

Her mouth wis fuul o chuckie-stanes –
'God bless this ship and all who sail . . .' –
an we wir laughin wild is wains
it muck on oor yerd-owner's tail
fae where he'd slipt on ile an fell,
the day we launched the San Miguel.

The botil smashed. There came a hush
sae lang an wide it felt like noise,
tae wee Joe yellt, 'It waants a puush!'
then, like it waited fur his voice,
the giant edged oot fur the swell,
the day we launched the San Miguel.

A roar rose up sae strang an fierce,
loud fit tae crack the cranes above,
an many throats choked many tears
bit nane cid hide the powerfa love
thit burnt in aw, is in masel,
the day we launched the San Miguel.

Pride ran sae deep it near wis pain
an me, ma fethir bae ma side,
watched whit oor hauns hid built, oor ain,
the ocean noo take fur its bride,
an take fae us pert o oorsel,
the day we launched the San Miguel.

Ther's men drag coal up oot the mine,
ther's men drag rhymes up oot thir soul,
ther's men build buildins, taw an fine,
bit in this big crule, sweaty hole
we built a beauty oot a Hell
the day we launched the San Miguel.

From *A Clydeside Lad* by Bill Sutherland, 1990.

THE LAST SHIP

In this opening extract from George Blake's The Shipbuilders *the launch of a ship signals the closure of the yard.*

It was all over. The ship *Estramadura*, taking the water like a swan, was safely launched. And here was the party at cake and wine in the boardroom, garrulous in reaction from the strain.

Leslie Pagan knew that he ought to have been particularly pleased, but he felt empty and lost; and that worried and puzzled him. He was not, he reflected, a chap given to thinking much about his states of mind, and to be thus aware of detachment from the people about him was like feeling the first symptoms of an on-coming cold. Odd, indeed, to be standing thus before the big fireplace, ostensibly chatting to little Mrs Moles, the Consul's wife, and yet to feel remote from it all, a mere spectator of the ceremony that succeeds the launching of a new vessel. Had the woman suddenly broken off her chatter and challenged him to repeat her last remark, he could not for the life of him have done it.

Perhaps it was natural that his mind should be on the ship. (A glance through the window across the tangled derricks and litter of the yard assured him that they were getting her safely to the fitting-out berth, the tugs nosing like little animals at her bow and flanks.) She was a beauty; to the making of her he had brought a passionate concern. Then, God knew, that last anxious business of her launching had been a trial for him, as it always is for every builder of ships. (Remember the *Daphne* that went over from the stocks at Linthouse and carried scores of good men to death in the Clyde.) For the man with the responsibility, the pretty ceremony of breaking wine on steel plates had been an irritating irrelevance.

But it had gone well. The *Estramadura* was safely launched. Little Mrs Moles, after much giggling and a display of girlish ignorance, had raised the bottle in her gloved hand, cried the brave name aloud, and let the silken ribbons swing. A thin metallic sound of splintered glass, a small spin of foam, a wet smear on the sheer bows of the ship – and then the awful moment when the hammers thudded on the chocks and drag-chains rattled, and it seemed that she would never move; then moved ever so slowly, then seemed to stop, and at last slipped away, roaring and at a speed that brought the heart to the mouth, to take the water with a rush, plunge wildly once, shiver a little, then come to rest – safely

Greasing the ways prior to the launch of *Yamuna* at Yarrow's in 1949. (Scottish Maritime Museum)

Right: Preparing the launch ways at Yarrow's. (Scottish Maritime Museum)

The launch of HMS *Keppel* from Yarrow's in 1954 by Lady Madden. (Scottish Maritime Museum)

Bottom:
The launch of *Rocafuerte*, a river boat for Peru, at Yarrow's in 1954. (Glasgow Museums)

launched and water-borne. Now they had her snug in the fitting-out basin, and Leslie Pagan saw with his mind's eye a flickering film of her progress towards completion, saw her steam out at length, all white paint and yellow funnels, for her trials over the measured mile at Skelmorlie.

And little Mrs Moles, kittenish on this great day of her life, was still talking, while he said 'Yes' and 'No' and 'Oh, indeed!' mechanically.

Distraction came at last.

'Excuse me a moment,' he said hurriedly. 'My father . . .'

The old man had stood up and was rapping on the polished mahogany for attention.

'Ladies and gentlemen, will you see to it that your glasses are charged?'

A lovely figure of an old gentleman, Leslie reflected, the recognition coming on a wave of emotion. Seventy-eight, but tall and straight as a soldier; clean-shaven, with only a hint of the old-fashioned in his double-breasted buff waistcoat, his stock, and a suspicion of whisker, still ruddy like his thick strong hair, before his ears. A gentleman of the old school, indeed – though his grandfather had been a ploughman and his father had spoken nothing else but the broad Scots tongue.

Son watched father with the detachment that had so strangely come upon him. He saw him immobilise the hurrying waiters with a glance, marked the familiar grasp of the lean hand at the left lapel, heard the small preliminary cough. And he knew what the speech would be.

It was well-delivered this day of the *Estramadura*'s launching, but it had a new power to depress Leslie Pagan. Lord, how the old man lived in the warm security of the past, in the greatness of glories departed! Clydebuilt . . . the grand old theme, but a bitter one in a year of doubtful grace.

Yes, they had built beautifully in Pagan's – clippers in the day of such beauties, swift steamers for coastal routes (for they left the bigger stuff to others), destroyers of grace and speed, yachts of moving loveliness. There were the half-models of them on the walls, as the old man's white hand indicated: a fine flotilla, created by men who had the art of the thing in their blood, mighty craftsmen before the Lord. It was a fine story to tell, and no one could tell it better or more lovingly than his father, who had lived through the most splendid chapters of it – but was it not near an end?

There was not a single order on the books.

From George Blake's novel *The Shipbuilders*, 1935.

The engineering firm of McCrindles in Ardrossan was not a conventional shipyard and the boats it built had to be lifted from the dock into the water. Here the fishing boat *Renown* is being launched in 1986. (North Ayrshire Museum)

FLAGS
&
BUNTING
GROCER

CHAPTER FIVE

BEYOND THE YARD GATES

You did not stop being a shipbuilder when you left the yard gates. There were so many workers in the industry that it was inevitable that the men who worked together lived beside each other and often chose to spend their evenings and holidays with each other as well.

The hierarchy of the yards in many ways carried over into everyday life. The lower-paid workers typically lived in a 'single end' or a 'room and kitchen' in the poorer tenement buildings, while the better-paid tradesmen would live in larger two- or three-apartment tenement flats. The head foremen and managers lived in large salubrious tenements or terraced houses, while the yard owners tended to have large town houses and, as often as not, a large mansion out on the Clyde coast for the summer months.

The strict social hierarchy within the yards could also be clearly seen on the outside in shipbuilding communities such as Partick, Govan and Clydebank. The poorest workers lived in tenements overlooking the yards while the better-paid lived progressively farther away from the yards, with the employers living well away from the dirt and noise of the yards.

Often shipyards were created on greenfield sites, such as at Linthouse, Clydebank and Burntisland, where there was little or no existing housing. In these cases the yard owners usually took it upon themselves to build new housing close to the yard. This was not altogether altruistic on the employers' part as workers living just beyond the yard gates were less likely to be late than if they had to travel long distances. The employers also profited from the rents they collected.

The two great passions of shipbuilders were football and drink, both of which were indulged in almost as much within as beyond the yard gates. Football was always played at lunchtimes in the yards. Often shipyards had their own football teams and the competition between the yards was intense. The bigger yards even had inter-departmental football leagues.

Football, of course, was not the only sport that shipbuilders enjoyed, and the yards' recreation or welfare clubs were the focus for boxing, badminton, bowls and many other sports. Many special interest clubs were also set up by the workers. There were photography, gardening, chess and model-making clubs, and some yards had pipe bands as well as amateur dramatic and choral societies.

The annual two-week summer holiday, the 'Fair fortnight', was the highlight of the year for many shipbuilders. The traditional holiday was a trip 'doon the watter', with poorer workers taking a day trip on a steamer on the River Clyde while the better off would take a week or two's lodgings at Saltcoats on the Clyde coast or in the island towns of Millport or Rothesay. The fact that there was no such thing as holiday pay until the 1950s, however, meant that for many the Fair could be a rather dismal two weeks.

Many yards organised camps during the Fair for the apprentices and younger workers. In some cases the camps were organised jointly by a number of yards, and this lent a competitive edge to the various sports and entertainments that were organised. Popular destinations were Arran, Bute and the Isle of Man.

As well as camps, most yards had annual outings and family days, staff dances, Burns suppers and Christmas parties. All these activities created a sense of pride and belonging in the industry and helped to bond the workers and their families into what was a real shipbuilding community.

Previous page: Shipbuilders on their way home from the Ardrossan dockyard in 1924. (North Ayrshire Museum)

LET FREE

V. S. Pritchett describes the scene as the men come out of Harland and Wolff's Govan yard.

You are standing outside the gates of the yard. A line of empty trams is waiting there. Squads of buses are parked in the side turnings. Presently the gates slide back, and with the roar of a football crowd the workers rush out. Two or three thousand of them come pelting out, shouting, their metalled boots clattering on the cobbles. They blacken the roads. They pack the trams and buses, men whose skins are yellowed and greasy with the fume of industry, who have been deafened by pneumatic tools, who are soaked by the sweat of the forge, who have scorched their boot tips as they drew the steel frames from the furnace, or ruined their overalls on the welding frame, they swarm in the streets; they own the city.

V. S. Pritchett in *Build the Ships* of 1946.

THE SMELLS OF SLUMDOM

MacKelvie and Connor walked down Moore Street towards their homes. Moore Street was the link between the respectable quarters of South Partick and its slum area adjoining the river. It was a busy street, giving entrance to the subway and leading to the ferry. It was also well supplied with public houses. The red-leaders were conspicuous in their paint-soiled clothes at this late hour of a Saturday afternoon. Everybody was clad in Saturday best: Saturday being an even more important day to be dressed than Sunday. Some of the slum girls were more flashily dressed than the girls from the better working-class homes. A number of them were recognisably prostitutes, making for Hope Street and Sauchiehall Street to find clients amongst the lecherous and hot-blooded section of the middle class.

The subway entrance breathed out its stale decayed air. Immediately beyond, where they turned into Walker Street, a warm odoriferous waft of slumdom met them. It was not a smell that could be escaped. There were identifiable odours of cats' urine, decayed rubbish, infectious diseases, unwashed underclothing, intermingled with smells suggesting dry rot, insanitary lavatories, overtaxed sewage pipes and the excrement of a billion bed-bugs.

MacKelvie met the waft with twisted nostrils. In the heat, Walker Street smelt fouler than ever. But he said nothing. Deep down he knew that his whole existence was foul. He knew that he did wrong to bring children into such an abomination; that he did wrong to tolerate calmly its very existence; that he should drag the whole place down, destroy it. He could not mention this feeling to Bill after their recent talk in the tramcar. He felt uncomfortable, uneasy. Most days he got out of it for a spell. It was his wife and children who were continuously cooped up in it with no chance of escape. Even if he had to slave at the bottom of a dock he got a change of air. He recalled the fields on the opposite bank from the yard – a wide expanse of sunshine and green grass.

From James Barke's novel *Major Operation*, 1936.

SHIPYARD TENEMENTS

On the other hand the tenements near the shipyards have mostly a clean and orderly look; and one can still feel (though they have degenerated a great deal since shipbuilding virtually stopped) that the people who lived in them led for many years a self-respecting existence and had a tradition. And immediately behind some of the shipyards one may come upon green fields dotted with trees. Shipbuilding does not pollute the air or ravage the soil as coal-mining does, and the comparative cleanliness of this work gives the shipyard worker, I think, a peculiar self-respect, or did at one time, when there was something for him to do.

From *Scottish Journey* by Edwin Muir, 1935.

A TYPICAL TENEMENT

The effects of the employment slump in so far as they affected the tenement close of 35 Vale Street were interesting. It is possible to live in such a tenement without being on speaking terms with any of the other dwellers. Jean only spoke to the people beside her though in her country fashion she passed the time of day with such others as she might pass on the stair.

Two families lived on a landing. On the top flat lived Patrick and Mrs Calligan. Patrick was a whisky traveller and his one daughter, Peggy, was a schoolteacher. They were not affected by unemployment. Beside them, but not

Workers are let loose from Duncan's shipyard at Port Glasgow. (Imperial War Museum)

Opposite: The hooter sounds and the workers stream out from Harland and Wolff's Govan yard. (Imperial War Museum)

V.H

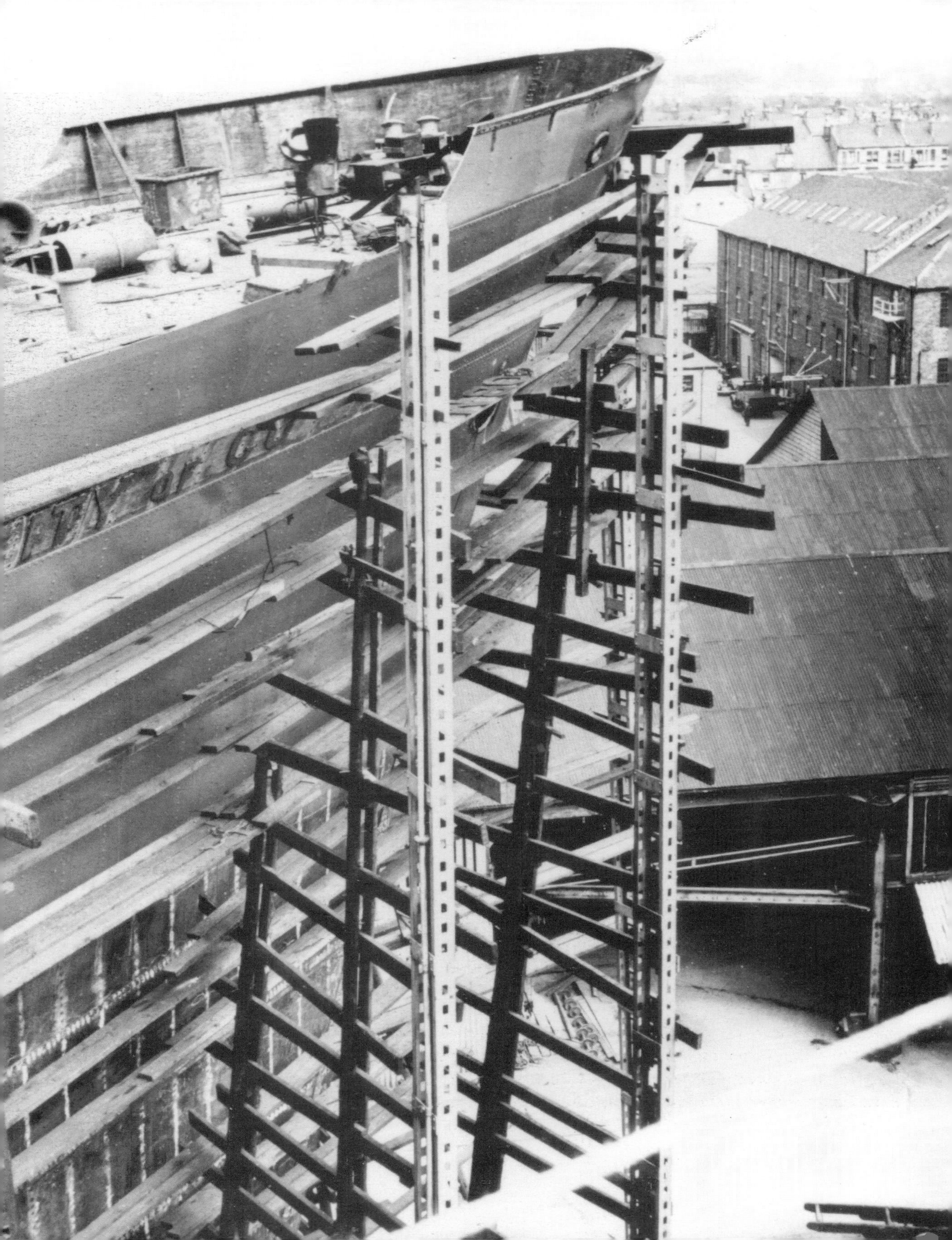

on speaking terms, were John and Mrs Campbell. John had a safe enough job as a tram driver, but his two office-working sons were unemployed.

There was no unemployment on the second flat. Robert Strain was a newly married grocer: his neighbour, George Brownlee, was a charge hand in a public house. But two of his daughters, Annie and Jenny, who had been trained as typists, were unable to get jobs.

On the first flat, beside David and Jean, were Edward and Mabel Millar. Edward was an engineer and had two small daughters. He was unemployed – and his wife was pregnant.

On the bottom flat, Michael Kearney, a foreman riveter, was hanging on to his job at half-pay by the skin of his teeth: his two sons, engineers, were unemployed. Beside him, Sarah MacAllister, a widow, had only one son working. Her younger son, a shipyard clerk, and her typist daughter were unemployed.

Shipyard tenements overlooking the workshops of Harland and Wolff. There was little escape from the yards for the families who lived here. (Imperial War Museum)

Thirty-five Vale Street was typical of any other number of any similar street in any working class district.

From James Barke's novel *Land of the Leal*, 1939.

RIVETERS' BUILDING

You might remember at the top of Hamilton Street . . . the Riveters' Building. That was the first tenement building in Govan with indoor toilets, bathrooms, you know. Definitely a superior building, you know, what would be known as a town mansion. And only the riveters could afford to stay there, because of the high rents, so it was known as the Riveters' Building.

Pat, a foreman shipwright, speaking in *Made in Govan: An oral history of shipbuilding on the Upper Clyde 1930–1950*, 1991.

Opposite: The bow of the *City of Colombo*, being built at Barclay Curle, towers above the tenements of Whiteinch, showing just how much the shipyards dominated the shipbuilding communities. (Glasgow Museums)

HOME FOR DINNER

Normally my father didn't come home for the three-quarter hour dinner break allowed, preferring to take a 'piece' for lunch and have his dinner in early evening. Dinner in working-class homes always referred to the mid-day meal. When he did come home, with his work a mile or so away in Helen Street, the sequence in our house and numerous others around mid-day, might have gone something like this. Stephen's horn would sound at ten to twelve and mother placed the potatoes on to boil. After ten minutes had elapsed Fairfield's horn was heard, and mum would know they would be boiling and salt could be added and Dad would be leaving his work on his bike. After a further ten minutes a third blow from another yard indicated that the potatoes should be ready for pouring, and Dad ought to be in the street or coming up the stairs. As he finished eating, yet another blast, in this case the 'ten minutes to go' start warning of the first of the earlier sequence of blows, told him he had another five minutes before he needed to leave on the return journey. He worked regular overtime and the early evening visit home for his tea was a hectic operation, with a shorter break of half an hour, which, with ten minutes' travelling each way, left little time for eating.

From George Rountree's memoirs, *A Govan Childhood: The 1930s*, 1993.

DRINK

Not every shipyard worker rushed home for his tea. For many a diversion to the pub was an all too regular occurrence for their wives' liking.

Leaning on a handle of the smoke-board Julia Haig stopped stirring the big black pot of soup to listen. Behind her the kitchen table, sheathed in pink oilcloth and with its folding leaf up, was set for four. Julia prided herself that her family's dinner was always ready and waiting.

As the first steam siren blasted its signal from amid the tangle of cranes and derricks visible from her three-storey window she glanced at the brass clock wagging on the room's widest wall. The clock responded with a throat-clearing whirr of springs and obediently clanged out twelve grudging chimes.

Julia smiled faintly. Every time she heard the shipyard hooters she remembered The Clincher, a Glasgow street-character's classic rejoinder to a departing rivet-heater. 'Maybe that, Mac,' bawled The Clincher to the figure disappearing in the big gates, 'but daft or no' daft nobody needs to blaw a whistle to tell me when I'm hungry and when I'm full. Only a bloody Black Squad man's as daft as that!'

Julia was the kind of woman who understood that kind of wit.

Easing the smoke-board up a few inches she brought each plate over separately and ladled the soup out of the iron pot. It was soup made of carrot, turnip, leeks, parsley, barley and peas and thickened with the juices and marrow of a big meaty ham-bone. The steam and smell of it filled the kitchen with a cloying fug.

Julia did not notice the fug. She did not feel hungry for the soup either. Constant cooking four times a day over the heat and smoke of the wide, black iron fire-range had left the finer edge of her appetite permanently dulled.

Julia's own idea of delight was a solitary cup of tea at midnight and a wee soda scone garnished by the knowledge that her man was working, that everyone was safely in bed and that her room and kitchen was as tidy as brush and shovel and floorcloth could make it. If she had wider ambitions she never confessed them.

But she had other standards for her family. And as a clatter in the little lobby that led to the stairhead heralded someone's entry she returned to the pots flanking the rib-boxed fireplace, and with a fork vigorously mashed a cooked mixture of potatoes and carrot. Without turning her head she said: 'Wash your hands, Ella – and put on a pinny before you sit down to that soup.'

'Och – soup again, Maw!' Ella's little doll face wrinkled and the blue bows at the end of her two fair plaits bounced with a petulant wriggle. 'I don't want soup.'

Julia continued stooping before her sooty cavern. She did not look round. Giving the mash a final stir she shifted her pots around the hobs to the best advantage. She gave a sausage and mince stew a shake and lifting a square tin tea-caddy decorated with pictures of King George V and Queen Mary from the mantelpiece swiftly measured out three teaspoonfuls into a big brown enamel teapot. Filling the teapot from a boiling kettle she laid it before the fire-ribs on a highly polished steel slider-edge.

Still frowning with an eight-year-old's temper Ella tugged open a brown cupboard door beside the iron sink and dried her hands on the towel hanging inside. As she dried them she irritably pushed aside the dishcloth hanging from the same nail and put out a rebellious tongue at the cups and plates and spare pots stacked on the three shelves inside. The edges of the shelves were decorated with crinkly pink paper attached by drawing-pins.

'Some day,' said her mother, 'you'll stick that tongue so far out you'll not get it back in again.'

Ella twitched her nose quick like a rabbit and stalked sullenly to the table. Sitting on the near-side chair she clasped her hands determinedly in her lap. Without turning away from her watch on the fireplace her mother said, 'You sup that soup, my lady, and no more of your nonsense.'

A girl bringing her father's lunch to him at John Brown's yard. (Imperial War Museum)

'Well, you *know* I don't like soup!' whined Ella.

'You don't like a lot of things,' said Julia briefly. 'Was Colin not in front of you?'

The child flicked her spoon peevishly. 'I don't know where he is – I never seen him.'

Unhurriedly Julia turned with the stirring fork in her hand. Without heat she said: 'I'll take my hand off your jaw if you speak to me like that. You eat up that soup and if you dribble any of it on that good frock I'll warm your behind for you. . . . I'm not your father, y'know.'

Resignedly Ella dipped her spoon. After two mouthfuls rancour faded from her face and she asked normally, 'Is my daddy not late?'

From Hugh Munro's novel *The Clydesiders*, 1961.

RUSHING THE GROWLER

There's nothing like the drinking goes on now that there was when I was a lad. I doubt there's many left in the yard who even know what 'rushing the growler' means.

There was drinking on and off the job then, and there was so much of it that it was the regular recognised job of the oldest boy to be sent out to buy whisky for the men. And that was what they called: he was sent out to rush the growler. It never crosses anybody's mind to try that today. There's a different attitude to drink altogether. In the old days I put a lot of it down to the way we were paid by the squad. All the money was in one big poke, and the men always adjourned to a pub to pay out. The money was divided out on a table and a lot of it was in the publican's pocket before they went home. It stood to reason. Even the man that didn't want a drink was more or less forced to have one.

Joe Curran reported in the *Lithgow Journal*, Autumn 1964.

A HALF AND A HALF

It was while working in the outside squad that I came to understand more fully the people on Clydeside, as I was frequently travelling with one or other of the fitters, and working very closely with them. One of these men was a drinker. Not that he drank too much; he just enjoyed it, and not being married, his spare cash went on booze. The first time I was working with him, he introduced me to the traditional Scottish 'half an' a half' – a measure of whisky taken neat in a very small glass, followed by a half pint of good, strong Scottish bitter as a chaser.

We had arrived to start on a repair job just as the pubs were opening. He swore me to secrecy, explaining that he worked better with a few drams inside him but did not want the bosses to know. I had never drunk much until then; my spare cash only allowed me an occasional beer. Scottish pubs in the 1940s, certainly in the towns, were dull and very uninviting. They were really just drinking parlours, frequented only by men. You rarely saw a woman inside one, and if a woman entered, even accompanied, it was usually assumed that she was of easy virtue, or worse.

The pub we went into on the Dumbarton Road was so forbidding that you

A view over Govan showing the shipyards of Fairfield and Harland and Wolff and the community that lay behind them. (Glasgow Museums)

immediately wanted a drink to cheer yourself up. Jim set up the first round. Realising my ignorance, he showed me how you downed the dram of whisky in a gulp, tipped the dregs into your beer, then gently chased the golden liquid until the two met up and gave you a warm glow inside. My stomach and throat were completely unprepared for this potent liquid coming at them in a huge gulp, and I was coughing and spluttering before I could get the beer to my lips. Jim thumped me on the back, and said, 'Take the beer, lad. Wash it doon. Yer'll soon get the hang o' it.' He ordered the same again. I took the second one more gingerly; I was not even sure that I liked whisky. By the time I had finished my third 'half an' a half' on an empty stomach, my head was spinning. By the time we reached the engine room of the ship to begin work, I was having great difficulty focusing, especially when it came to finding the right spanner for various nuts. At one point, Jim told me to lie flat and reach down between the gap in the metal deck plates where we were standing, and loosen some nuts on the lower part of the pump. Putting my head and shoulders down through the gap was nearly the end of me. I lost my grip, slipped further down, and Jim and another engineer had to grab me before I went any further. As I was dragged up through the narrow opening, my wallet, containing all my important documents and what little money I possessed, slipped out of my pocket and landed in the bilge water. I was advised to let them go, but I was not going to lose such precious items so easily, especially the hard-earned money. To hell with the state of my head, I asked the two men to hold my ankles as I eased my whole body down through the gap. Hanging at full stretch, I could just reach the bilge water and managed to scoop up my valuables before they sank or floated away. It was some time before they dried out, and some time before I drank so much again, especially on an empty stomach.

From Nicholas Parsons' autobiography, *The Straight Man*, 1994.

SHIPBUILDING FAMILIES

I had a lot of friends as a young lad, who were all in shipyards. . . . And it was quite common to be sitting talking in somebody's house to each other about what we were doing in work. And the women of that family would join in as well, and talk quite knowingly about 'A' brackets and double bottoms and bulkheads and all the rest. The conversation had been ongoing all their life with their menfolk, and they picked it up as commonplace. They could go into the shipyard and start to build the ships themselves: they knew so much about it. And when I first heard it, it quite surprised me, because I didn't come from a shipbuilding family myself, and I didn't hear this conversation in my own house. But when I was up in Tony Sharkey's, Robert Smith's, or these sort of people, their mums and dads spoke about shipyards as if they were out the back street, you know. In fact, Robert's house actually looked into the yard, you know; that's how close it was.

Pat McCrystal, a foreman shipwright, speaking in *Made in Govan: An oral history of shipbuilding on the Upper Clyde 1930–1950*, 1991.

A VICTORIAN FAMILY HOME

The homes that the bosses lived in could hardly have been more different from those of their workers. Here John G. Inglis remembers his grandfather John Inglis' house in Dowanhill, Glasgow.

Four Princes Terrace was quite a large stone-built terrace house in the Victorian style and faced north which meant that the front of the house got no sun and in the sooty air of Glasgow at that time the bright clean sandstone soon became blackened and looked rather forbidding.

Downstairs there was a semi-basement kitchen and staff bed-rooms, etc. Like so many similar houses the 'ground floor' was approached up five or six massive stone steps and the front door was kept locked. Every caller, every son till long after coming of age and every tradesman or messenger boy had to ring one of the two bells marked 'Private' or 'Tradesmen' and each time one of these bells rang below stairs a maid had to climb the stairs and answer the door.

On this ground floor were the dining room, the parlour which faced south, the spare bedroom where lady callers deposited their cloaks, the pantry and the schoolroom with its four desks made at the shipyard and a piano. There was also a small cloakroom for coats and hats where a row of polished black boots sat each morning and where carpet slippers were donned on returning in the evening. It had a washhand basin but no 'loo' which meant using Grandfather's bathroom one up for the privileged or the one two stairs up – nearly sixty stairs – for the sons and their friends. The hall was very dark and made more so by the front door panel which instead of translucent glass was filled with a stained glass portrait of King Robert the Bruce in his cave watching the spider.

The first floor contained a double drawing room with folding doors to divide it for smaller parties. The complete room ran the full depth of the house and had large bay windows at either end. It contained a Steinway concert grand piano and an organ made specially in Paris and here the family string quartet, quintet and even sextet performed all the classical repertoire for these combinations of players. Grandfather like his own father Anthony had a magnificent bass voice and his 'Drinking Song' and 'Oh ruddier than the Cherry' were something to be remembered and treasured.

On the same floor as the drawing room were the Grandparents' large bedroom and dressing room and the nursery whilst on the top floor were the four bedrooms for the 'Boys' and also the billiard room which for many years was the only place where smoking was allowed apart from the post-prandial cigars in the dining room. The cold and rather uncomfortable billiard room was really the sons' lounge after they had become too big for the nursery, but as a child I often listened to tales of football matches in the nursery in which my mother and her sisters and the Hamilton girl cousins took part. From all accounts these were lively occasions with no quarter given and formed either a tribute to the solidity of the house or the soundness of the Grandparents' post-prandial snooze.

From John G. Inglis' memoirs, *Inglis, Glasgow: The story of a shipbuilding family*, 1977.

A NEW HOME

Many of the bosses preferred to live in the country, far from the dirt and grime of their shipyards. All up and down the Clyde coast mansions were built for the wealthy shipyard owners.

During the past months Bessie and I have looked at several country houses, Fallowside, Melrose; Muirburn, near Strathaven; Tour near Kilmarnock; Dalmore at Row, etc. We have done this because the Knowe has been very noisy since the spar yard in front was started, and will get more noisy and smoky, and I sometimes thought I should like a place with farms and some shooting, but the places for sale are generally in very bad order, requiring great repairs. . . . During these months Seafield at Ardrossan has been for sale in consequence of the late Bryce Douglas' death. Bessie has always liked it. The house is nice, the garden well sheltered and the accommodation considerably more than the Knowe.

When I bought the Knowe in the spring of 1885 I thought we had reached our ultimatum in the way of residence, and I still like the place very much. The

Seafield House, the seaside home of Joseph Russell, shipbuilder at Port Glasgow. (North Ayrshire Museum)

house has every convenience we want, the garden is very pretty and the place is within our financial capacity.

I look forward to Seafield with some anxiety as to society and Church.

The place was sold for £5,000 to a Mr McClure of Glasgow who hoped to re-sell it to a syndicate but failed to do so and thus it came back on the market. Bessie had made the matter the subject of special prayer and I hope that it will turn out well. Bryce Douglas paid £7,500 for it and spent, it is said, as much more. I have paid £4,500 for it.

Extract of 19 January 1893 of the diaries and papers of Joseph Russell 1834–1917, Shipbuilder, Port Glasgow, held at Glasgow City Archives.

SATURDAY RELEASE

His heart leaped when the foreman popped his head over the half-door of the store about eleven and called on Danny to run across to the engine-shop with a message to the foreman there. For this meant a licensed escape from the yard at a vital hour – and Danny had just remembered his need of something necessary to his enjoyment of the afternoon.

In their wisdom the Magistrates of that part of the world in which Pagan's was situated had long ordained that public-houses should open at ten and close at noon on Saturdays. The ordinance was based on the theory that the working-man should not be tempted to squander his wages on strong drink on his way home, and had no doubt a bearing on public behaviour at the after-noon football games; but as the artisan had for many a day past been paid on Fridays it was only an interesting anachronism of local administration and bore hardly on such as Danny who desired refreshment in anticipation of other enjoyments. So the foreman's gruff order rejoiced him. It was easy to slip into Mackenzie's, between Yard and engine-shop, swallow a quick half and half-pint, buy a flat half-mutchkin of whisky for the pocket and the cold vigil on the terraces, and time his return to the store almost as the whistle boomed the signal for the week-end release.

Thereafter there was nothing in the world for him but the Game. He hurried home, hurried through his washing and changing and eating, and, as if all the claims of family and hearth were nothing now, was out on the streets again half an hour before two o'clock, a unit of one of the streams of men converging from all parts of the city and from all its outliers on the drab embankments round an oblong of turf in Ibrox.

From George Blake's novel *The Shipbuilders*, 1935.

THE FUTURE AT THEIR FEET

These boys have the future of industry in their hands, and at their feet. This at least will never change. I don't care how much the yards are streamlined these boys will always, but always, grab a ball in their lunch break and knock it stupid. This old place has as many notices forbidding football as it does football players.

From the Scottish Television documentary about Fairfield's, *The Bowler and the Bunnet*, narrated by Sean Connery, 1967.

FOOTBALL

In those years of my youth I was anxious to learn, and I certainly got every opportunity. I was Timekeeper, looked after the Stores, and at the Cost Books all in turn, and there wasn't much about the construction of engines and boilers that I didn't know – at least I thought so. In addition to my daily work I had evening classes to attend, and altogether I had a busy time, but Saturdays then, as now, were devoted to football and cricket. We had a John Elder Football Club and a Cricket Club – with playing ground in the Dock Park free of cost. I was the Treasurer of the Clubs. The Engine Draughtsmen were also great at football in those days. Every dinner hour there was a migration to the Dock Park. On wet days they played in the corridor of the Old Office.

From George Strachan's retirement speech *From Ticket Boy to Director*, 1921.

THE SPORTING GROUSE AT STRATHALMOND

The Scotstoun Marine Welfare Trophy football final took place at Strathalmond Park on the evening of Monday June 2. Results – welders 5 – platers 2. The following 'graphic' account was written (with tongue in cheek) by Danny Bill, manager (!) . . .

'A lively ball and over-enthusiasm spoiled what should have been a cracker as both teams were studded with has beens, was beens and never had beens who all quickly settled to the slow, lazy pace to which they were accustomed.

'However much to the amazement of the platers, for some unaccountable reason the welders managed to score from a misdirected balloon effort from Conlon.

'The platers immediately gave their dead bones a rattle, and had some very near misses, but worse was in store for them.

'A welder called Kennoway fell on to a ball which went into the net, to put the welders two up.

'This angered a character called Danny who threatened the platers to such an extent that, believe it or not, they scored through Johnson with a glorious cross high ball which stretched the welders' goalkeeper to at least two feet or 606mm behind the line, but the referee was looking the right way at the time and had no hesitation in awarding the goal.

'The shock caused Danny to collapse, to be revived by a stimulant from a bottle labelled Grouse.

'This conditioner was really good, as some of the platers' team collapsed and were immediately revived and rejuvenated with a drop from the same bottle.

'They also seemed braver than ever, and McComish managed to struggle another ball into the net. At 2–2 the play raged from end to end and so did the fans.

'Thanks to a strong referee with a good pea in his whistle, two players, one from each team, were given their marching orders.

'However, during the interval the welders' team were fed their "Bob Martins" by "Big Bad John Magee", which seemed to work wonders as they soon scored again with an acrobatic goal by McLeod using Taylor's shoulders to add height.

'Norville took advantage of the fact that the sun was in the eyes of the platers' goalkeeper to add number 4.

'By this time the platers were anxious to adjourn for refreshments and carelessly gave away a penalty which Conlon converted.

'A great night was enjoyed by all, the highlight of the evening being the presentation of prizes by Alex Pettigrew – who for once was smiling.'

From *Keel*, the newspaper of the Govan Shipbuilding Group, July 1976.

A SHIPBUILDER'S SPORT

The sporting passions of the employers, however, were of an altogether different nature.

In September 1930, as guest of Sir James and Henry Lithgow who, incidentally, were keen yet friendly competitors of Burntisland, I shot grouse over their Ducal moor in Renfrewshire. The previous evening I stayed with Sir James and Lady Lithgow at Gleddoch House. I was intrigued by a caterpillar-type train operating on a narrow gauge railway for conveying the 'guns' and their equipment around the moor to the locations of the various shooting butts, in its course, riding over heather knowes and bridging yawning gullies and tumbling burns. There were eight vehicles with tramway-type seats; lockers for coats and other accoutrements; cloth-lined drawers for guns; dog kennels; a van containing lunch comestibles: then an open truck for the game. The petrol engines in front were operated by James; Henry controlled the brake mechanism at the rear. The

The works football team from the Ayrshire Dockyard Company at Irvine. (Scottish Maritime Museum)

Below:
The 100-yard dash at the Ardrossan shipyard's annual sports day in the 1920s. (North Ayrshire Museum)

Members of the Scott family enjoying a day out on their steam yacht *Carola*, which was built at their shipyard at Bowling. (Scottish Maritime Museum)

railway, with the various bridges, was an ingenious contraption but it did not flatter the ability of the Lithgow brothers as civil engineers! Thanks to its convenience we took part in six drives. In each there was something of interest, whether it was the initial flush of grouse planing over the butts; the bird that doubled back over the beaters; the wily one that sheered off to dodge the wing gun on the line, or the intelligent dogs after their suppressed excitement hunting the scent of fallen birds and bringing them to hand. The bag totalled 127 brace of grouse and sundries. It had been 'grouse shooting without tears' and an enjoyable experience.

From Wilfred Ayre's autobiography, *A Shipbuilder's Yesterdays*, 1968.

THE PICTURES

Apart from football, another weekly treat for many a shipbuilder, especially those with wives or girlfriends, was a trip to the pictures.

They took up their positions in the queue outside The Sun, though their favourite house was The Western Mecca. MacKelvie was not a fan and was attracted to a picture by the appeal, or otherwise, of a title. Tonight his choice was limited. There was no choice other than a choice of variation. *Ginger in Love, Purple Passion, Love Deferred* or *She Sinned for Love*. None of these titles attracted MacKelvie or his wife. What did determine their choice was a short comic entitled *Tenderfoot Tim* featuring Slim M'Gurk. Jean MacKelvie thought they might get a laugh at that however bored they might be with sinning for love.

The shade from a block of tenements cooled them from the heat of the sun. The air was warm and sultry. By the time the first house came out at a quarter to nine the queue was round the corner into Dumbarton Road. With a patience exceeding the patience of dumb domesticated animals the crowd waited hoping they would get a seat but quite resigned, should that luxury not be forthcoming, to stand. The Saturday night had reached that dreadful point when, failing admittance to *She Sinned for Love*, there was no other way in which to spend the night. In a quarter of an hour the stimulation of alcohol would be denied the citizenry.

MacKelvie and his wife were fortunate in securing a seat. The atmosphere was foul and oppressive. MacKelvie felt there was something wrong with spending such a night in such an atmosphere. But his wife had to get a break sometime. This, wrongly or not, was the best break she could get. Jean felt it was a break. She was not enamoured of the sophisticated love-making of the foolish Hollywood puppets. Nor did she enjoy the fantastic exploits of the celebrated Slim M'Gurk. But for nearly two hours she was able to forget she lived in Walker Street . . . able to forget its sounds, smells and meannesses. This constituted a break in her weekly darg: her seven-day battle with existence.

From James Barke's novel *Major Operation*, 1936.

THE DANCING

A trip to the dancing was another popular weekend treat for the courting shipbuilder.

She was a wonderful partner, perfect in every movement, instinctive and effortless in anticipation. They danced in silence until, abruptly, Colin asked, 'Come here often?'

Equally cryptic she said, 'No.'

They covered half the length of the hall with a couple of reverse turns before he said, 'Where d'you usually go?'

'Paisley Town Hall.'

'Come from Paisley?'

'No.'

'Where do you come from?'

'Burnford.'

He stepped back from her and cocked his head. She had pale, boyish features and neat black eyebrows. Her straight jet hair was cut in a bob so close and smooth it seemed to have fitted round rather than grown on her well-shaped head. He had an impression of a white slender neck disappearing into a high-bodiced, simple red frock. 'I don't know your face,' he confessed.

'I've had it for years.'

'Oh – wise girl!' and they both laughed.

'What's the attraction in Paisley?' he quizzed as the band resumed after the first of the two customary encores.

'My pal likes it there.'

He looked to where the red-head was gliding along but talking animatedly in the arms of McBride. 'Is she giving the home town a break tonight?'

'Oh, that's not my pal,' the brunette followed his glance. 'My regular chum couldn't manage to the dancing tonight and Lily asked me to come here with her.'

'Funny I don't know you. What did you say your name was?'

'I didn't say.'

They laughed again. But by the end of the encore he knew her name was Ann White. She and her friend were assistants in a multiple store.

From Hugh Munro's novel *The Clydesiders*, 1961.

THE RECREATION CLUB

Because of the big influx of employees, in March 1920, we inaugurated a recreation club. This was an obligation we felt we could not evade. It was financed on a part contributory basis. We acquired a sports ground and laid out appropriate facilities for cricket, football and tennis, each with their separate pavilions. These were well patronised and appreciated by various kinds of employees and followers. Opportunities for playing golf, bowls and badminton were organised. At a later stage, we acquired a commodious institute with rooms for billiards and reading. These amenities were warmly appreciated by our employees, particularly those whose homes were still in distant places.

From Wilfred Ayre's autobiography, *A Shipbuilder's Yesterdays*, 1968.

THE OFFICE STAFF DANCE

On the evening of Friday, 26th December last, the staff of the different Departments in the Office together with their friends held their Annual Dance.

The Committee, determined to provide an even better function than last year's, engaged the large Ballroom in the Grand Hotel where fully 220 people assembled. The Dance commenced before eight o'clock and was kept up in the liveliest of spirits throughout the whole evening.

A quintette orchestra supplied by Messrs Govan Brothers rendered a programme of the latest in Dance music and were repeatedly called upon for encores.

As luck would have it, the Taxi-drivers' strike began on the day of the Dance but although some of the revellers arrived late, the inconvenience caused in no way damped down their enthusiasm.

The artistically designed programme was the work of one of the Draughtsmen and displayed twenty-one appropriately chosen dances. A remark made in the local Press regarding the selection of the dances was probably near the mark – 'the Dances seemed to admirably suit the "modern steppers" as well as those of the older school.'

There is no doubt about the social qualities of our staff, but much of the evening's enjoyment was due to the Master of Ceremonies, Mr Kenneth MacKenzie, who worked right hard.

The announcement of the last Dance at 2 a.m. was received universally with regret. Owing to the foresight of the Committee the company were relieved of their Taxi-strike worries, as two special tramcars were in waiting to convey the majority to within easy reach of their homes.

From the *Linthouse Works Magazine*, March 1920.

Shipbuilders letting their hair down at the Lithgow's staff dance in 1959. (Glasgow University Archives)

ANNUAL OUTING OF THE FOREMEN AND OFFICIALS

Under favourable weather conditions and amid hearty cheers four motor charabancs left the main gate of Linthouse on Saturday, 23rd August, at 1.30 p.m.

As they turned to the right on to the Govan Road, a boy supporting the corner of the aeroplane shed remarked to his companion, 'Is't the Band o' Hope away fur a pic-nic.'

'Naw,' the other replied, 'It's only the heid yins at Linthoose oot on the skite.'

So modest and retiring did the company appear that except for this stray remark no one would have guessed that it had anything to do with shipbuilding and engineering.

The Party, proceeding along Govan Road at about twelve knots per hour, soon reached Paisley Road via Hillington Road, and then going through Crookston and various by-roads, found itself at Nellie's Toll on the Kilmarnock Road.

Here the company sat back and began to enjoy a bit of real country scenery: with rolling moors on either side showing purple in the Sunshine, intersected with streams standing out like streaks of silver, the cars climbed to the highest point of the road, where, in the distance, the peaks of Arran could be seen, and still further on, peeping over the Ayrshire hills, 'Paddy's Milestone'.

Soon a signpost on the left indicating 'To Galston' appeared and a few miles along the road a stop was made to refresh the engines and allow the company a chance to view the country.

One worthy member of the staff, an ardent student of nature no doubt, proceeded to the side of the road the better to look at some fine Ayrshire cattle grazing in a field: unfortunately, some thoughtless County Council had ordered a ditch to be dug there; the said ditch, as time went on, had become overgrown with grass, etc., and, but for the fact that our friend's co-efficient of fineness is roughly estimated at .999, he might have completely disappeared: happily, he was 'salved' by willing hands and soon all were in their places once more and the charabancs under way.

Soon, on the left, Loudoun Castle, the seat of the Earl of Loudoun, came into view and then the village of Galston. This was skirted and, by turning to the left, Newmills was entered and so on to Strathaven arriving at the Crown Hotel about five o'clock, where the company numbering about a hundred did ample justice to a very splendid tea.

Mr John Ferguson occupied the chair, and in a few well-chosen words said how glad he was to see such a fine turn-out and expressed the regrets of a number of the Shipping Company's Representatives at their inability to be present; but he extended a hearty welcome to those who had been able to come. He felt sure, he went on to say, that the company would be proud to see with them on such an occasion Mr A. Murray Stephen, Mr Fred Stephen's eldest son, who had now been demobilised and had made a start in the works; he took the opportunity of giving him a hearty welcome to Linthouse.

After tea, the company adjourned to the Public Park where most interesting sports were held. A start was made with the hundred yards race; then followed the three-legged race in which no one under three feet six was allowed to link up with anyone above seven feet, competitors to understand that crawling was forbidden: then came the egg-and-spoon race, a race for those over forty years of age, and the wheelbarrow race.

A special race was arranged between the Shipyard and Engine Shop Representatives, the weights of the competing parties being taken into account when arranging the handicaps: taking this into consideration, the company was not surprised at the Engine Shop Representatives coming in second. Nevertheless it was a close and exciting finish.

The event of the day, the Tug-of-war, came next. Four captains were chosen – Mr Ferguson, who, as the programme announced, 'would punch' his men if they did not win; Mr Firth who would put the 'screw' on his men if they did not win. Mr Sampson – 'And Samson called unto the Lord and said "Strengthen me (and my men) I pray Thee".' Mr Currie whose powder would be given before starting, and who, should his men fail at the first pull, would address them in a manner calculated to inspire all with fresh vigour.

Each of these gentlemen chose eleven members of the company. Mr Sampson's 'call' must have had the desired effect, as his team left the field unbeaten. This is not to be wondered at when one saw his choice, Messrs David Brown, Alf Horsburgh, William Sinclair, Charles Brown, William Johnston, Hugh McLean, David Donnelly, David McCrindle, Dan McKay, John Graham, Robert Leitch.

The company then returned to the 'Crown' where the presentation of prizes was made. These were numerous and valuable and were greatly appreciated by the recipients.

A few special presentations were made including one to the chairman for his untiring efforts at all such meetings; his took the form of a very fine steel engraving of his Majesty the King suitably framed.

A hearty vote of thanks was accorded the Committee for its splendid arrangements and to the chairman for the genial way he had carried out his duties.

After 'Auld Lang Syne' was sung followed by the customary three hearty cheers, the party resumed their seats in the conveyances which were again in waiting. These were soon filled and a start was made for home, travelling via Chapelton, East Kilbride, Busby, Pollokshaws and Dumbreck, arriving at Govan about ten-thirty. The arrangements for the comfort and enjoyment of the company were admirably carried out and great credit was due to the Committee who arranged one of the most enjoyable and successful outings the Foremen and Officials of Messrs. Alexander Stephen & Sons, Ltd, have yet had.

From the *Linthouse Works Magazine*, October 1919.

The Lithgow staff bowling match in 1962. (Glasgow University Archives)

THE CLYDEBANK FAIR

It was that magical time of year again, the first fortnight in July, The Clydebank Fair. Two weeks off work with three weeks' wages to spend. Now in 1957, Spain and Majorca were just dots on the map, while 'doon the watter' was the standing order for Maw, Paw, and the weans. However not everyone could afford the luxury of a holiday, and the next best thing was to go on the 'Fair Sunday' bus run. In 1957 the destination was Dunoon. Now, while most men were partial to a generous refreshment, some didn't drink at all, and these were usually detailed to run the bus and keep good order. At the end of a very enjoyable day, it was to one of these 'officials' that a pub owner called out, 'There's a guy in here, very drunk, he's sound asleep, does anybody know him?' He was recognised immediately. 'That's wee John Ticketts, he's a plater in John Brown's, he must have come down on another bus, don't worry, we'll get him home safely!' On their arrival they announced, 'We've brought yer faither hame!' His daughter stood silent for what seemed like an eternity, and then burst into uncontrollable laughter. 'What's so funny?' asked Jimmy Elgin in his best shop-steward's voice (shop-stewards are like polis – they're never off duty!). 'Nothing compared to how funny it will be in the morning when Dad wakes up – you see, he and Mum only just went to Dunoon on Saturday morning . . . to start their fortnight's holiday!' The word spread like wildfire, and with razor-sharp precision, the shipyard satirists went into overdrive and a new nickname was soon to be launched on the Clyde which would bring many a wry smile to the faces of old-timers for years to come when asked by new apprentices, 'Why do they call that plater . . . "Return Ticketts"?'

From Alfred Forbes Smith's *I Belong to Glasgow*, 2000.

A WORKS CAMP

Many of the Clyde engineering works and shipyards, including Beardmore's, went on an annual camp to the Isle of Man.

The members who attended our 1926 Camp have been heard to describe it as 'our best' so far, and, while this may not be altogether true, it justifies the remark made in an earlier issue that if we but maintained the high standard of our past holiday camps all concerned would be more than satisfied.

The camp was an undoubted success, due no doubt to the excellent behaviour and loyal support of every member.

The following were outstanding features in the camp programme:-

A charabanc tour round the island, visiting all places of interest.

A swimming gala in which the Beardmore contingent won the relay race and other events.

A fancy dress parade in which Beardmore won the first three places for fancy dress. The parade which was organized on behalf of the Lifeboat Institute and the local hospital, collected the sum of about £14 for these deserving institutions.

Not the least attractive feature of the programme was a night spent at sea with the Scottish fishing fleet. Although mal-de-mer 'hove to' occasionally, the night

Crowds of people enjoying a trip 'doon the watter' on the *Queen Alexandra* in 1924. (North Ayrshire Museum)

Left:
The Lithgow's Club annual outing gave shipbuilders and their families a chance to relax. (Glasgow University Archives)

The annual outing of the staff from Scott's shipyard at Greenock. (Glasgow University Archives)

was voted a most enjoyable experience; all concerned were greatly appreciative of the kindness shown to them by the crews.

Dancing knows no season and our camp was no exception. In addition to other dances, a special dance carnival was arranged by the camp party for the Friday evening and provided the *pièce de résistance* of the Peel season.

The various sports of football, golf, tennis, swimming, etc., etc., were enjoyed to the full. In addition to other successes the Beardmore Football Team won the camp championship.

From the *Beardmore News* of September 1926.

HOLIDAYS AND RESTARTING

At one of the Welfare Committee meetings the question was raised regarding the length of the New Year Holiday, and it was suggested that three or four days were sufficient. On the other hand it was stated that no matter how long the Holidays were the majority of the men would take a day or two longer than the official Holiday. On the 8th of January we were curious to know if such would be the case. It was.

On further inquiry we learned that it was 'just custom'; we were told that 'the men had always done it'; that 'if the Holidays were of a month's duration or longer, the same thing would happen.'

There seems to be no real reason for such a state of affairs. Most of us from our early schooldays hated the first day's work after the Holidays, and the day or two extra that is taken may just be the 'putting off of the evil day', a Holiday habit that will go on until Doomsday, we suppose. It is a pity, though, especially for the womenfolk whose household expenses run high these days.

From the *Linthouse Works Magazine*, March 1920.

AFTER THE HOLIDAYS

All the black squads used to gather outside the yard gates the morning you were supposed to start work after a holiday. Then somebody would 'toss the brick'. If the brick landed on its end then we'd start back. It's a funny thing but for a few days the brick never seemed to land the right way up! People drifted back to work as their money ran out. This ceremony was just to remind the bosses that they didn't own us – that they needed us just as much as we needed them!'

From Alan McKinlay's oral history of John Brown's shipyard between the World Wars, *Making Ships, Making Men*, 1991.

CHAPTER SIX

CHARACTERS AND CARRY-ONS

Shipyards were renowned for the interesting characters who worked in them. The humour of the yards is legendary. The fantastic stories and the running jokes that spread through the yards, the tales of the strange goings-on and the high jinks that the men got up to have been passed down through generations. It also seemed that just about everyone in the yards had a weird or bizarre nickname often conferred by some joker as the result of an incident or physical characteristic.

As well as the comedians there were also a great many poets, artists, musicians and writers whose talents could often be seen and heard inside the yards. The sheer number of people who worked in the yards meant that of course there would be a proportion of talented individuals employed in them, but shipyards certainly seemed to have more than their fair share. Some who went on to find fame and fortune outside the yards include Billy Connolly, Alex Ferguson, Gus Macdonald and Nicholas Parsons. These examples give an added gloss to the romance of the yards, but it was really the men who stayed behind who made them so special.

Although many of the characters were humorous and their exploits amusing, there could also be a dark side to some of the yard characters. There were some seriously 'hard' people in the yards and violence was common. A great deal of underhand dealing also went on. Petty pilfering was endemic. You could get virtually anything you wanted from a shipyard. The Queen Mary *must have been fitted out at least twice, given the number of Clydebank homes that claimed to have furniture or other fittings from the liner. The usual way to get things home from the yard was down a trouser leg, which obviously limited the size of what could be smuggled out. Shipyard workers are nothing but ingenious, however, and it is said that one Clydebank kitchen was beautifully fitted out with the latest formica tops, all made up out of three-inch strips.*

Scrap metal was the most popular thing for stealing. Big money could be made from it, and in some cases there were organised gangs who ran quite elaborate scrap-metal rackets. In an attempt to counteract this wholesale plunder of the yards, gate-men, watchmen and even special shipyard detectives were employed, but they were able to find only a fraction of the material that disappeared out of the gates. The poor wages, terrible working conditions and lack of job security meant that the workers felt little guilt at all this stealing. Indeed, for many it was not simply a matter of supplementing their wages but also a matter of pride in getting one over on the bosses.

However, the culture of deception and corruption could be found among some of the bosses as well, although they tended to be involved in slightly more subtle rackets. Common scams were fiddling the piecework tallies, claiming wages for non-existent workers or demanding back-handers for putting choice jobs the way of certain people.

Needless to say, this corrupt behaviour did not do the industry any good in terms of productivity and profitability and contributed in no small way to the demise of shipbuilding in Scotland. In the modern efficient industry of today such practices have largely gone by the board. There are certainly fewer colourful characters than there used to be, but the fact that shipbuilding is still such a passionate and emotional industry means that it will always attract workers who are just that little bit out of the ordinary.

Previous page: Workers enjoying a break among the drag chains. (Imperial War Museum)

WONDERFUL STORIES

There are all kinds of wonderful stories of enormous feats of strength. The reason that they grew up is a very interesting one. Because a shipyard is such a noisy place – if you think of thousands of men hammering, and people doing all kinds of jobs and hammering about with steel, and what they are hammering is like a big steel drum because it's hollow and they batter away and the noise is horrendous. Conversations do not take place. Everything is done with body language or mimed words, you know, so when the lunch hour came along, or the breaks, it was a grand opportunity, after you had been forcibly quietened for four or five hours, to come out with the boasting and the great tales and all that kind of stuff. Out of that grew a kind of mythology, a kind of bravado, macho tale-telling where you were the hero and this was the tale that you were actually going to tell. These sort of things always permeated in the shipyards. When anybody ever told a good story it would eventually come down through the generations and be embossed and embellished.

I suppose one of the best examples of how exaggerated they actually got, because they grew in the years, was – I had an uncle who was a riveter and it was always supposed to be that your uncle Jimmy, the strength that man's got is unbelievable, and once when he was riveting a ship – and just to explain the basic process, the rivet is put into the hole and there's a guy who stands at the back of the rivet with a hammer called a holder-on to stop it flying out the hole – and he took a draw on his Woodbine, and that uncle hit that rivet so hard that it went down one deck, penetrated another deck, went down through another deck, hit the tank top, bounced and ricocheted straight through the side of an armour-plated ship that was twelve and a half inches thick, flew across the Clyde and killed two sheep that were grazing on the Cart.

That was the sort of great mythological stories of strength there were, and there was always the tale-telling and the idea of comedy, and the patter merchant, and that sort of stuff grew up out of that need to communicate when there was the occasional silence.

Tom McKendrick speaking on the video to accompany his exhibition *Iron* at the Collins Gallery, 1997.

LUNCHTIME DREAMING

During the meal hour a long stretch of blue sky floated up from the east. Brian and Sannie sat on a bench on the top deck, their cans of tea and sandwiches separated by a vice which Sannie used as a prop for his elbow while he chewed and swallowed mechanically. Brian dreamily gazed down at the river, so smooth and sleek looking from this height, and let his gaze drift lazily across to the fields on the other side. Here, where he sat, was a maze of steel cranes, plates, girders, machinery, all strangely silent now. And yet just across the water there were cows browsing below a farmhouse, and above that a belt of trees. Men worked over there in the peaceful fields all day, while here was a soul-tormenting riot of sounds, smells and fatiguing drudgery. But the meal hours were golden intervals of rest and quiet. Brian loved these meal hours with old Sannie Stuart. If a ship

The lunch breaks were a great opportunity for joking and story-telling. Photograph by Cecil Beaton. (Imperial War Museum)

passed Sannie could tell you where it came from, how many engineers she carried, her type of engines, and a hundred and one answers to a hundred and one questions.

From Edward Shiels' novel about Beardmore's Dalmuir yard, *Gael over Glasgow*, 1937.

THE CHARACTERS

My two best workmates were Helen's cousin Ian Morrison and John Gray. John's father, George, was the boilermakers' convener during the UCS crisis, and Ian's dad, Jim, was a liner-off for the sheet-iron department. John, Ian and I were known as the 'A' team as we were always together. While working on a ship we used railway wagons as departmental offices cum changing rooms and canteen. We had this helper working with us who was nicknamed 'Super-chicken'. He used to fall asleep on the job regularly. One day, while he was sleeping during the tea break, someone poured salt on his tongue as he slept with his mouth open, and he never even stirred. The characters were the one thing that kept you sane. There was 'Wullie the dug', who used to creep up behind you, bark and grab your ankle, and it didn't matter how many times he did it to you, you always jumped. Then there was 'The Doonhamer', whose trade was a shipwright. He always walked about with his maul over his shoulder, and when no one was looking he would smash things up with it. One of his jobs was to go out on the river after a launch and undo the wire connecting any timber and bring it ashore. He was sculling in a clinker-type boat, which means using one oar through a rowlock at the centre of the stern. While I was working on a ship in the next slipway to one where a ship had just been launched, I went up on the deck for a smoke. There was The Doonhamer, standing on his boat in the middle of the river, waving his bunnet and shouting for help as he had lost his oar.

There was a plater known as 'The Paratrooper' who told the story of flying over the desert during the Second World War and spotted a Woodbine cigarette on the sand so he landed to get it.

Our department had a sheet ironworker called 'Monty' who always wore a red beret and kept his money in a handkerchief. When he got his pay on a Friday he would sort out his cut and put it in his hankie.

Another character was a plater called John Mitchell who was known as 'The Talking Horse'. John was also a keen beekeeper and used to sell honey in the yard. Whenever there was a mass meeting John would plan his bombardment of the shop stewards, as he would call them. No matter what the meeting was about John would have something to say.

At every mass meeting he's there
To shout abuse at the chair.
You hear the lads cheer
When they see him appear
With the speech the last week he's prepared.

From Jim Collins' unpublished memoirs.

BALDIE

I was sent to work with a man called 'Baldie'. His real name was Archibald Deas. He was a middle-aged man with a very pale face and bushy black whiskers something like Lord Palmerston's. His chin and upper lip were clean shaven, and there was a suggestion of the monkey about him. He was very strong, and I never knew him tired.

Although I was no prude, I had been shocked at first by the blasphemy and obscenity of the workmen, but that feeling soon wore off, and when I started as Baldie's mate I had acquired considerable proficiency in the use of bad language: but Baldie's was a revelation, and I feel it is a pity that his conversation is unprintable. His figures of speech and his mixture of incongruous adjectives and nouns showed a sort of genius. He was an excellent workman, and besides teaching me to be an expert swearer he showed me how to use a hammer and chisel and a file almost as well as he did himself. He was always cheerful, and even at six o'clock on a cold winter morning he would begin the day by saying, 'What do you think the wife said to me last night?' and then would follow an account of a probably quite imaginary conversation in which Mrs Deas showed a freedom of speech and a turn for repartee which would leave the newest of new women breathless.

From W. G. Riddell's autobiography of 1932, *Adventures of an Obscure Victorian.*

PLAYING TRICKS

The test engineers for whom I worked were real gentlemen, and always treated me with respect (even their pin-up calendars were taken down). They very rarely swore in front of me. As in all industries, there were the usual characters. Paul kept bees and sold the honey. He also made up a concoction of different blends of honey, filled small jars with it, and sold it at Christmas time as a hangover cure. We called him 'Buzz'. He detested the Royal Family, was very politically minded, and supported the Scottish National Party, the Labour party and the Tory party, whichever one agreed with his opinions at the time. His teacup was 'boggin' as it was only washed once a year, when Alistair gave it a 'spring clean' at the Fair. (Honest!)

Alistair was a member of the Theatre Guild and was an actor on and off stage. When he was going on the sea trials he asked me to post a birthday card to his wife and to be careful to send it off in plenty of time, as he had drawn a diagram inside the card to show her where her present was hidden.

Bobby was an apprentice and liked to play tricks on people. He would sellotape the buttons down on the cradle of the telephone so that when it rang and I lifted the receiver the phone kept on ringing. One day he played a stupid joke on one of the typists. He got a fish's head (don't ask me why) from the canteen, put it in a brown envelope, and sent it to her anonymously through the internal post. The typist went completely hysterical, thought there was a contract out on her, and nearly called the police. Bobby had to own up and was summoned to the manager's office, where he was severely reprimanded. He was very lucky not to have been dismissed.

From Ellen Robertson's memoirs, *Sappy Sooracks and Burnt Sugar*, 1996.

MAIMING AND MAYHEM

I started off as a general apprentice in Yarrow's Shipbuilders' Training Centre in Scotstoun in 1978 where you had a 'shot' at various methods of maiming oneself and other new recruits before specialising in your chosen method of mayhem for the next four years. I wanted to be a spark because I thought that was the best shout for 'homers'. Not to be – everyone wanted to re-wire houses after hours. No-one realised at the time that being an electrician aboard one of Her Majesty's warships also entailed hauling cable from one end of a frigate to the other, plus the odd bit of soldering once you arrived there. No, I was assigned to the 'black squad' or welder/burners. 'Mee-maw, mee-maw' meant someone had been set alight on purpose and everyone joined in the chorus until the hapless individual realised that it was indeed them that was alight.

After six months or so they needed draughtsmen. I had O levels. Apparently these were required, why didn't they say at the start? I was a Draffy – after a

Opposite: Workers larking about on the keel of a ship at Duncan's shipyard, Port Glasgow. (Imperial War Museum)

fashion. It was Jam/Buzzcocks/Elvis Costello, etc., in the canteen. . . the same at home. . . then the same again when I was supposed to be working. I will not be remembered for my skills with a Rotring pen. But I did love ships. Something to do with the fact that the 'Salty Highway' outside the office window could connect me with any and every part of the globe – a fixation for a sixteen-year-old with itchy feet. The yard's camaraderie and larger than life characters proved invaluable as an education. I still write about it.

From Kevin McDermott's text for the exhibition *Over the Wall* at the Vennel Gallery, 2001.

THE GREAT ENLIGHTENER

Two old cronies were sharing confidences, and Rab began. 'Man Jock. I jist wish I could coont a wee bit better; the ither Setterday I gied the wife ma' skin instead o' her pey.' Realising the struggle Rab would have had with the pay, Jock suggested the purchase of a Ready Reckoner: 'wi' it coontin' wis as easy as fishin'.' The great enlightener, even at a cost of fourpence, was indulged in, but even after a whole night's poring, the intricacies of arithmetic still stood unrevealed. Jock was chiselled about the matter, and confronted with his recommendation. He scanned the mystic page, but it was as big a maze to him; however, not to be beat he exclaimed, 'Nae winner ye canna' mak' it oot; it's last year's Ready Reckoner they've palmed aff on ye.'

From Mat H. Lion's observations in the *Linthouse Works Magazine* of September 1921.

THE ENTERTAINERS

Connolly talks about his years in the Clyde shipyards in the way that some literati conjure up their golden days at Eton or Oxford or Cambridge. 'I was so happy there,' he says. 'I fell right into it. Loved it. As soon as that gate shuts, a shipyard becomes a complete wee town. You could buy shoes, cigarettes, transistor radios, cheap booze. It was an amazing place.' 'It's an uncomfortable job at times,' he explains, 'wet, damp, cold. You weren't allowed a fire because the heat might buckle the metal. And the guys were forever peeing over the side so there was piss everywhere.'

But the yards had their compensations. Like Jimmy Lucas and his friend Dalgleish, two of the funniest men Connolly ever knew. 'They even sound like a variety act,' he observes. 'One was a plater and the other was a joiner. They used to tear me up. I wish they'd gone into show business.' Then there was the blacksmith who kept his fag bobbing about in front of his face on a wire attached to his helmet. And 'The Great Voltaine', a labourer who used to entertain the troops at dinner time dressed up in a silver-painted welder's helmet, and a cape decked out with light bulbs. 'He had a helper who walked about behind him with a battery, lighting the bulbs up. "Think of a number," Voltaine would shout. "Thirteen," somebody would say. "Correct. . . ." He was bloody great.' Connolly still delights in the repartee of the yards; the manager who tried to discipline a man caught with an illicit can of tea was told to piss off. 'So the manager says, "Do you know who I am?" And Wullie McInnes turns to his mate and says, "Hey Jimmy . . . here's a f—— disnae ken who he is . . ."'

From George Rosie writing in the *Sunday Times Magazine* of 23 February 1975.

GO FETCH

When I started out as an apprentice in the shipyards, I was terrified of all the older blokes. They used to say to me: 'Go and get this and fetch that,' and I'd do it. And one time they said: 'Can you go fetch this frae the Stowaway's Locker?' So off I went. 'Eh – excuse me, could you tell me where the Stowaway's Locker is?' 'Aye, son, doon there turn right, keep on past the paintshop and you'll see it.' Off again. 'Er . . . is this the Stowaway's Locker, please?' 'Naw, son – doon past thae benches there, turn left and ask again.' The place never existed, of course. It was all a big joke at the expense of the apprentices. So after I'd been there a few months one of them asked me to fetch some carborundum, which you have for sanding stuff down. And I thought: 'Carborundum' – that doesn't sound real. It must be another of their wee jokes. So I said; 'Naw, cannae fool me this time.' They didn't know what I was on about.

Another time, one of the welders sent an apprentice to get him twenty Embassy tipped. 'Aye, OK – what if they don't have any?' 'Och, just get me anything, son.'

He came back with two hot pies.

From Billy Connolly's *Gullibles Travels*, 1982.

THE BIG IMPERSONATOR

In the pattern shop, smoking was strictly forbidden because of the wood all around. There were two small outside lavatories at the rear of the building, which were often used by one or two apprentices sneaking off to have a smoke, or what they called 'a wee drag'. On one occasion, when I went out to the loos I opened the door of the first one to find three of my fellow apprentices puffing away. I said, 'Oh, I'll go next door.' They replied, 'No, no, come in, Nick. Quick, shut the door. D'yer wanna fag?' I said, 'No, I want a pee.' They said, 'Well, go ahead. Don't mind us. Next door's busy.' It is difficult enough to relieve yourself comfortably with three people closely watching, but it was made worse by one of them suddenly saying, 'Hey, Nick, gie us one of yer impersonations. Gie us Charles Boyer.' It was an incongruous situation. I was standing there with my boilersuit open and fly buttons undone, putting on the deep voice and French accent of the great cinema heartthrob, speaking the words he delivered in an emotional farewell scene with Bette Davis in the film *All This and Heaven Too*: 'No, no, my darling. Don't move. As I see you standing there, with the light on your hair, and your image in the mirror behind. This is how I want to remember you . . .' I finished, did up my fly buttons and made to go. 'Hey, Nick, that was great. Come on now, gie us yer Jimmy Stewart.' They would not let me go. Squashed between the three of them, I did a passage from *Mr Smith Goes to Washington*. I then had to give them their favourite, W. C. Fields. It did not compare with the Glasgow Empire, but they were a very appreciative audience. I gave them William Bendix, Max Miller, and had just launched into an impromptu script in Winston Churchill's voice about being closeted in an outside loo with three young characters discussing the war effort when there was an almighty banging on the door. It was forced open and there was an irate Jock Cunningham, minus teeth, purple with rage at this unforgivable waste of the firm's time. He rounded off an almost continuous string of expletives with, 'Get back to yer bench, yer big impersonator. Yer here to make patterns, no make yon buggers laugh.'

From Nicholas Parsons' autobiography *The Straight Man*, 1994.

SANDWICHES

'When I came in here I was a boy and there was all these big men, tough characters, and you sure as anything didn't want to be a shrinking violet around them boys. The humour in here was, still can be, very rough at times. If you have any wee thing noticeable about ye, they're on to it. The banter never stops. You'd have to have that in an industry as tough as this. Men died in these yards, remember, it's a dangerous industry. People fell or were crushed or got burned.'

He reeled off a list of names. The Pig. The Paratrooper. Pinky and Perky. Nicknames. He smiled then and told me a story about a man who was taken ill in the yard a few years back. 'Right away the boys called an ambulance, comforted him and made sure he was looked after. The ambulance came and everybody waited on word from the hospital. See, as soon as it came, the word

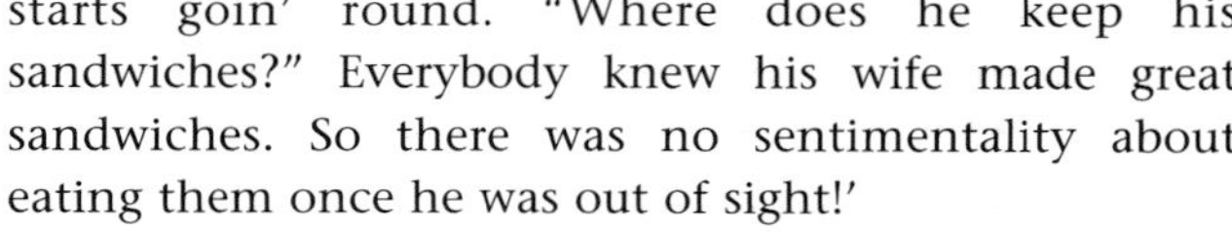

starts goin' round. "Where does he keep his sandwiches?" Everybody knew his wife made great sandwiches. So there was no sentimentality about eating them once he was out of sight!'

Two apprentices at Harland and Wolff. (Imperial War Museum)

From Fergal Keane's *A Stranger's Eye: A foreign correspondent's view of Britain*, 2000.

THE NAME GAME

Did you ever hear of the Haddie Choker, Qua Qua, Cherry Blossom, or the Derry Hangman? Of Dummy Bolt, Eachiboe, or Passage West?

Not only have you probably heard of them you may even be able to identify the men, for men they are, or were.

For these are a few of the nicknames given to men in the Clyde shipyards. Some were conferred on men at Govan, at Scotstoun, at Clydebank. In yards now vanished and in those still building.

For instance, take Sludgieguts. He's alive and working not five minutes from the Clyde Tunnel. The term is descriptive – his waistline demands roomy tailoring!

Haddie Choker – a shipwright who came from the North East of Scotland.

Pick a Plank – an old shipwright who spent his lunch break looking for all the straight planks to use, leaving the bent ones to others.

Metal Polish – he always carried a tin of polish in his tool box and cleaned his tools carefully at the end of the day.

Volga Boatman – sculling a lifeboat down the basin, he was carried by the current downriver and had to be rescued by the launch.

Iron Duke – as broad as he was tall (5'2"!), always on iron work. He used to talk to the bolts as he worked with them.

The Ghost – a yard security man.

Deen and Dour – two lads who joined their yard together, one from Aberdeen, the other from Aberdour.

Cherry Blossom – his boots were brighter than a Guardsman's and he always carried a cloth to dust them over as he worked.

Qua Qua – a Highlander whose name (Farquhar) and whose voice prompted his mates to imitate him.

Eachiboe – a Gaelic-speaking instructor whose mixture of the auld tongue and plain English earned him, too, an imitative nickname.

Derry Hangman – not sinister, just a man from Derry whose clothes didn't fit, but hung loosely from his frame.

In and Out Charlie – he changed yards as often as his shirt.

Mouse – at only 4'9" in height this old character could creep into the smallest places.

Passage West – a very old man, he hailed from a village of that name in Ireland. He had a superstition that no ship could sail off safely unless he was there to cast off her ropes.

Dummy Bolt – when putting two bolts in a beam, he always put in a 'dummy' – that is, one without a nut.

Urgent George – he always marked his jobs 'urgent' so that in fact, they were always left to last by the men who received the instruction!

Dock George – working in the same yard, this distinguished him from Urgent George because he worked in the basin.

Declivity – worked on the slip all the time, but happened to carry one shoulder lower than the other due to surgery.

Dillinger – an avid patron of detectives and gangster films. Also a safety officer.

That's enough to be going on with. From time to time we'll run some more nicknames from the lore of the Clyde shipyards, and try to run some of the more printable yarns which they provoke.

From *Keel*, the works paper of Govan Shipbuilders, November 1975.

James Mathew, a rigger, in Lithgow's East Yard in 1958. (Glasgow University Archives)

THE PAPE

As Tommy MacLeod made his way home at the end of his shift he was accompanied more often than not by Danny Boyle, who lived in Crown Avenue. Danny was the other riveter on the squad, the left-hander to Tommy's right hand, and he also 'kicked wi' the left foot', an expression that indicated that he was a good Catholic boy. 'Left of foot, left of hand and left of nature!' as Tommy used to say. Because of this his nickname was, without offence being intended or taken, 'Danny the Pape', which over time had been shortened to 'Pape'. Tommy and Danny Boyle would separate where Second Avenue met Kilbowie Road, where Marion waited every night for her father, while Danny walked on up the hill to Crown Avenue.

'Night, Tam, see ye in the mornin',' Danny would say.

'Aye, bright an' early, Pape,' Tommy would respond, clasping his daughter's clean hand in his huge, rough, filthy paw.

'It'll be the golden rivet the morra then, Tam. Ah feel it in ma bones.'

'Me tae, Pape, the morra without a doubt. It's the golden rivet for us an it's you an' me for the good life. Night, Pape!'

'Da,' Marion would ask, 'whit's the golden rivet?'

'It's a secret, hen!' Tommy would whisper, his eyes darting here and there for eavesdroppers. 'When me an' Pape find it we'll let you see it first, a'right?'

But she of the inquiring mind couldn't let the question of the golden rivet go and took it to her mother as Jean was going through the ritual of cleaning out the fire.

'Whit's the golden rivet?'

'Where did ye hear o' that?' Jean asked, poking the ashes through into the ash can below.

'Da and Pape talk aboot it every night, bit Da won't tell me whit it is.'

Jean turned round to face her daughter with the expression Tommy called her 'shocked missionary face'. 'Well, first of a', Marion Katie MacLeod,' she said sternly, 'you will *not* call Danny Boyle "Pape". Is that understood?'

'Da calls him "Pape".'

'Ah don't care if the Pope hissel' calls him "Pape", you *don't*! Understood? The last thing we want is you goin aroond copying anythin' that daft Da o' yours says or does, or ye'll end up as daft as him. Danny Boyle is Mr Boyle tae you!'

'Well why does Da call him "Pape", then?'

'Holy Jesus, Mother of God!' said Jean in her own mother's Irish accent.

'Mammy, Jesus wasnae the Mother of God.'

'Ah know that fine!' Jean retorted, struggling up from her knees with the ashes from the fire. 'An' don't think Ah don't know where ye heard *that*! Whit Ah'm sayin' is there isnae always a reason why your Da does or says anythin', an' jist because he does, disnae mean you havtae dae the same, does it?'

Marion's brow furrowed, trying to work out where this conversation was going and why. 'But' – 'Marion, will ye let it drop? Listen; it's wan thing for your Da tae call Danny Boyle "Pape" but quite another for you to call him "Pape". That's a' ye need tae know!'

Opposite left: Jimmy Smith at his job as a counter-sinker at Harland and Wolff. He was also a famous centre-forward with Rangers Football Club. Many footballers ended up in the yards during the wars so that they did not get called up to the front and could continue to play for their teams. (Imperial War Museum)

Opposite right: J. Dover of Glasgow at work as a welder at Yarrow's in 1945. He was also the goalkeeper for Dumbarton Football Club. (Imperial War Museum)

Marion gave the matter some more thought and decided to abandon the 'Pape' issue till a more auspicious moment. 'An' whit aboot the golden rivet, well?'

'Whit golden rivet?'

'The golden rivet Da and Pa— Mr Boyle talk aboot.'

'Och, Marion, Ah *tellt* ye! Ah don't have an explanation for every daft thing your Da comes up wi'! Noo run away oot an' play, Ah've tae get the dinner oan in a minute!'

Marion made her way to the door, deep in thought, then she turned back. 'Mammy?'

'Holy Jesus, Mother of God! – an' nae smart answers! Whit is it *noo*, Marion?'

'When Ah'm aulder will Ah get tae call Mr Boyle "Pape"?'

'Aye,' said Jean heavily, 'when ye grow up an' you're a riveter in Broon's, ye can call Danny Boyle "Pape". But for noo it's Mr Boyle, OK?'

From Meg Henderson's novel *The Holy City*, 1997.

SNIFTER

Snifter's Christian name had been lost since a certain frosty morning years ago, when he and his mate spent two hours working in a small tank; and the man had reckoned that the boy's sniffs were equal to his respiration. The joke spread quickly, and Snifter's explanations offered to a group of jibing apprentices, that he had a cold and forgot his handkerchief only added a smack of truth to the legend. The apprentices immediately set to work and calculated the total sniffs for the two hours and their relation to the revolution of the turbines they were fitting; and what would be the result if each sniff equalled 0.005 horse power, and the two forces were placed in opposition. Someone had begun the sum, chalking it on a bulkhead. Huge sprawling figures: 'Let X = total sniff horse power' and below that a jumbled equation offering a conclusion of '100,236.257 cubic sniffs'. Tanks, bulkheads, casings were disfigured with involved mathematical problems with .005 as a constant factor; logarithms began on a staging twelve feet up and finished on the engine-room floor. Brian, and another young journeyman, who had since died on the Gold Coast, had tried it out in trigonometry, with angles and arcs jumbled all over a condenser. The joke went on like this for months. That was years ago and Snifter was now an efficient young journeyman. But Snifter he remained.

From Edward Shiels' novel, *Gael over Glasgow*, 1937.

THE WRITING ON THE WALL

Despite the title I have chosen for this scribble, it has no reference whatever to a certain incident in Jewish history except perhaps in its wider application, but refers particularly to a demoralising habit indulged in by a few, to the confusion of many. We need not be moral missionaries or purists of a very high order to be shocked and scandalised by some of the things we see inside a shipyard.

Chalk markings and writing of an indecent character and sketches that are too vile to be named stare us in the face in all their vulgar aggressiveness from bulkheads and casings or anything in fact that presents a surface suitable for the purpose.

It is a pity that men or boys should be so foolish as to sacrifice hard-won attainments upon such corrupt amusements, or turn their God-given talents to such vile purposes.

Nor, on the other hand, is it creditable to those who profess to be of 'purer eyes' to refrain from using their influence to eliminate the evil.

I am convinced, however, that the majority of workmen look upon the practice with the loathing it deserves but adopt an attitude of indifference, preferring not to speak of it. If such a policy effected a remedy it were worthy of commendation, but I fear the reverse of that is nearer the truth.

'To the pure all things are pure' is an aphorism that appeals to all, and one that naturally presents itself to those who confront themselves with the question 'Am I sincere in my aspirations or am I just a hypocritical humbug?' The purity of things in themselves can never be for a moment in doubt, but none, not even the most licentious, can have the temerity to say that vile writings or indecent drawings can have any tendency towards purity or towards the uplifting of the human race.

It has to be admitted that, wherever a community of men are congregated for the purpose of carrying on large undertakings embracing the employment of many different trades, there is bound to be among their number a certain proportion of evilly disposed persons. But why, I ask, are those who are few in number permitted to write and sketch at their pleasure things that are repulsive and abominable to the majority? That, I believe and as many perhaps would remind me, is a question of long standing and not easily answered, but I am sure,

Two riveters at work. On the ship is one of the less offensive slogans that could be found chalked on every ship in every yard. (Imperial War Museum)

Bottom:
Chalk drawings could be found everywhere in the shipyards. This photograph was taken at Ailsa Troon in 1998. (Author's collection)

and many, I know, will agree with me, that there is hope for improvement in turning the searchlight of public opinion upon the undesirable thing.

'Shipwright' writing in the *Linthouse Works Magazine*, October 1919.

A WESTERN SCENE

It was a western scene, it was a bar-room with all the men, the cowboys, and the carts, etc. I done it in coloured chalk. That was a good thing about the yards, you'd all that steel to play about with. So when I finished it I drew a white chalk frame around it and it looked no' bad, you know. So when the red leaders came in, that's them that painted the bulkheads an undercoat, they painted right round it, and it was like a wall with this picture sticking right out. And everybody trotted up to see this, you know. So one day we were sitting at our dinner and I turned round and the manager was up, and my head foreman welder, and the under-gaffer, and this man, Mr McLaughlin. He said 'Are you the fella that did this?' and I said 'Aye,' and he said, 'Well, don't do any more, there are too many men leaving their jobs to come up and see this.'

Stephen Conroy speaking on the BBC Radio Scotland programme *Clydebuilt*, 1990.

THE CARTOONIST

In the winter we would build a canopy out from the stationary mobile crane, put seating under the canopy and site a salamander heater out from it. Anyone waiting for a lift from the crane would sit under the canopy to get a heat until it came to their turn. A crowd of us used to gather there and the patter was wonderful. There was an engineer's helper called Bobby Stirrat who was a painter and decorator to trade. Bobby was brilliant at doing cartoons, and I remember him doing one of his squad sitting round the salamander. The last I heard of Bobby he was painting film sets, and I'm sure his name will have appeared in the credits.

From Jim Collins' unpublished memoirs.

THE INK BLOB

A number of elderly gentlemen were still drawing plans of immaculate conception at the age of 65 or 70 years of age. These plans were works of art and took months to complete. One such draughtsman drew the superstructure steel deck plans for all ships built at the yard. He was a nice old boy, ponderous in the extreme as well as being a creature of habit. To enliven the somewhat staid proceedings of the office, one bright spark of an apprentice bought a very life-like blob of ink (made of tin plate) from a local Joke Shop.

The latest work of art to emanate from Old Willie's hand – the Promenade Deck plating plan – was within a day or two of completion. Young Jimmy placed the blob midway along the plan and the office awaited with interest old Willie's return from his lunch. As usual, he walked slowly up the office to his bench while buttoning up his brown dust coat. Arriving at his bench, he then carefully unlocked his drawer full of drawing instruments and sat down on his stool. It was at this point he saw the ink. Extracting some blotting paper from his drawer, he carefully tried to mop up the ink but only succeeded in moving the blob along the plan. The whole office erupted into laughter. Willie was nae amused. The next day, Jimmy placed a real blob of ink on the plan, but Willie was not to be taken in a second time and swept the blob away with his hand. The Promenade Deck plating plan was very late indeed in being issued to the yard!

From George H. Parker's *At the Sharp End!: A shipbuilding autobiography*, 1992.

Opposite: Shipyard workers admiring a swan family at Irvine. (Scottish Maritime Museum)

A SWAN IN THE HOLD

A pair of swans nested for three or four years behind the privy. An incident I vividly remember happened one night I was working late with Johnny Gordon relaying the flooring planks in the hold of one of the dumb barges. A squad of

riveters were riveting the holes which were always left for drainage up to the launching. And a man, Harry Wilson, was a holder-on inside the hold. Nat Montgomery was a caulker waiting to finish after the riveters, and he lifted the female swan off the nest and with one arm round her wings and his other hand holding the neck. He carried her up the ladder and dropped her into the hold, then pulled up the ladder from inside the hold. Well the swan was flapping up and down until it got airborne. Harry Wilson thought the swan was after him and was running up and down looking for the ladder.

From a recording of John McCash, who worked at Peter McGregor's shipyard from 1912 to 1916, held in the oral history archive at the Auld Kirk Museum, Kirkintilloch.

STEALING APPLES

We had to work a great deal of overtime on that ship, as the foreman was rather a muddler. When I remember how little work was done at night, I am often amused to read how much harder people worked then than now. One night we were berthed alongside an American liner which had been discharging apples all day. About midnight it was arranged that I, being the most innocent-looking, should entertain the night watchman with some of Baldie's stories, while the others hoisted a barrel of apples out of the hold and got it on board our ship. It went off very well, and we had apples to eat for a long time, but a thing like that can be done only once, and some plagiarists were caught red-handed a few months later and dealt with by the police.

From W. G. Riddell's *Adventures of an Obscure Victorian*, 1932.

The long-service employees of the Ardrossan Dry Dock and Shipbuilding Company. Between them they had a total of 856 years' service. Old Mr McCallum in the centre of the front row had been with the company for 61 years. (North Ayrshire Museum)

A DAY OUT

Another incident which might have had a disastrous ending was in connection with a steam pinnace belonging to Sir William Collins, an ex-Lord Provost of Glasgow. We wintered her for a year and she was laid up on the ground at the end of the Dock. Well, one Spring Holiday the Head Foremen in the Engine Shop thought they would like to have a day out, and they had it. They put the boat into the water and off they went down the river; landed at Dumbarton and found everything so nice there that they wouldn't go any farther. One of the old boys, John Hope (or 'flannel feet' as he was called), had had enough and he came home by train, but all the others were enjoying themselves, and on the return journey, late at night, a Tug ran into the pinnace just off Linthouse and all of our Engine Shop Head Foremen were in the water in the drowning stage, when they were rescued by the men in the Tug. It was a terrible experience and a 'wag' in the Shop – a poet – wrote a long lingo of poetry on the trip. I regret not having retained a full copy, but at that time who could have foreseen a gathering such as this. I do however remember one verse, which read –

'They took Brimstone Bob as Engineer,
To drive and keep a' things richt;
And to sit in the bow when the nicht grew dark,
For his nose would dae for a licht.'

Brimstone Bob was a fitter in the Shop and he certainly had a nose.

From George Strachan's retirement speech *From Ticket Boy to Director*, 1921.

THE MOTOR BOAT

D'you remember when they stole the motor boat. When they were nearly finished, they had to put them over that side, and seemingly they had got a rope, and they went to the other side, and they pulled it – through the night, they pulled it away, and they never got that boat to this day. Out of this world. It must have cost thousands of pounds. They were dragging the dock – they thought it had sunk. They come in and dragged the dock. An Admiralty boat, you know. Oh, you've no idea. They'd take the sugar out your tea.

Anon, speaking in *Made in Govan: An oral history of shipbuilding on the Upper Clyde 1930–1950*, 1991.

THE GATE-LEG TABLE

In the meantime there were other pressing problems. Eric, he of the thriving gate-leg table export business in Brown's, had taken an order that was proving difficult to deliver. Getting gate-leg tables out past the guards on the gates was always successful, thanks to the ingenuity and co-operation of his workmates, but in a rash moment he had agreed to make a big, fixed-leg table. And he had made a fine job of it, everyone agreed, rarely had workmanship like it been seen outwith the big liners like the *Queens*. The problem was how to get something of this scale past the guards at the gates who were employed by the management to cut the level of pilfering from the yard. The matter had been exercising the finest minds in the yard for weeks, and Tommy MacLeod's especially, as Iain had assisted the master craftsman in the making of the table.

'Why is it ony o' your business?' Jean demanded.

'Jeannie, Jeannie,' he sighed, 'wan o' these days somebody's gonny hear ye askin' things like that, an' it'll look bad for me! As ma mither aye says, "It's Us an' Them". Noo that would be reason enough, but oor Iain here helped tae make this table, so that's another reason. But the main wan is that Eric has an order tae fill an' we canny let the customer doon, noo can we?'

'Well, Iain shouldnae have got involved!'

'Eric's his boss, wumman!' Tommy replied, shaking his head.

'An' Ah still don't see why you, the great Tommy MacLeod, should have anythin' tae dae with this. Ye're a bloody riveter for God's sake!'

Tommy threw his hands out to the rest of the family, appealing for the support of his audience. 'Have Ah no' jist explained a' that?' he demanded. 'Whit merr can Ah say tae make the wumman understand?'

As the weeks passed the logistical difficulties of how to get the table out of the yard were discussed back and forth, plans were assessed, discarded and thrown back, until the night Tommy arrived home with the light of genius burning in his eyes.

'Right, Jeannie lass, all hands tae the deck! Ah need your auld pinnies an' things.'

'Aye, Tommy, Ah'm sure ye dae, but Ah'm wearin' ma auld pinnies an' things.'

'Noo, Jeannie, we've nae time for your impression o' Auld Maggie the Martyr, jist get yersel' busy an' help the War effort! Ah've had an idea!'

'Holy Jesus, Mother o' God!' Jean moaned. 'We're a' done for noo, he's had an idea!'

Tommy's solution to the great table problem was, like all brilliant ideas, astonishingly simple. The now famous table was so big that each leg was supported by a small castor, in other words, it was mobile and could be pushed out of the yard. The next thing had been to think of items that could be legitimately wheeled out, and that was where Tommy's spark of genius came into play: a bridal party.

When women were leaving work on the last day before getting married, they were traditionally dressed up as babies by their workmates, dummies in their mouths, frilly bonnets on their heads and a chamber pot, a chanty, on their laps. They would then be pushed out of their workplace and through the town in a pram, their friends singing songs as raucous and risqué as possible. Every male they encountered, even if they had to be dragged out of all the pubs en route, was forced to kiss the 'baby' and drop a donation into the chanty for the pleasure. Then the blushing bride would be returned home, usually several hours later, red about the face but with a little bit extra with which to start her married life. If such a bride could be found and the rest of the work-force invited to join in, then the plan could proceed, Tommy decided, and if there was no one about to marry, a volunteer would be press-ganged. An idea so simple that it had to work, but for Tommy it was too simple. 'If somethin' is tae be done,' he said, 'it's tae be done well,' and when no genuine bride-to-be was found, he decided that the volunteer bride should be male. He had been determined to give the starring role to the biggest, ugliest, dirtiest man in the yard, but even Tommy had to toe the line somewhere, so he reluctantly settled for one of the less muscled apprentices. What he needed now was female clothes, and as he was gathering Jean's, others were finding camouflage material for the table itself.

When Friday came around the plan was put into action. They would exit through the smaller gate near the Town Hall rather than the bigger, better-policed one along Dumbarton Road. The 'bride' was dressed and made up by the women in the cleaning shop and the bridal carriage assembled, covered by purloined sheets and tablecloths and decorated with streamers of crepe paper in different colours. When the hooter sounded to mark the end of the working day a heavy entourage surrounded the table with the blushing bride on top and pushed it through the yard, all of them shouting, cheering and singing, and the unsuspecting guards laughingly waved them through.

It was too easy for Tommy though, the lack of challenge was almost an insult. He decided that the guards had to be tested, so to everyone's horror he halted the procession in its tracks, and insisted that the two guards had to kiss the bride and give a donation. One by one they were encouraged to climb on top of Eric's table, kiss the unfortunate apprentice and throw some money into the chanty on his lap. And no quick peck was accepted, Tommy insisted that only the most passionate of kisses would be allowed, as it was, he commented, 'probably the last chance the poor lassie will get'. Only when he was satisfied did the bridal party proceed past the gate and on into the safety of the town. As a parting gesture he greeted both the guards warmly in Gaelic and slapped each of them on the back for being such good sports. Eric's mammoth table was delivered, the apprentice was allowed to keep the cash in return for losing his dignity, and honour was satisfied all round.

It was a victory, one-up for 'Us' in the constant war between 'Us an' Them', and there were precious few of those.

From Meg Henderson's novel *The Holy City*, 1997.

TONS AND TONS OF LEAD

At one time there was a wee shed outside where they kept flanges, and the maintenance were in there. And in that store they also kept the lead for the lead boiler. Well, there was tons and tons of it. It was all in ingots. And there was this lad that worked in the maintenance at that time. He had an old ramshackle bike, and everybody used to kid him about this old ramshackle bike. He was working for six or seven months, and a job come up, and we needed the lead for the lead boiler. They went to it, there was nane there. This fellow had been taking an ingot each night in this old ramshackle bike, putting it in the saddlebag. He shifted tons and tons of lead. It was only when they went to get it that they realised what he'd been up to.

Anon, speaking in *Made in Govan: An oral history of shipbuilding on the Upper Clyde 1930–1950*, 1991.

FISHING FOR SCRAP

'I was hiding on the dock and I saw Mr Farr fishing.'

'Fishin', b'God! Where wis this?'

'The Dock Burn.'

'Ah!' He nodded with satisfaction and turned to Dosser. 'And whi' did ye catch this time?'

'Enough to make it worth me while,' announced the wizened little man. He undid his long ragged coat and from its many deep interior pockets produced a gleaming haul of gunmetal valves, small brass flanges and white-metal facings.

The watchman was impressed. 'Things are lookin' up, eh?'

'Oh, they are surely,' Dosser agreed. 'As apprentice quality in that place is going down. I'm glad to say.'

I laughed. 'If you'd waited you could have had one of mine.' The scrap-fisherman was alert to my potential. He beckoned me to sit down beside him. 'So! Are ye on the brass-work, then? I have a great interest in the non-ferrous range; whether it's made into anything or not. I mean, why should you go to the bother of working on a piece, scrapping it and throwing it in the Burn where I have to trawl for it – when ye could jist give me it?'

'Don't listen tae him, son, or ye *will* be wantit' by the polis.' Dosser was offended. 'Am I not tryin' to save that shipyard money?'

'*Save* them money?'

'Certainly – on labour costs.' The young man laughed and Dosser, nodding at the appreciation, went on, 'They have to pay these boys, y'know, for the time they spend on the work they scrap.' He turned earnestly to me. 'You see that, don'cha, Billy?'

From Tom Gallacher's novel *Apprentice*, 1983.

SAGGING POCKETS

The money that was proffered in the cap came from scrap. I never knew what scrap was, only that it was something secret, that it involved stealing and that you made money from it. When my father came home straight from work with his pockets sagging to his knees, then he was in scrap. For years, I longed to see it, but he was too smart for me. As soon as I appeared in the lobby he said to me:

'Here, buzz off, quick smart. Intae the kitchen, go on!'

I had been thinking that I would suddenly thrust my hand into his pocket to feel what was inside, no matter if I did get a slap. But he never let me get within touching distance. He went straight into the lounge-room and shut the door. Sometimes I pressed my ear almost into the wood trying to interpret the strange noises I could hear on the other side, but almost immediately my father would shout out:

'Hey Rose, make sure Big Ears isnae at the keyhole,' and my mother would come and lug me off. The next day I would rattle the handle of the big press in the lounge. That's where he would put the stuff from his pockets, but he always kept the key on him. I looked in every drawer in the house, on top of the wardrobe, and tried every key I could find, even those that were palpably unsuited to the lock. One or two days later the door would be open, but I knew then that it was no use looking. Whatever had been there was gone. I felt in every corner of the press, but it was always empty, except for two of my mother's irons, heavy ones, that she only used for sponging and pressing. When my father came home he always knew I had been looking and would ask me:

'Well, how has old Nosey Parker been today? Turned up anything yet?' Then he roared with laughter, and his little eyes shut with glee. I would punch him and feel in his pockets:

'Tell me, tell me, Da, honest ah'll never tell anyone, ever. What dae ye do in the press? Ah want tae know.'

'Aye, ah know ye want tae know,' he would say, grinning delightedly, 'but that's something ye'll never know,' and he'd point his two fingers at my face, 'because ah'm too smart for ye, see.' He was, too! But I found out just the same.

One night my father hadn't come home and it was very late. I thought my mother would be angry, but instead she was worried.

'Ah've a feeling something's up wi' your Da,' she kept saying. There was a knock at the door, and when I opened it a work-man stood there.

'Is your mammy there, hen?' he asked me. 'Ah'm Chris Cullen from Stephen's, Mrs Lavery,' he said to my mother when she came to the door. 'Big Bob's been held up but he asked me to bring ye his pay packet.' He held out the envelope and started to leave the close in a hurry:

'Ah've got tae get home myself, Missus,' he said as my mother started to question him. 'He'll be home later. He said no' tae worry.'

My father didn't come home later. Instead, a policeman came to the door. Detective Lynch from Orkney Street police station and he would like to inform you, Mrs Lavery, that your husband Robert has been detained at Orkney Street Station pending trial for the theft of scrap iron from the shipyard of Alexander Stephen and Sons. Bail can be arranged for ten pounds and you can visit your husband tomorrow morning at ten o'clock.

. . .

I stared down at my shoes and said nothing. My mother too sat in silence, thinking, of concrete things, however. She jumped up suddenly, knocking her chair backwards with a clatter onto the patched linoleum.

'Here, ah just thought a' something. Pour me oot another cup a' tea, ah'm goin' tae get the irons. They might come an' hae a snoop aroon here,' and she went off in a hurry into the lounge-room, yanking open the door of the big press. I could hear her scrabbling around inside it and in a minute or so she was back, carrying the two big flat irons that I'd seen inside the press each time I'd been rummaging around, seeking evidence of my father's secret activities. She laid the irons down on the floor beside the smaller ones that she normally used for pressing.

'They might just catch on your Da was using them tae weigh the scrap,' she said. 'Oh aye,' she went on, noticing the look of surprise on my face, 'ye never

worked that out, did ye? Your faither had a wee see-saw affair that he used as a scale: the irons on one end and the scrap on the other. That gave him a rough idea of the weight because the weight o' the irons is stamped on them. 'Of course,' she added, 'that was only when there was nae big deal on at the yard. Ah mean, ye don't make much from these wee crumbs o' copper an' lead your Da was carrying hame in his pockets. Ye need a truckload tae make any money.'

'A truckload,' I said, rolling my eyes in astonishment.

'Aye, an don't make your eyes roll like that. They'll stay fixed one day an' then ye'll be a right sight. Aye, he paid the gate-keeper to let the truck intae the docks, and the crane driver to unload the scrap from the ship, an' of course the truck driver got a fair whack because he took the most risks. But the bloke who usually drove the truck got sick, an' that's why that new man took his place. A right squealer he was. The old yin would never hae put anybody in. It was that foreman who tipped off the police. Your Da told me he deals in scrap himself an' he wanted it a' for himself.'

From Mary Rose Liverani's memoirs, *The Winter Sparrows: A Glasgow childhood*, 1976.

John Currie drilling a hole in the bottom shell of a ship at Lithgow's yard in 1959. (Glasgow University Archives)

BUNG

'Is this your kid then, Johnny? Fine wee chap. Takes plenty dough to keep 'em goin' these days, eh, Johnny? . . . Now – me and the boys was just talkin'. We were hopin' you'd change your mind about comin' in wi us. If it's only a matter o' steppin' up the bung, Johnny – just say what you want an' we'll see what we can do. . . .'

John looked at him distastefully. The ring was dead keen to get him: a welder working for long spells near the keel of the ship where all the dirt and refuse gathered – he could hide stuff among the rubbish till they were ready to take it away. And his wife's uncle was a gateman who might be persuaded, for family reasons, to turn a blind eye on what was being carried out.

John had always steered clear of big theft, thinking you were bound to cop it sooner or later. It must be big stuff they were after this time – probably brass portholes by the dozen, since nothing smaller would pay off enough. They'd give him his whack for a week or two, but then his share would be cut, and if he tried to break with them the pressure would go on. Only last year Bill Carey, one of his mates, had got a prison sentence because he'd been made a scapegoat for the ring.

From Margaret Hamilton's short story *Bung*, 1978.

DUMPLINGS

TAM: I was going for . . . I was getting supplies.

WUMP: What? Steel plating an that?

TAM: (*mutters*)

RONNIE: Eh? Timber . . . copper piping . . . tartan paint maybe?

TAM: Currants!

ALAN: Eh?

TAM: I ran out of currants . . . for . . . (*mumbled*) my dumpling.

RONNIE: For your what?

TAM: Dumpling. I've been making dumplings . . . in the tea-urn.

ALAN: Tam what are you on . . .?

TAM: I've been going daft, sitting about down there. I'm a welder, I can't do anything else . . . since this started I've been going like a train. My production's way up and I've kinda got ahead of myself. I've got time on my hands, waiting for everybody else to catch up. And you're all . . . he's . . . I can't do anything. When I'm not welding I've taken to making dumplings . . . for the boys . . . they give me a few bob for the currants and flour . . . they're good.

WUMP: Well, well, Alan, we've got ourselves a right entrepreneur here. That's a right wee scam he's got going there.

RONNIE: Tut-tut, Tam, a capitalist in black's clothing.

TAM: No, no. I don't make a profit. I just wipe my arse.

WUMP: You're putting me off these dumplings, Tam.

TAM: I mean I just cover my costs.

ALAN: Much?

TAM: Eh?

ALAN: Much does it cost to make a dumpling?

TAM: Two bob.

ALAN: Ten new p, and you sell them for how much?

TAM: Two an' a tanner.

ALAN: Twelve and half new p. That's two and a half new p profit.

TAM: Aye, but I have to buy new cloots and I break the odd bowl.

ALAN: Ah! Replacement overheads. What do you think, boys?

RONNIE: It's a very serious offence. Possible profiteering, misuse of company time, misuse of company equipment. Mounts up.

WUMP: Mind you, it's a first offence. And he's a very good timekeeper usually.

RONNIE: And a very good welder.

ALAN: I'll tell you what I'm prepared to do, Tam. You increase your productivity in this venture , maintain current costs and sell your product at, let's say, fifteen new p, with the percentage profit going into the strike fund, and we'll say no more about it.

TAM: Eh?

RONNIE: Maybe get Davie to build you a wee stall at the front gate and sell them to the public. UCS dumplings, they'll go like hot cakes!

From Frank Miller's play *Work-in*, 2001.

A SWEET RACKET

'Money?' McClint stirred.

Clutha side-mouthed: 'He's yapping about a bonus racket, Menie bust it up.'

'How?'

Clutha squinted cold-eyed at the riveter gaffer: 'Want me to sing?'

'As long as I'm listening.'

Clutha shrugged. 'Snaphead,' he said, 'has been a ship's gaffer of riveters in Alma's for half a lifetime. From the moment a keel's laid until the last rivet is knocked down, he is the man who hires or fires the squads who nail her together. He is the bloke who hands out the jobs – the good and the bad.'

'A little big shot?'

'Riveters,' went on Clutha, 'are mostly pieceworkers. It makes a lot of difference to a pieceworker if the gaffer's nice to him – or if he's nice to the gaffer.'

'Everybody got a square deal from me,' growled Snaphead.

'Like hell they did. What about "Snaphead's Lilies"? Do you think the Clyde doesn't gurgle? There was no secret about them. Every catch-boy and plater's marker from Finnieston to Renfrew Ferry made jokes about them. Time after time I myself saw the nice cushy number – the straight shell berths, the open bulkheads, the well-screwed-up deck seams – go to the same dozen or so squads. And the dour men, the sticklers for principle who greased no palms, had to battle away with the hoby-hammer work and acrobatic stuff down among the chain lockers and bilge bottoms. You can kid the management, Snap, but you can't kid men with red lead in their veins . . . I could see what was going on all right – have done for years – but it was none of my business. I'm only paid to watchdog time and material around here, not morals.'

'Keep women out of this,' said Snaphead sullenly.

Clutha lifted one eyebrow at McClint. 'This is the type they make gaffers – then they wonder why they've strikes.'

He looked down his nose at Snaphead. 'I'm talking about big greasy pints slipped quietly across the counter for you. I'm referring to the half-mutchkins and bottles of whisky left slyly in the corner of your wee market hut.'

'Market?' quizzed McClint.

'The open space in every yard where riveters generally meet and team up their squads.'

'I hope you're enjoying yourself,' jeered Snaphead. 'But you're a long way from this yet,' and he jerked a head to Menie's body. Ambulance men were strapping it to a stretcher now preparatory to slinging it through a hatch on a crane-hook.

Clutha looked at the corpse. Everybody else waited. In that moment it was oddly quiet in the stokehold. There was a raw rustiness about the atmosphere

Watchman George Letson patrolling Lithgow's Kingston yard with his dog, Rolfe. (Glasgow University Archives)

that chilled the bone, and the damp seeping up from the mass of water filling the ballast tanks lent a tomb-like note to the least sound. Even the continual cloth-capped heads, popping and peering curiously down from the ranks of staging buttressed and stepped up to the gloom and shadows of the fiddley bulkheads, seemed disembodied and ghostly. The hammering and clatterings of work resumed in neighbouring holds and upper decks had a theatrically distant ring absolving the outer world from any participation in the stokehold's chill cameo of death. Only Clutha, with his rusty old bowler tipped forward on his brow and his hard sombre eyes brooding on the mask of Menie's gruesome face, seemed unaffected by the general aura of morbid anticipation.

'No,' he said casually at last. 'Not such a long way from Menie as you think, Snap. You got ambitious. More. You got greedy. The drams and the back-slapping weren't enough. You got Matt Glaur, the last piecework counter, in tow. You parcelled out the jobs and he parcelled up the tallies. It was a sweet racket. It meant fat paypokes for the Lilies and cash back-outs for you and Matt.'

From Hugh Munro's shipyard detective novel *Who Told Clutha?*, 1958.

CHAPTER SEVEN

THEM AND US

Shipyards were places of great social conflict. The fundamental difference was that between the workers and the bosses. The bosses were primarily concerned about their own profits and treated the workers essentially as disposable cogs in their machines. With their comfortable houses, big cars, and strict bowler-hat dress code, they did little to build bridges with their workers.

Originally, the bosses had absolute power over the workers and they did not shrink from using it. In many ways they abused their power by inflicting random acts of management on the workers, just to show them who was in charge. Workers could be fired on the spot for the slightest reason, wages docked at the least excuse or cut as soon as profits looked like falling. No wonder a deep-rooted hatred of the bosses was bred among the workers.

The issue that typified the conflict between the workers and the bosses most was that of tea breaks. Officially there were no tea breaks in the yards, but the men would boil up their cans on the riveters' stoves or under a burner's torch as best they could. If they were caught brewing up by the foremen, they could be summarily sacked for wasting company time. Tea breaks therefore became a great point of principle on both sides, but essentially they developed into a rather pointless game of cat and mouse between the workers and the bowler hats.

These attitudes inevitably led to militant trade unionism in the yards. The ideals of socialism and communism were embraced with great fervour among the workers, and political agitation became a common feature of shipyard life. The heady days of Red Clydeside during the First World War strengthened the power of the unions, and gradually shorter hours and better conditions were won for the workers.

The bosses naturally tried to resist the power of the unions and blatantly discriminated against the union leaders. This served only to make the workers even more militant, and strikes became a regular feature of the industry. In many cases the original cause of a strike would become lost in the eternal battle between workers and bosses. The bosses often retaliated against the workers by imposing lock-outs so that no one could get in to work. With no wages coming in, the men were effectively starved into backing down and returning to work.

Religious conflict was never far away in shipbuilding. The large numbers of Irish immigrants and Highlanders who came in search of work in the early days ensured a heady mix of Catholics and staunch Protestants in the yards. Sectarian slogans were found everywhere, chalked all over bulkheads and on workshop walls, and discrimination on religious grounds became simply a fact of life. Much of this friction was resolved in good-natured banter, but inevitably, when tensions became unbearable, violence would break out.

Previous page: Archibald McInnes drinking tea on a ship at Harland and Wolff. He had worked at the yard for 45 years and presumably had managed to avoid being caught taking tea all those years. (Imperial War Museum)

The rigid caste system that developed among the different categories of workers also led to conflict. The attitudes of the different working groups were deeply inbred, and although there may have been genuine grievances over wages or conditions, a lot of the resentment existed simply as a matter of principle. These attitudes also stemmed from shipbuilding's early days when each craft jealously guarded its own area of work. As new construction methods were introduced, there would be a jockeying for position among the different trades to ensure their own survival. It was this fight for survival

that led to the great demarcation disputes, when a fraction of an inch could move a job from the domain of a sheet-metal worker to that of a plater, or from a coppersmith to a plumber.

All these conflicts of course played a massive part in the decline of the industry. Who knows what might have happened if the bosses had been a bit more enlightened, the workers a bit less militant and attitudes a bit less entrenched?

Workers going up the gangway of a standard ship under construction at Harland and Wolff during the First World War. A manager and a military observer look on. (Imperial War Museum)

Opposite top: A shipyard engineering workshop. The bowler-hatted managers are keeping a close eye on the workers. (Imperial War Museum)

Opposite bottom: A ship's plumber at work on a pipe. The size of a pipe determined whether a job was to be done by a plumber or a coppersmith. (Glasgow City Archives)

WORRIES AND PROBLEMS

My father strongly recommended to me that if I wanted a quiet peaceful and happy life I should not become a shipbuilder. He said that if I did become a shipbuilder I would spend all my life having money worries and problems with unions. I didn't believe him at the time, but he was absolutely dead right.

Sandy Stephen speaking on the BBC Radio Scotland programme *Clydebuilt*, 1990.

THE BOWLER AND THE BUNNET

When times were good the bosses made money. When times were bad the workers went hungry. The stone tenements of Govan, as enduring as Clyde ships, were outliving their pride and decaying into slums. There was a blight on the place. World trade was in decline. There was less for everybody, and by now bosses and workers were each sure the others were getting too much. The bosses' answer was to keep down wages. The workers had built their unions to guard against just that. And the unions, dozens of separate unions, each guarded its privileges with savage fervour.

It was a fight to the death. And this is the death: Harland and Wolff, one of the proud names in Clyde shipbuilding, is a graveyard. And there are others: Henderson; Simons Lobnitz; Blythswood; Hamilton; Inglis; Denny's of Dumbarton. These shipyards have gone under with millions of pounds' worth of orders, and with some of the best workers in the world. There are some things you can't cure with deflation.

When it's your job to sack a thousand men at the stroke of a pen you can't be sentimental about the men. When it's your job to take the sack at the drop of a hat you can't be sentimental about the boss. To the worker's bitter eye the situation looks clear. The boss takes the gravy when the going is good and when things look bad he sells out and takes his money, and vanishes. And that is the crux. The gulf is complete: the gulf between the bowler and the bunnet.

From the Scottish Television documentary about Fairfield's, *The Bowler and the Bunnet*, narrated by Sean Connery, 1967.

THE HATS

It was an old yard, wide and spacious, with shops and huts and boxes built in the most convenient way that had suggested itself to the original builders. There was the engineering shed, the platers' shed, the blacksmiths' shop, the general store and the quarters for the plumbers, joiners and electricians. And in each of these quarters the foreman, and in some cases the leading hand, had a box or private office. It was possible to spend a very pleasant lifetime dodging about from one howff to another – if you were a foreman, a leading hand, a manager or a member of the staff. Having tea in one box, a smoke in another or a game of cards or a round of bawdy stories. Naturally, of course, if you were a workman you had to work.

Being Saturday afternoon, the yard was quiet and peaceful. Only such squads stood by as had work to do on *The Sunflower*. Some joiners, a few electricians, the black squad and a squad of red-leaders.

A group of young managers pose in front of a ship at the Ailsa yard in Ayr in the 1920s. (Scottish Maritime Museum)

In the sunshine the yard looked like a decaying scrap-heap. The buildings were patched and repaired and there was nowhere to be seen evidence of paint fresher than ten years. But inside the ramshackle buildings modern and up-to-date machinery was installed enabling Bilslaw's to turn out a first-class job – as jobs go.

Of the small crowd that were gathered round the dockside there were only two hats in addition to Willie Donald. Foreman-joiner Simon Forbes, Foreman-electrician Sandy Bain. In the sun their bowler hats shone grey with dust. A foreman might dress much as he liked but his headgear had to be a bowler hat, symbol and survival of the Holy Victorian Empire and Scottish Presbyterianism.

From James Barke's novel *Major Operation*, 1936.

SHEER MALICE

Work in a shipyard is a brutal experience. You're standing on deckplates that might be an inch thick but it disnae matter how thick your boots are, the cold really does penetrate it. And there was a really bad severe winter – everybody decided they were going to get oil drums and batter holes in them and get old bits of wood and driftwood and things like that and light fires. And this battalion of managerial staff appeared on the scene with bowler hats and big sticks and just systematically went about the yard putting out these fires. It was just a sheer malicious act of cruelty and these bizarre things actually happened. The working conditions were absolutely abysmal.

Tom McKendrick speaking on the BBC Radio Scotland programme *Clydebuilt*, 1990.

RUNNING SCARED

The characters who were among the workforce were legion, not the least being the managing director, John Coleman, a 16-stone energetic Irishman who, with his bowler hat on and dust coat flying, went through the yard every morning at starting time like a dose of 'Epsom Salts'. If you had a vantage point like a crane or a ship's bridge, the spectacle of J. C. shooting in one end of the plating shed or paint shop and dozens of workmen stampeding out the other was something to behold.

From Thomas MacLean's memories of his life in the Ardrossan shipyards, published in Catriona Levy's *Ardrossan Shipyards: Struggle for survival 1825–1983*, 1984.

TURNING BACK THE TIDE

Shipyards are not the easiest of places in which to supervise labour. The joiner's shop, plumber's shop and other trade shops were the exception. Elsewhere and particularly on board ships, the labour force was dispersed and located within various compartments. Management tried hard over the years to ensure that the labour force started and finished work at the proper time. They never succeeded. Nor did they succeed in eliminating tea-breaks. Managers and foremen were posted at strategic points all over the yard to try and keep the men at work on ships' gangways, at shed entrances and the like. The men however stopped work at 15 minutes before the end of the shift and slowly and silently made their way off the ships by various means. They joined their mates at ground level, who by 10 minutes before the end of the shift, were gathering force as they shuffled nearer to the main gate. Had they been permitted to reach the gate, there could well have been a serious accident.

Thus it came about that the last line of defence was the shipyard manager, my father, or in his absence, his assistant. At around 10 minutes to twelve o'clock, he would emerge from the office, in full view of a large crowd of workmen now some 50 yards from the gate. He would start to walk slowly towards them, while extracting his pocket watch from his waistcoat. The technique apparently was to try to catch somebody's eye in the front row, glare at him and keep walking forward. The front rank began to turn and move backwards, forcing their mates to do likewise. The whole crowd then retreated into the comparative warmth of the platers' shed, where they remained until the whistle blew. This was a daily procedure and the tactic only had to fail once to cause serious injury to the shipyard manager. It never did.

From George H. Parker's *At the Sharp End!: A shipbuilding autobiography*, 1992.

Hugh Ferguson, a piecework clerk, clocking in at Harland and Wolff in 1945. (Imperial War Museum)

PLAYING WITH FIRE

The following extract gives an example of the many irrational acts of random authority that certain bosses used to indulge in.

One day Mr Murdoch came into the boiler-shop and took me over to a little oil-furnace which was used for heating rivets. It stood in a dark corner of the works, and the floor all round it was saturated with oil. He asked me in a casual way if I knew how to handle the extinguishers, and I replied that I did, meaning to read the instructions later. He took a box of matches from his pocket and bent down and lit a piece of cotton waste. I think he started a much bigger fire than he intended, for he had to jump back when the whole corner blazed up.

'Put the fire out,' was all he said.

I had a wonderful piece of luck. I tucked an extinguisher under my arm. It was an unwieldy thing, and I nearly dropped it. I noticed a brass knob on the side and I hit it with the hammer. A jet of liquid squirted out of a nozzle, and when I played it on the flames they died down at once. It was like a piece of magic. If Mr Murdoch had known how surprised I was, he would have got a shock, but he was as pleased as a boy with a new toy and left me all smiles.

He went straight to Rigby and asked him if he knew how to use the extinguishers and, of course, Rigby said he did. He then lit another fire and told Rigby to put it out, but Rigby was a little fellow and he could not manage the extinguisher. He dropped it, and the fire did a good deal of damage. I was in great favour after that for a time, and it amused me to think how little I deserved to be; but in future I was more careful about my statements to Mr Murdoch, for he was so ruthless and so unexpected that one never knew what he would do next.

From W. G. Riddell's memoirs of 1948, *The Thankless Years.*

ASTRONOMICAL

In 1919 Grandfather, not long before he died, sold the controlling interest to Lord Pirrie of Messrs Harland & Wolff, saying to the family that in his view shipbuilding on the Clyde was finished. This opinion arose mostly from the growing power of the unions. He had campaigned for years from about 1880 onwards against the unions victimising individual members or non-members and also against their limitation of the number of apprentices. In a lighter vein he said at one meeting – 'A new cure is the endeavour to discover how men's wages can be increased without increasing the price of the product. It is not so difficult as it perhaps looks at first sight to raise wages and decrease the price of the product. All that is required is that men should be paid for what they do instead of for the flight of time. A workman has got nothing to do with the world turning round. It will turn round quite well without him and I do not see why he should base his claim for remuneration on that astronomical fact.'

From John G. Inglis' memoirs, *Inglis, Glasgow: The story of a shipbuilding family,* 1977.

The foremen of Denny's shipyard at Dumbarton. (Scottish Maritime Museum)

KEEPING TIME

At 7.25 every morning the first hooter sounded at Brown's followed at 7.30, the official starting time, by the second, and the closing of the main gates. At the timekeeper's wooden hut each man was given a small, round, brass disc with his works number stamped on it. But the hut was a good ten minutes' walk from the main gates, and the only way the entire work-force could get through on time was if those who arrived early also passed through early – for no extra pay. A man's working time, and so his pay, began as he picked up his metal check, not as he entered the gates, so if you missed the 7.30 a.m. starting time because of the inevitable queues at the hut, you were deemed to be late and were therefore 'quartered'. This meant that men who had been on company soil for ten minutes had fifteen minutes deducted from everything they earned, basic pay, piecework and overtime. So in the perpetual battle between the management and the workforce, a new strategy was worked out. The men who arrived early refused to collect their metal checks until 7.30 on the dot, and the queues that built up were so huge that a great deal of time, and therefore money, was lost processing the workers. This brought the practice of 'quartering' to an end, not because of its basic unfairness, but because the way the men hit back cost the company money. It was a victory though, one of the few the workforce managed to force out of the management.

When work finished for the day the men were held wherever they were, even on board half-built ships, until the hooter sounded. Then they would scramble in their thousands down the gangplanks to get home, with accidents avoided only by luck. As they pushed and edged forward the gates would remain firmly closed until the last possible second. You could see them as you passed, crowded behind the gates like cattle, then bursting forth to freedom when the hooter sounded. Yet to hear the grand speeches on launch day, you would think the bosses held the men in the highest esteem; they were the skilled tradesmen who had built the most famous ships sailing the seven seas, as well as the reputations of the yards. It was the law of the yards; words were cheap, but men's sweat, men's lives, were cheaper.

From Meg Henderson's novel *The Holy City*, 1997.

SCREWING THE MEN FOR EVERY LAST PENNY

The works were on the north side of the Clyde, and all our ships were fitted out there, but shortly after my appointment a new dock was opened on the south side and, to relieve congestion, one of our ships was berthed there after the machinery had been put on board. She was a fairly large vessel, and there was still three weeks' work to do before she was ready for sea. Duff, the cashier, and Fleming thought of an ingenious economy, with which, as a newcomer, I was credited.

It had always been the custom to provide the workmen with ferry tickets when they were sent to work on the other side of the river. These tickets cost $^1/_2$d, but the firm bought them in bulk at a much lower figure and the expense was trifling. Fleming told Boyd to discharge all the men before the ship was taken across the river and re-engage them next day on the other side, as this would save the firm the expense of ferry tickets.

I knew nothing about this, as Fleming still ignored me, and I heard nothing about it until I was stopped on the street next forenoon on my way to the ship. A slightly drunk riveter stood in front of me and began to take off his jacket.

'If you're a man at all,' he said, 'put up your hands, for I'm going to knock daylight out of you.'

I was very surprised, but I laughed and asked him what the trouble was.

'I always thought you were a gentleman,' he said, 'till you played this dirty trick on poor working men. But I'm going to see Jimmy Murdoch himself about it, and we'll see how long your plan to make us pay our ferry will stand.'

When I reached the ship, I found Boyd at the gangway. No one had turned up, and he was in a frightful temper. I had difficulty in persuading him that I knew nothing of the scheme. I went back to the works and insisted on seeing Mr Murdoch. He said he knew nothing about the new arrangement and agreed that it was insanity.

The order was cancelled, and the men got their ferry ticket. They went back to work, but they sulked for a long time.

From W. G. Riddell's memoirs of 1948, *The Thankless Years*.

RASCALS

You were supervised by what you called the hat men, the bowler hat men – rascals. If you were caught taking tea it was deemed as a sacking offence. There was one foreman, he gave you a warning, but the likes of big Willie Walker, if he caught you taking tea he sacked you on the spot. He was a very ignorant man. He would take a walk round the yard occasionally just to noise the men up, particularly at the furnace where you'd be making tea. He'd stand at the furnace, everybody scattered, all the cans would be laid out at the furnace, stand for maybe ten minutes, then he opened the furnace doors up, then let the cans boil up, melt down, give a laugh and slip back to his office.

John Stewart, an ex-plater, speaking on the BBC Scotland EX:S programme *Iron*, 1997.

TEA BREAK

Another character worth mention was 'Big Bob' the riveter. Bob's sole aim was to hammer in rivets on piecework and woe betide anyone who prevented him from doing so, but alas he lacked a certain measure of refinement. One day at the unofficial tea break Bob was boiling his black can on the rivet fire when 'Puggy' (J. Muir, the under-manager) caught him and said, 'Now, Bob, you know you're not allowed to drink tea.' Bob replied, 'Youse huv tea in yur oaffice!' to which Puggy replied, 'Yes but I take it for my health' (meaning he had a drink of liquid to help him swallow angina tablets). Whereupon Big Bob pushed his face into Puggy's and said 'And dae ye think a take it tae poosin masel'?'

From Thomas MacLean's memories of his life in the Ardrossan shipyards, published in Catriona Levy's *Ardrossan Shipyards: Struggle for survival 1825–1983*, 1984

John Miller, a burner, having a drink from his tea can at Yarrow's shipyard. (Imperial War Museum)

COOPER'S TEA

There was this one time in the yard, the foreman caught a rivet boy heating up the cans on his stove.

'Whose tea is that?' asked the foreman.

'Cooper's Tea,' replied the boy.

'Well, you tell Cooper that I want to see him right now.'

You see, Cooper's was a popular brand of tea at that time and so the boy hadn't lied. He just ran off leaving the foreman standing. That kind of thing happened all the time.

From one of Charlie Kirkwood's many tea-break conversations with the author.

CAN O' TEA

Chorus
The champagne flows, the wine glass glows.
The shipyard gates'll have to close.
They say it's all because of me.
And I cannae hae ma can o' tea.
Dowra ya the day ma can o' tea.

For forty years and fourteen mair
The men that work with Donald Blair
They've aye had a middle of the morning plan
They stop at ten to boil their can.

But Donald he was awful wise
Although he always closed his eyes
He never ever gie'd us leave
So he'd a trump card up his sleeve.

This morning Donald came to me
He pointed to my can o' tea
Then he let out an awful roar
Said he 'Young man get out that door.'

But the men said I'd been victimised
For the Union I had organised
So when I laid down my can o' tea
A thousand men marched out wi' me.

RULED BY FEAR

There was never a warm relationship between my own trade, the shipwrights, and the platers. They were always at war with each other. There was always a querulous rapport between the shipwrights, who were mainly responsible for the general marking off of a ship, and the service trades, who they required to come and to burn and to drill and do these various functions. There was always bickering about that sort of thing. But across the trades, there was usually quite a good relationship. . . . There was a common bond when it came to 'Them and Us', but there was no doubt among the workers who the enemy was, and that was the management. . . . We were all very well aware in my time that we were ruled by fear. We were ruled by the fear of losing your job, so you did not back-bite to the management; you did not back-bite to your foreman. That threat, although it was never said, was certainly implied. It was ever-present, and the thing to remember was that if you cleared your pitch in the yard, you could always leave. But the danger was you would never get back again, and that was too easily done. I knew quite a number of people who were actually black-balled on the Clyde.

Pat, a foreman shipwright, speaking in *Made in Govan: An oral history of shipbuilding on the Upper Clyde 1930–1950*, 1991.

STRIKE ACTION

Of course a strike is a very serious matter. It is not only costly in terms of wasted man hours, but is very damaging to the company's reputation. Shipowners naturally do not take kindly to delays to their new building caused by unconstitutional action by a group of trouble-makers. Despite the pressure applied by shipowners for the swift settlement of a dispute, I do not recall a single instance when a section of the labour force was awarded a pay rise as a result of strike action. As I was to learn myself some 25 years later, a strike by shipwrights immediately prior to a launch can be the most embarrassing of all. On a number of occasions, Caledon ship sponsors had to content themselves by naming, but not launching, a ship.

While a strike was in progress and the yard closed, my father would come home in the evenings, pace round and round the dining room table, muttering 'They've taken me on again. They've not won yet and they are not going to start now.' Had the strikers known how worried he was they might well have held out longer.

From George H. Parker's *At the Sharp End! A shipbuilding autobiography*, 1992.

A FIREBRAND

The socialist devotion of the workers naturally riled the bosses and often led to victimisation, as this extract set during the First World War shows.

'Care to have a look in the boiler-room, Miss MacAndrew?'

She assented, and was invited to crawl through a cavity low in the hull. Above her rose cavernous walls that shut out the sky and engulfed as in a tomb the human figures crouched on the steel and wooden boardings. Deafened by the piercing noise that filled the hollow, she emerged breathless and excited. As she stood resting, the glare from an acetylene welder lit up the face and neck of a workman near at hand. His eyes, faintly bloodshot, were dark with fatigue. His reddish brown hair was tumbled, and his boldly chiselled features looked set and defiant in the startling white lights.

Rickets went over to the man and addressed him. For a second the faces of the two were sharply focused in the glare – the one querulous and elderly, bags of loose flesh blurring the contour; the other young, defiant, Greek in its shape and purity of its outline. Rickets came back to where she stood.

'A pest that fellow,' he murmured. 'Keir Hardie has a lot to answer for on Clydeside.'

'Is *he* a Socialist?' she asked, nodding vaguely towards the figure now bowed over some mysterious task in the darkened yard.

'One of the worst. I hope he'll get his neck broken one of these days, then we'll be shut of him.'

Mr Rickets' voice was low with rage. He looked as though he would like to smash something, but that young man did not look as though he would be easily broken.

'Why don't you sack him?'

Mr Rickets dug a heel in the ground. For a second he appeared too agitated to speak, then he regarded her with a smile he intended to be conciliatory.

'Have you never heard, Miss MacAndrew, of a body called a Trade Union? If we sacked Steve Wilden we'd have the whole pack of 'em downing tools, and she's got to be finished to make room for another. So long as this war lasts there'll be a call for ships, more ships; and if we aren't done in for lack of labour it'll be full steam ahead for the Clyde yards.'

'And when the war ends?' she said curiously, 'What then?'

'We'll not speak of that', he said in hushed tones. 'Sufficient unto the day –'

From Dot Allan's novel *Deepening River*, 1932.

BLACKLISTED

Matt McGinn certainly found out what could happen to union activists.

In Harland and Wolff's in Finnieston I was enjoying my job as a storeman. Among other things it was intriguing to find how many things the mind can take in. There were a quarter of a million items there stored and it astonished me that within a month of starting work you could pick up an order sheet at the desk from the engineering workers who wanted liners of screws or bolts, and within a couple of minutes you could have found the item from among all those and have it in the hands of the worker wanting it.

But I wasn't destined to spend a lifetime there. The gaffer did not like it when I made an attempt to get the storemen into a Union, as all the tradesmen were.

I was not the only one the gaffer did not savour. There was a harrier there called John who would have made it impossible for any gaffer to like any other worker grafting alongside him. Besides John, all of us others were like tortoises. He ran from Shettleston, of whose Harriers he was a member, to Finnieston, a distance of some five miles, every morning. He ran from Finnieston to Shettleston at night when he had finished work even on overtime nights and he ran all day at his work.

So anyway I would have gone, but the gaffer did not want to say anything direct about the Union organising. He waited till I was up a ladder outside his despatch office where I was singing 'Old Man River, That Old Man River, He must know something but he don't say nothing.' Then he came rushing out, a round-figured man in brown dungarees and similar coloured hat.

'Cut out that singing,' he bawled.

'Why should I stop singing,' says I. 'I'm happy.'

'You're happy,' he says. 'You're sacked. And I'll have you blacklisted throughout the Clyde.'

'For singing?' says I.

'Aye,' says he. 'A lot of fucking Darky songs.'

Come to think of it, Harland's and me were never designed to be friends. Six months I was with them in their Govan yard and we didn't get on well together.

The charisma wasn't there in my relationship with their head timekeeper, for example, who one day walked into the platers' shed and kicked over the brazier fire, sending burning coals sprawling at the feet of the men. A nice chap he was and it was just his wee way of showing his slight disapproval of the men having been boiling their cans a few minutes before dinner time. It was a pity mind you that it left some of the men without tea for their 'lunch' but these things happen. After trying unsuccessfully to get some of the men nonetheless to complain that it wasn't precisely the way they liked to be treated I decided to go it alone. Well not exactly alone. I was after all the 'Burners' Helpers' Shop Steward'. (How low can you get?)

'I would like to see the head timekeeper please,' I spoke to one of his aides. 'And who are you?' said he without looking up from the desk where he was scanning over some papers. 'My name is McGinn. I am the Burners' Helpers' Shop Steward NUGMW.' 'Oh,' he said, most impressed. 'And what do you want to see him about?' 'Well,' says I. 'He's after kicking over a fire in the platers' shed, to which I cannot object, although I should imagine your insurance company might, but the men's tea and sugar and cans were kicked over in the process and I want to demand an apology; either that or police proceedings are going to be taken on the grounds that he was thereby interfering with the men's private property.' 'Aye well,' said he staring smirkily into my face, 'I'll leave word to that effect.'

It was now well into the dinner break and there was a meeting about to be held outside the gate at which I was due to speak and when I did get up I was ranting on about the management having taken up the game of 'kick the can' and generally lambasting this Napoleonic attitude of a haughty and dangerous wit.

At precisely three o'clock that day Sammy Wylie the burner and I were heating up our cans for tea, when a bowler hat popped up from the side of the boat and a voice quietly said, 'Up you two go to the office and collect your cards.' Quietly we went and did collect. The money and cards were lying waiting and made up to the penny. As we were walking out of the office, another bowler pulled Sam aside, 'Hold on a second, Mister Wylie.'

I waited outside for Sam who came out with a disturbed look on his face. 'They've asked me to start in the morning,' said Sammy. 'I'm no' gonnie dae that.' 'Look, Sam, for Christsake, they're out to get me and they'll have done it one way or another. Just you start in the morning.'

Around this period I worked in another Clyde shipyard which shall remain un-named in case Sir Eric Yarrow gets angry but there I was in the lofty and mind-boggling position of a Plumber's Helper and would you believe it held the post of Plumbers' Helpers' Shop Steward. I'll get to the top of the Trade Union movement yet.

Nothing very exciting happened there except that this time I did not feel so terribly alone when the time came to part company with Yarrow's. There were seven members of the Communist Party in the plumbers' shop who were all active selling the *Daily Worker* of a morning and what not, and one day the Management pounced and sacked the seven of us, throwing in five Catholics for good measure and so no one could possibly accuse them of discrimination.

From Matt McGinn's autobiography in *McGinn of the Calton*, 1987.

THE APPRENTICE STRIKE

Apprentices had been treated appallingly by employers for years. They were often seen as cheap labour and were paid off once they had served their time. They were not able to join a union so they took matters into their own hands.

The 18th March will go down in history as one of the most important days in the history of Clydeside. The reason for this is the fact that 70 apprentices of Messrs Lobnitz's (Renfrew) came out on strike.

This was the start of one of the biggest strikes the Clydeside has ever seen, the present figures being 12,800 boys concerning 116 firms.

On Wednesday March 31, Fairfield's (Govan) came out on strike. This strike concerned 500 boys.

By Saturday the 500 had changed to 5000 boys by which 60 firms had no apprentices bar a few SCABS.

Over the weekend 90 per cent of the firms in the Clydeside area came out.

On Monday, John Brown & Co.'s apprentices joined the strike, 100 per cent. This was the final link in the chain; apart from a few small firms every apprentice in the biggest firms on the Clyde was out.

In spite of having no previous experience of strike leadership, great organising ability was displayed by the apprentices who elected a committee composed of 160 delegates from every department of the shipyards and shops and an elected executive committee forming the central leadership.

The Trade Unions indicated their sympathy with the boys from the start and have since given us their full support in all matters.

Journeymen refused to do boys' work, therefore not only have we the unions behind us but we have the men also.

From *The Clyde Apprentice Strikers' Bulletin*, Issue No. 1, 1937.

BLACKLEG

By no means all shipbuilders were militant unionists, and this led to further conflict between strikers and strike breakers.

In the morning David found a crowd round the gatehouse but there was also a large detachment of police keeping a path clear to the entrance. David did not hesitate: and amid boos and cat-calls and vicious threats he walked up between the line of policemen and lifted his check.

Douglas, the manager, was standing inside the gate.

'Well, Ramsay,' he said, 'you're remaining loyal to the firm?'

'Weel, I'm willing to work as long as there's work for me.'

'That's the spirit,' said Douglas. 'You're a sensible man and we'll see that you don't lose by it.'

He went down to the riggers' shed but the door was locked and there was no sign of MacHaffie. The yard was almost empty. There was no sound of any work in progress although there were small groups of men gathered here and there. He went back to the gatehouse and reported to the yard manager.

'I suppose there'll be work for us to do, Mr Douglas?'

'Oh yes, certainly. Certainly there'll be work: but don't worry for the moment. We want to see how many men have come in and after that we'll decide just what's to be done.'

David went into the gatehouse and got the key of the riggers' shed. He did not want to stand idly about and, truth to tell, he was beginning to feel misgivings. He was tidying up the riggers' shed when MacHaffie came in from a conference of foremen with the management.

'Weel, David,' he said, 'you turned out, did you? Weel, it could have been worse. Some of the foremen have no men in at all. There's no' an electrician or a plater or a riveter.'

'There's no' much we can do at that rate?'

'No: nothing at all. Douglas says we've to take what men we've got and clean up. But that's only talk. They'll keep us here doing nothing so long as the strike lasts so that they can give the impression that the strike's no' solid. Don't be surprised if you see a notice in the papers that we're carrying on as usual.'

'Weel, that's one thing we'll no' read in the papers for there's nane.'

'What! No papers? There's bound to be a paper, Dave!'

'No: not a paper. They're all out on strike too.'

'That's bad. There'll be hell to pay before all this is finished. I hear they're setting fire to the buses at Parkhead. The next thing you'll see is that the military'll be called out and there'll be some o' them shot. Though, if I had my way o' it, I'd shoot every damned ringleader and trade union official without a trial. And that would put an end to their strike.'

'Weel, that would be a bit drastic, Fred. But they could at least put them in jail.'

'Jail! Jail's a damned sight too good for them. I tell you, this will cost the country millions.'

'Aye . . . Where's it going to end?'

'Oh, God knows. You're asking me. But I wouldn't be surprised if it had collapsed by the afternoon.'

But the strike didn't collapse that afternoon: if anything, the spirit of the strikers was more militant. The men had not got out for lunch and the management, after consulting with the police, decided that it would be unwise to let them out at the usual stopping time. According to the police a big crowd was due to assemble at the work gates and threats had been made that all the police in Glasgow wouldn't save the blacklegs from their wrath. And as the police had more trouble on their hands than they could cope with they could not offer the management any guarantee of safe conduct for their men.

When David did not come home at his usual time, Jean became very alarmed and begged Andrew to go down to the gate and see if there was any sign of him. Andrew protested.

'I told you what it would be, mother. My father's mad to go against the strike. Whether he's in a union or not makes no difference. He's a blackleg: and even if he is my father I couldn't blame the workers if they opened his head with a brick.'

From James Barke's novel *Land of the Leal*, 1939.

RELIGION

Undoubtedly religion was a very important factor in our shipyard, I tended to avoid completely being involved in religion but I knew there were problems that existed. There were some departments where the foreman refused to have a Catholic in the shop and there were others where the reverse applied but on the whole we tried to keep a very fair balance and when there was somebody who was being promoted his religion wasn't even taken into account.

Maurice Denny speaking on the BBC Radio Scotland programme *Clydebuilt*, 1990.

UNDERHAND AND SECRETIVE

It was a very difficult thing to pinpoint because it was all sort of underhand and secretive. It was one of these things known but difficult to prove. In a place like

The engineering apprentices at the Lobnitz shipyard in October 1936. A few months later these boys led the famous apprentice strike of 1937. (Scottish Maritime Museum)

Clydebank, which really kind of sprung up in the last hundred years out of nowhere, you had a big Irish immigration population, you had northern Scots population moving down, and of course when the Irish thing moved across then the religious problem moved across with it. So it was an imported thing, and it grew up with the town. I mean at one time I think there might have been thirteen or fourteen Orange Lodges in Clydebank and the Orange band walk through Clydebank was really quite extensive and massive.

Tom McKendrick speaking on the BBC Radio Scotland programme *Clydebuilt*, 1990.

SECOND-CLASS CITIZENS

It was not uncommon in Harland and Wolff in Govan to build a ship in two halves: the Catholics on one side, and the Protestants on the other. Don't forget, Harland and Wolff came from Belfast where there's been, unfortunately, this sad religious divide, and it was brought very slightly to Govan. In fact, in Govan, outside the shipyard there was an almost invisible line where the two gangs, one Catholic, the other Protestant, met and knocked hell out of each other. But they never used razors or any weapons. It was all a stand-up fist fight.

No, no. You found that the bosses in Belfast would appoint some managers from Belfast, and they in turn would make themselves known to that section of the community, so they would be friendly towards them. Roman Catholics in Harland and Wolff were second-class citizens. They were doing the most repulsive jobs, and I really mean it. When the tide came in not only did you have human waste, but also condoms and come what have you, being washed in, and they're working up to their knees in this. Whereas the craftsmen, the electricians, the painters, the plumbers, the carpenters: they were just that little bit above them, and of course the only way you held your job was by being good at your job. If you were good at your job, even the bosses who would prefer someone of a different religious persuasion, they had to say, 'Well, at least he's good at his job.'

Andy, a shipwright, speaking in *Made in Govan: An oral history of shipbuilding on the Upper Clyde 1930–1950*, 1991.

DIFFERENT CASTES

There are strongly marked differences between the members of the Clyde black squad and the engineering sections. The engineer has long been regarded by the black squad as a more brainy type and socially superior, but the black squad's way of acknowledging this superiority is anything but flattering to the engineer, who is made to feel like a despised aristocrat. It is, of course, the horny-handed toiler's usual attitude to the white-collar worker, though in this case the latter is often collarless and is seldom ornamental in get-up. He does, however, have his overalls cleaned regularly, a thing no member of the black squad could do without losing caste.

From J. J. McCall's article in *Scotland's Record*, 1946.

DEGREES OF POWER

. . . the men were insignificant and identical, except that the foreman wore a suit – and a soft hat which, apparently, he never removed in public. He ruled his department from a little wooden hut. It was like a small garden shed set indoors, leaning against the soaring whitewashed wall which rose sixty or seventy feet to the glass roof.

Immediately outside 'the box' was a long trestle table in front of a bank of filing cabinets. That was the domain of the foreman's chief assistant, the charge-hand. He was responsible for all the working drawings that came to the department. The charge-hand had no real power but was an invaluable intermediary and was a great retailer of information in both directions. Then there were senior journeymen who all wore caps and junior journeymen who rarely did until they were thirty, or were blessed with premature baldness. Then came the apprentices in strict order of their year, from fifth to first. Last were the servants of all these – the labourers. I never discovered if they had their own pecking-order because if there was anything that the youngest apprentice wanted done, even the oldest labourer would have to do it.

From Tom Gallacher's novel *Apprentice*, 1983.

DIPLOMACY AND THE DRAUGHTSMAN

In T. M. Watson's play a shipyard plater is horrified to hear of his daughter's interest in a draughtsman. While this is essentially a social comedy it does highlight the serious issue of the deep-rooted antipathy felt between the men who worked in the yard and those who worked in the office.

MRS G. You're lookin' real tired the nicht, John.

MR G. An' sma' wonder. There's anither boat in. Anither alteration. (*Irritably*) The drawin' office again. They're never content unless they're changin' somethin'. Draughtsmen! Ugh!

MRS G. Ye shouldna girn sae much at the drawin' office, John. Ye ken weel enough they've just tae dae as things dae wi' them. (*She pours out tea.*)

MR G. Girn! Wumman, if ye kent hauf o' whit I hae tae pit up wi' frae that same drawin' office, ye wad wonder hoo I wasna daft. (*Pulling on slippers and rising.*) An' whit dae draughtsmen ken aboot boats onywey. (*Crossing and sitting at left side of table.*) Ceegaurs and spats are mair in their line.

(MRS G. *replaces teapot on hearth.*)

MRS G. (*soothingly*). I ken a' aboot it, John. A foreman plater's job is nae bed o' roses. I was just tellin' Mrs MacNab nae later than this mornin' that I never kent the 'oor tae expect ye hame. Aye, she's an understaunin' wumman that, John. A' she said was, 'Mrs Gartshore, yin hauf o' the world disna ken hoo the ither hauf leeves.'

MR G. (*beginning his dinner*). It's no' for the want o' speirin' onywey. But whaur's Annie the nicht?

MRS G. Buyin' some bits o' things in the toon. She's been oot a' day.

Group photographs of shipyard workers virtually always show members of a particular trade. The trade is clearly more important than the shipyard. Here we see the caulkers at Ardrossan shipyard in 1929. (North Ayrshire Museum)

Middle:
The blacksmiths of Ardrossan shipyard around 1910, proudly showing off the tools of their particular trade. (North Ayrshire Museum)

Bottom:
The carpenters at the Ardrossan Shipyard in 1898. (North Ayrshire Museum)

Mr G.	Umph! She's never done buyin' somethin'. Is she expectin' onybody, dae ye think?
Mrs G.	She never said and I never asked her. But dinna ask me what that lassie's expectin'. She's past ma comprehension.
Mr G.	Aye, Jean, the young yins nooadays wad pass onybody's comprehension. (*Shaking his head.*) I've been thinkin' a lot aboot Annie lately. Ye ken, Jean, Annie's just a wean, an' weans sometimes get queer notions intae their heids.
Mrs G.	Aye, an' whit notion hae you got in yours?
Mr G.	(*sharply*). I've just been hearing that Annie's been seen gallivantin' aboot the toon wi' a masher.
Mrs G.	Weel, weel, whit aboot it?
Mr G.	Whit aboot it? Ye staun there hearin' this aboot yer ain dochter, an' a' ye say is – Whit aboot it? (*Striking table with his fist.*) I'll tell ye what aboot it! I believe in lettin' young folk hae their fling, bit gallivantin' aboot the toon wi' a masher is mair than I'll staun.
Mrs G.	And whaur did ye hear ony sich rubbish? In the yaird, I'll be bound.
Mr G.	(*rising*). Aye, in the yaird. An' it's a fine thing for me – me – a heid foreman, tae hear sich stories aboot ma ain lassie. Guid kens what the world's comin' tae at a'.
Mrs G.	John, Annie's a level heided young wumman, sae dinna fash yersel'.
Mr G.	Dinna fash ma'sel'! Wumman, dae ye ken that that damned masher's a draughtsman?
Mrs G.	(*in pleased tones*). Ye dinna tell me that?
Mr G.	(*explosively*). A draughtsman! I wadna hae cared a make had he been a candy-man or a Salvation Army drummer, but there's naethin' mair obnoxious tae me than thae puir abject meesarable specimens o' humanity ca'ed draughtsmen.
Mrs G.	Wheest, John, the neighbours'll hear ye.
Mr G.	Wumman, imagine the dochter o' John Gartshore bein' seen oot wi' yin o' thae flat-fitted, flat-heided eediots wha dinna ken the stern o' a boat frae a wooden leg. Ah tell ye, Jean, I wad raither see her mairrit tae an undertaker.

From T. M. Watson's play *Diplomacy and the Draughtsman*, 1926.

THE BASTARDS

'The bastards,' he whispered.

Inside him distrust of sedentary men smouldered to madness. His fists bunched, and behind his rust-bleak eyes an impulse to smash the grey glass throbbed temptingly. In the hinterland of his mind obscene epithets revolved. He'd throw them through the shattered glass at their pasty silly faces. They would be shocked and scurry for the police. One of their own kind, steeped in barbers' lotion and hypocrisy, would sit on the Bench and wag his fat shiny head in horror.

He'd get thirty days and everybody would lick their lips and pretend to be sorry for Julia. And in the Paddy's Arms Big Mick would accept another schooner of stout from one of the creepers and declare: 'Ach, shure, I didn't want to pay the poor bugger off but didn't he cry me out of me name? What man that is a man could stand for that, now?'

And all the Tims and Dans around would chorus: 'By the holy jaize, Mick, you were very dacent, very dacent indeed. It's a God's blessing you didn't lift a hand and strike him to the ground yourself. . . .'

The window shot up so swiftly and silently it caught him grimacing.

The face that stared out was unimpressed. Nor did it comment.

With a flick Haig tossed across his slip. The clerk picked it off the polished counter and read it. His expression never changed. Middle-aged, he had washed-blue eyes, grey hair bushy above the ears and a completely bald crown that arched from brow to nape. He wore a severe suit of sombre grey and a high-winged collar so prim and tight it propped his long chin at an angle. His name was Meldrum and he was an earnest lay preacher who spent Sunday evenings standing in the centre of a forlorn but resolute little circle of followers advocating the sure spiritual rewards of repentance to embarrassed and unwilling, but tolerant, audiences of tenement corner loungers. Rumour was strong that Meldrum could have been Chief Cashier years ago had his conscience not forbidden him to join in the whisky drinking of managerial conferences. With envious cynicism Haig doubted the truth of this and – at this moment – despised Meldrum's white hands, white collar, douce suit and everything about him with a bitter contempt for all things allied to the trappings of administrative authority. He conveyed his hostility by a brash, unwinking stare.

Meldrum remained unshaken. The tragedy of men being fired or laid off was so much part of his routine that he seemed immune to the passions involved. He glanced over the slip again, glanced back at Haig and moved out of view.

The rigger found himself gazing vacantly at the crowns of two clerks perched on high stools bent over high, sloping desks. They did not look up. He could see their inward-turned toes propped on their spars – one, despite the camouflage of high polish, was distinctly down-at-heel and he could see the frayed turn-ups of their well-brushed trousers. Yet he felt no kinship. To him they were two sheltered specimens of a soft breed whose activities could hardly be classed as real work and whose semi-indolent existence was supported entirely by the sweat of hard-grafting chaps like himself. The shine on their trousers and the cracks in their boots was not proof of poverty but contemptible brands of their willingness to trade truth for a place at the rich man's table – any place, so long as they sat and were mistaken for hosts.

When, at last, they raised their heads and gazed woodenly at him he read patronage and rebuke in their detached survey. That they were bored or tired never occurred to him. Or that the open window exposed them to a draught relatively more uncomfortable than a hard wind whistling between icy keel-blocks on a frosty morning.

He interpreted their glances as an expression of resentment at his invasion of their tidy, ledger-built castle. Arrogant behind his own dirty face he saw their clean ones as an affront. And automatically hated them.

From Hugh Munro's *The Clydesiders*, 1961.

PAY DIFFERENTIALS

One aspect of the shipyard I didn't agree with was that in common with all yards the 'Boilermakers', i.e. platers, riveters, caulkers, and welders, had a wage of 50% in excess of the finishing trades, i.e. engineers, plumbers, joiners, carpenters, painters; this situation was inherited from the era when a ship was just a shell and the internals were very simple and unsophisticated which didn't give the finishing trades much muscle. I would not detract from the skill of the 'Boilermakers' but it did not outdo that of the finishing trades. This problem was resolved in the middle sixties when the shipyards of this country saw the writing on the wall and tried to re-equip and modernise when among the other changes such as dropping many of the lines of demarcation, all tradesmen irrespective of union received the same wage. The classic example being in the days of demarcation when it took three different trades to fit a port light to a ship side or bulkhead and after reorganisation one tradesman performed this job.

From Thomas MacLean's memories of his life in the Ardrossan shipyards, published in Catriona Levy's *Ardrossan Shipyards: Struggle for survival 1825–1983*, 1984.

JUST A HELPER

I started work in Fairfield's on the twenty-fifth of November and nearly caused

Two engineering draughtsmen from David Rowan marine engineers in Govan. The antipathy between the yard workers and the office workers was intense. (Glasgow City Archives)

a strike on my first day. My title was sheet ironworker's helper. While standing on the shop floor as everyone was given their jobs for the day, the shop foreman, Willie Coleman, asked me if I had just started. On my reply he then told me to wait until everyone else had been attended to. Eventually he took me over to a guy called Willie Hart and said to him, 'This is Jim; he's just started, he can work along with you.' After standing around like a statue for ten minutes or so while Willie had his head down studying a drawing, he said, 'Do you want something to do?' I said, 'Yes,' as he handed me a drawing and said, 'Make up these lugs – there's the flatbar.' I looked at the drawing and asked Willie for a scriber. He went into his toolbox and gave me a scribe. I then said, 'Can I have a rule?' He shook his head and tumbled once again in his toolbox before giving me a rule. He didn't look too pleased and I didn't know why. I began marking off the lugs on the flatbar when Bert came up and said, 'What are you doing? You'll cause a strike.' I didn't know what was wrong, as I would have been quite happy working away. Bert turned to Willie and told him that I was a helper and not a sheet ironworker. We had a good laugh about it.

From Jim Collins' unpublished memoirs.

IT'S NO FAIR

They all want to go to the welding. This is Utopia this welding. I'll tell you another wee story. In 1966 they were going to pay off sheet ironworkers so the boilermakers said we'll take them in. Well, the blokes went and got trained. They wanted to volunteer because there was extra money there. OK. Fair enough.

Welder at work in 1955. Rivalry between the different trades was intense and the numerous demarcation disputes arose out of a need to preserve the rights of each individual trade. (Glasgow Museums)

They go to the welding, they are trained for the welding and the boat got tacked up. Fair enough. I say, tack all that up. About a month ago they wanted to send the same blokes to the welding. Ah no: we don't want to go to the welding. How no? We had enough of that the last time. *Because it's the same money*. They get the same money for sitting on their arse as for welding, so that they don't want to go to welding. Why not go to plating or some other trade? They all want to go to welding. See maybe I'm prejudiced that way. See I put you in here. Suppose it's a wee store or something, a vegetable store. You tack up the bulkheads, tack up that, tack up the stanchions and you walk out the door, you are finished. They send for the dumplings and they come in and they've to weld it all for the same money that you've been getting for playing yourself. It's no fair.

A Clydebank boilermaker speaking in 'The Oral History of Upper Clyde Shipbuilders', *Oral History*, 1974.

THERE IS A GREAT DEAL TO BE DONE

The use of labour in shipbuilding is wasteful; nobody who discussed the industry with us has challenged this statement. Partly this waste is due to shortcomings of planning and supervision, partly to the practices on which the unions insist and partly to the level of response and application of the individual participant which is itself conditioned by the first two factors. The planning and organisation of work could be improved but a solution depends on a substantial improvement in industrial relations and a raising of individual morale.

We do not regard this as the only major problem in shipbuilding. But both managements and unions must seriously and urgently review their attitudes with a view to overcoming the costly and debilitating lack of confidence which exists between them. The present situation has caused apprehension among the industry's customers and suppliers as well as among many in the industry itself and has been seen as one major reason for the failure to meet delivery dates. The importance of making full use of labour extends therefore beyond the contribution which it can make to cost reduction.

The time has come for those within the industry to stop blaming each other and for those outside it to encourage change and to applaud those who lead it. There is a great deal to be done.

The employers complain of restrictions on output as a result of meticulous insistence on craft demarcation; insistence on over-manning of machines; strikes at short notice, often just before a launching, by groups of employees to enforce a wage claim which cannot be granted without repercussions on the wages of other groups; the creation of shortages of workers by restrictions on entry and then the exploitation of the shortage bans on overtime or the insistence that all must work overtime if some are to do so; and bad timekeeping.

The unions for their part argue that the practices of which the employers complain are often based on agreements to which the employers were party, and on demarcations between trades which the employers themselves originated; that the industry is one which has been dominated by the 'hire and fire' attitudes of employers; that because of failure to keep open a channel of communication strikes are often the only way of securing speedy and serious attention to a grievance; that the employers have done far less than they could have done to give a measure of security and to promote safety and welfare amenities in yards; and that there has been on the part of many employers an unwillingness to consult the unions until serious trouble has developed.

A modern plate-cutting machine being operated at Fairfield's in the 1960s. The introduction of machinery like this was fraught with problems because of additional pay claims and demarcation disputes. (Scottish Maritime Museum)

We are not a court of enquiry into industrial disputes and we shall not achieve anything constructive by attempts to allocate responsibility for this state of affairs. The joint failure of both management and unions to tackle the problems of bad industrial relations resulting in the wasteful use of labour has cost the industry dear in money and reputation. The present state of affairs has hampered the work of managers, planners and individual workers alike; has kept costs up and deliveries late; and has in consequence tied the industry's right hand behind its back. We were therefore encouraged in our contacts at all levels in management and trade unions to find there were so many who were, at last, fed up with the situation. Too often however there is the suspicion that any new attitude on the part of one group in the industry will merely provide an opportunity for other groups to gain an advantage. Both sides of the industry must resist the temptation to seek short-term gains at the expense of the long-term interests of all.

R. M. Geddes, *Shipbuilding Inquiry Committee Report*, 1965–66.

FRIGHTENED

I always believed that management gave in too easily. They must have seen what was going to happen but were too frightened to face up to it. That's my opinion. They were frightened to have a face-to-face confrontation. That was what was required for the whole industry. Someone had to say: 'Look, this is the way it's going to be and if you don't like it then your jobs are going to disappear.'

Willie Clydesdale, welder and shop steward at John Brown's speaking to Ian Johnston and Lewis Johnman in *Granta 61: The Sea*, 1998.

CHAPTER EIGHT

THE YEARS OF DECLINE

The fortunes of the shipbuilding industry were notoriously fragile. Bust followed boom with predictable regularity, and inevitably it was the workers who were the first to feel the effects. By employing casual labour the bosses could hire and fire to meet these ever fluctuating needs.

Minor crises in the 1870s and 1880s saw some yards close, but the first major crisis in the industry came in the aftermath of the First World War. Many yards had expanded to meet the demands of the war and after the post-war building boom was over there was massive over-capacity in the industry. During the 1920s and 1930s yard after yard closed down. The bleakest period came in 1931 when work was stopped on the new Cunard liner being built at Clydebank and thousands of men were left to walk the streets. The fate of ship No. 534, as it was known, came to symbolise the decline of the industry, and the great rusting hull stood out as a beacon of despair.

The industry was eventually saved from this depression by re-armament and the Second World War, which saw the yards once more working flat out. This boom continued into the late 1950s, but by then there were major problems with the industry that couldn't be solved by simple belt tightening.

The yards had been running at full capacity to meet the demand to replace the shipping lost in the war. With the order books full and the money rolling in, many yard owners were unwilling to halt production in order to implement much needed modernisation programmes. Meanwhile, new foreign yards had begun to take full advantage of modern prefabrication techniques.

By the time the Scottish shipbuilders realised what was happening it was too late. Some of the yard owners decided to get out of the industry with their fortunes intact. Others struggled manfully on with half-hearted attempts at modernisation and increasing productivity. But the writing was on the wall, and yard after yard continued to close in the 1960s and 1970s.

There seemed to be a collective death wish among both the bosses and the workers in the industry. The bosses failed to anticipate changes in the world shipbuilding market, and their modernisation programmes, when they came, were often too little, too late and designed for the wrong kind of ship. There was a fatal arrogance about the shipyard owners. Clyde ships were the best, and everyone knew it, why did they have to change? John Brown's famously had no marketing department because they believed that 'People come to us, we're John Brown's'.

The failure to improve both working conditions and productivity played into the hands of the unions. The unions meanwhile abused their power, and strike followed petty strike with sickening regularity. Delivery dates were not met, technical difficulties began to mar the Clydebuilt reputation, and costs spiralled out of control. Not surprisingly, shipowners began to look elsewhere for their ships.

When the receivers were called in to wind up the ailing UCS shipyards in 1971, the workers could see that striking would be self-defeating and instead took it upon themselves to save the yards by starting the famous work-in. To a certain extent it worked. John Brown's was sold off to become an oil-rig yard while Govan was taken under government control as a precursor to the wholesale nationalisation of the shipbuilding industry.

Previous page:
The last ship built at the Ailsa yard in Ayr, ready to be launched in 1929. Like many yards it carried on for a time as a repair yard before finally closing down. (Scottish Maritime Museum)

In 2000 the Kvaerner group turned their back on shipbuilding, leaving hundreds of jobs under threat at Govan. (Jim Dunn)

Like so many schemes that had gone before, nationalisation was not the answer to shipbuilding's problems and yards continued to close. In 1988 Govan Shipbuilders was sold to the Norwegian Kvaerner Group. Great hope was put in the new owner, and despite early job losses the future looked rosy. But crisis is never far from shipbuilding, and in 1999 Kvaerner decided to withdraw from shipbuilding altogether. Only a fraught last-minute deal with BAE Systems saved the yard.

At the start of the twenty-first century, all that remains of the Scottish shipbuilding industry are the two BAE Systems' yards at Govan and Scotstoun, the small Ferguson's yard at Port Glasgow and a couple of fishing boat yards at Buckie and Macduff. Quite how long they manage to continue to maintain at least a semblance of Scotland's proud shipbuilding heritage only time will tell.

A BLEAK OUTLOOK

Events seem to be conspiring to render impossible the work of ship construction. For the second month in succession not one general trading vessel has been launched on the Clyde, and the output of the river has consisted of a few small craft of specialised types. Never before in the history of the river as the leading shipbuilding area of the world, has there been two such months. The vessels were, from an industrial point of view, insignificant, and their aggregate tonnage was pathetically small. No contracts for commercial vessels have been announced on the river since early in July, and unless there is an almost immediate improvement in industry none can be anticipated in the near future. Owners cannot place orders because tonnage built at present costs will not pay at present rates of freight, while costs cannot be cut any lower than they are. As if this were not enough, the overtime and nightshift dispute remains unsettled, and the few ironworkers for whom there is employment are walking the streets or emigrating. The Executive Council of the Boilermakers' Society continues to reject an agreement which is being operated by other shipbuilding unions, and, in consequence, their members cannot obtain employment in federated establishments. All this is leading to a stoppage of work more complete than has ever been experienced in the past, and one from which recovery will be an extremely difficult and protracted process. The need of the moment is the greatest possible measure of co-operation among ship owners, ship builders and ship constructors, in order to nurse the industry back to economic health and strength. Instead, there is the minimum of co-operation, and everyone concerned appears to be fighting for his own hand.

From the *Glasgow Herald* of 23 August 1923.

THE QUIET YARD

The midday hooter at Messrs John Brown's Clydebank yard on Saturday sounded to the casual ear no more fateful than usual, but its hoarse bellow was silencing a great shipyard for an indefinite period, instead of the normal week-end break.

For some time before noon groups of men stood about outside the main gate. They were time workers waiting to collect their lying-time. When the hooter sounded they entered the yard while hundreds of their fellow workers started to stream out.

The outgoing men, silent, sober faced, carried the tools of their trades, the ominous badge of the suspended workman.

Many of them were men who had been thirty and forty years in the service of Messrs Brown, and were carrying their kits out for the first time. Others had had the unfortunate experience several times in recent years.

The crowds of men quickly dispersed by train, tram and bus, and within a few minutes the gates had closed on the quiet yard.

Three thousand men had gone to swell the unemployment total.

From the *Daily Record* of Monday 14 December 1931.

THE EMPTY RIVER

It was in a sense a procession that he witnessed, the high, tragic pageant of the Clyde. Yard after yard passed by, the berths empty, the grass growing about the sinking keel-blocks. He remembered how, in the brave days, there would be scores of ships ready for the launching along this reach, their stems hanging over the tide, and how the men at work on them on high stagings would turn from the job and tug off their caps and cheer the new ship setting out to sea. And now only the gaunt, dumb poles and groups of men, workless, watching in silence the mocking passage of the vessel. It was bitter to know that they knew – that almost every man among them was an artist in one of the arts that go to the building of a ship; that every feature of the *Estramadura* would come under an expert and loving scrutiny, that her passing would remind them of the joy of work and tell them how many among them would never work again. It appalled Leslie Pagan that not a cheer came from those watching groups.

It was a tragedy beyond economics. It was not that so many thousands of homes lacked bread and butter. It was that a tradition, a skill, a glory, a passion, was visibly in decay and all the acquired and inherited loveliness of artistry rotting along the banks of the stream.

Into himself he counted and named the yards they passed. The number and variety stirred him to wonder, now that he had ceased to take them for granted. His mental eye moving backwards up the river, he saw the historic place at Govan, Henderson's of Meadowside at the mouth of the Kelvin, and the long stretch of Fairfield on the southern bank opposite. There came Stephen's of Linthouse next, and Clydeholm facing it across the narrow, yellow ditch of the ship-channel. From thence down river the range along the northern bank was almost continuous for miles – Connell, Inglis, Blythswood, and the rest: so many that he could hardly remember their order. He was distracted for a moment to professionalism by the lean grey forms of destroyers building for a foreign Power in the sheds of a yard that had dramatically deserted Thames for Clyde. Then he lost himself again in the grim majesty of the parade. There came John Brown's, stretching along half a mile of waterfront at Clydebank, the monstrous red hull of Number 534 looming in its abandonment like a monument to the glory departed; as if shipbuilding man had tried to do too much and had been defeated by the mightiness of his own conception. Then came, seeming to point the moral, the vast desolation of Beardmore's at Dalmuir, cradle of the mightiest battleships and now a scrapheap, empty and silent forever, the great gantry over the basin proclaiming stagnation and an end.

Even where the Clyde opened out above Erskine, with the Kilpatricks green and sweet above the river on the one hand and the wooded, fat lands of Renfrewshire stretching to the escarpment of Misty Law on the other, the sight of a legend – FOR SALE – painted large on the walls of an empty shed reminded him with the effect of a blow that Napier and Miller's were gone, shut down, finished, the name never to appear again on a brass plate below the bridge of a good ship. And he suddenly remembered that there lay on his desk at the office a notice of sale of the plant at Bow, Maclachlan's on the Cart by Paisley. His world seemed visibly to be crumbling. Already he had been appalled by the emptiness of Lobnitz's and Simons's at Renfrew, and the sense of desolation, of present catastrophe, closed the more oppressively upon him.

As they rounded the bend by Bowling, passing close under the wooded crags of Auchentorlie on the one hand and, as on a Dutch canal, past the flats of Erskine on the other, his eye was taken by the scene ahead. The jagged, noble range of the Cowal hills made a purple barrier against the glow of the westering winter sun. Now he was lost for a space in wonder that this cradle and home of ships enjoyed a setting so lovely. Through the gap of the Vale of Leven he could see the high peak of Ben Lomond, and his fancy ranged up those desolate, distant slopes. But then the dome of Dumbarton Rock, the westernmost of the chain strung across the neck of Scotland, brought him to think of the mean town at its base, and of Denny's yard in the crook of the Leven behind it, and of the lovely, fast, small ships they could build, and of the coming of the turbine. And another yard there, Macmillan's, derelict.

Past Dumbarton, the river opening to the Firth, the scene took on an even more immediate grandeur. The sands of the Pillar Bank were showing in golden streaks through the falling tide. The peninsula of Ardmore was a pretty tuft of greenery thrust out towards the channel. Dead ahead lay the mouth of the Gareloch, backed by the jagged peaks on the western side of Loch Long. A man could almost feel the freshness of the open sea coming to meet him over the miles of island, hill and loch; and Leslie Pagan marked how the fresher and larger waves slapped against the sides of the *Estramadura* and could almost imagine that the ship responded with quiver and curtsey to their invitation.

That openness of the river below the derelict timber ponds of Langbank, however, is deceptive; for still the channel must run round the end of the bank and close into the Renfrewshire shore. There are miles of waste space there over the shallows, and Glasgow is more than twenty miles away before a ship of size has more than a few feet of water between her keel and the bottom. Port Glasgow and Greenock look across miles of sand and sea to the Highland hills, but the yards there must launch their ships into narrow waters; so that the man who had built the *Estramadura*, scanning the shores, saw thereabouts an even thicker crowding of berths than he had marked on the upper reaches.

It was another roster of great names, older, more redolent even than those that had become namely about Glasgow with the deepening of the Clyde. Ferguson's, Duncan's, Murdoch's, Russell's, Hamilton's. . . . Even he could not be sure that he had them right; there had been so many changes. Out on Garvel Point, under the old marooned Scots mansion-house, stood Brown's – the 'Siberia' of the artisan's lingo. There came Scott's East Yard – was it not once Steele's, where the clippers were built? There came the Greenock and Grangemouth, once the artisan's 'Klondike'. Then Scott's Mid Yard; then Caird's, the last of the lot – closed down.

From George Blake's novel *The Shipbuilders*, 1935.

THE SILENT CLYDE

The strongest impression I received of Glasgow was one of silence. In the centre of the city people are still busy, or seem to be so; but when one goes down the Clyde, to what used to be the busy shipbuilding quarter, there is hardly anything but this silence, which one would take to be the silence of a dead town if it were not for the numberless empty-looking groups of unemployed men standing about the pavements. I noticed that even the children seemed to make less noise than they used to do, as if silence had seized upon them too: or it may simply have been that they were insufficiently fed.

From Edwin Muir's *Scottish Journey*, 1935.

ALIVE AGAIN

Cunarder 534 is alive again. Six hundred men are at work on the great gaunt hull which has stood silent and bleakly alone on the Clydebank stocks for 28 months.

Steel rings on steel, pneumatic riveters roar a challenge to the depression and men's voices eagerly exchange the language of the shipyards in a 'new world' symphony of industry which had a pipe music overture in the rosy dawn of April 3, 1934.

A Daily Record pipe band led Clydebank back to work on the giant Cunarder.

As the gates of John Brown's moved slowly back at 8 o'clock yesterday morning Dalmuir Parish Pipe Band invited by the Daily Record to make a national gesture of thanksgiving, strode with bold step, swinging kilt and streaming plaid, into the most famous of all shipyards, telling the world 'The Campbells are Coming'.

Cheering, laughing workmen crowded on the pipers' heels, and marched with gay steps and light hearts to their posts, keyed up to begin again the work they were reluctantly compelled to stop over two years ago.

A thousand men went through the gates. There was not work for all of them; but, in addition to the three or four hundred who received definite instructions to resume, there were places for still more, taken out of the daily 'market' from which men are chosen for a day or a week's work as the need arises.

The result near the close of the day was that over 600 men were working on Cunarder 534. There are more to come. By the end of next week about 1500 men will be employed, and subsequently 3500 at work.

The pipes called out Clydebank to see its men go back to work. The streets outside the gates were packed with people, but theirs were not the only eyes which watched the pageant of a new prosperity unfold itself.

Press and sound pictures were the eyes and ears of the world, recording on plate, celluloid and microphone impressions of one of the greatest days in the Clyde's history.

Every window overlooking the yard gates was crowded with men, women and children, and flags and bunting appeared here and there on buildings.

The men who gathered at the gates, ready for work, had eager eyes and a restless mood. Many of them wore brand-new dungarees on the grounds, no doubt, that the occasion demanded some sort of sartorial celebration.

From the *Daily Record* of Wednesday 4 April 1934.

BACK TO WORK

Once again Brian O'Neill marched with an army of workers, a solid moving mass of humanity, pressing close together through the gate of Brown's shipyard. The air was heavy with the smell of oils, paint and naphtha. Wonderful scent it was to Brian with its hundred and one vivid memories of pre-unemployment – his apprenticeship days and the colourful riot of experiences that was his in the old days in Beardmore's. It all came back again there, marching with his fellow tradesmen, in old familiar smells and noises. He was eagerly excited too. God, how many grey ages had passed since he had handled the tools? Files, scrapers, calipers, dividers, hammers, chisels; steel, brass, gun-metal, cast iron – would he have the old skill and knowledge of all this? And what kind of a job would he

The *Queen Mary* nearing completion at John Brown's. (Scottish Maritime Museum)

get? Oh, the thousand and one jobs and the thousand and one ways to begin and only one right way! Would he remember? There would be so many fancy gadgets in this *Queen Mary* too. Of course, the big jobs in the engine-room, landing and squaring up the turbines and huge gear cases, the propeller shafts, all this would be well ahead now. Still she was such a brute of a thing that they would have a small army of engineers connecting up the maze of piping, the hundred and one auxilliaries, fitting chokes and bolts – oh, there would be months of work yet. And with his father idle now labour took on a new dignity, a greater responsibility, with his wages now infinitely more important.

From Edward Shiels' novel *Gael over Glasgow*, 1937.

NOT YET THE END

Regret and resentment and nostalgia, however, are quantities as variable, incalculable, and irrational as the revolution of trade cycles. It does not even matter in the long run that prosperity on the Clyde is apt to be a symptom of war in the offing, since the shipbuilders of the Clyde happen to be particularly good at building men-o'-war. All the cards are stacked against the old order. Even while these new notions of trustification were influencing the board-room there invaded yard and workshop, by the same gate and at the same hour, the machine.

This may prove the most insidious influence on the character of the shipbuilding art. It clearly means the decay of craftsmanship. The lay visitor to any shipyard might well be most deeply impressed by the spectacle of a man, in stained dungarees and tweed cap, enthroned on such a metal seat as serves the driver of a mowing-machine. The levers in his hands so manipulate the edifice of which he is the crowning figure that the cutting points of punches can be brought precisely over tiny circles chalked on a thick steel plate. His infernal machine in position, he pulls another lever, and a large plate is thereupon perforated with a sufficiency of holes for rivets. By that single, almost automatic, act he puts out of employment a sizeable squad of men under the old dispensation. It has been reckoned that the use of the 'piano' punching machine may save as much as a month of time in the completion of a ship of size.

The tendency runs through every process of the industry. The old-style riveter with his brawny forearms has been almost completely replaced by equally strong men, but a smaller number of them, armed with pneumatic hammers. They may have to give place in their turn to manipulators of the welding arc with its livid, potent flame. Another machine, served by a man and a boy – and there is an irony in that very word 'served' – will make in the same time as many hatches as used to take fourteen craftsmen to put together. An affair more or less like a lawn-mower, pushed by a likely lad, will caulk the decks of a ship in half the time taken by a dozen of such good men as John Wood employed. Between 1920 and 1930 the number of men working in the shipyards of the Clyde – the men who 'wrought,' as their own good word has it – was reduced to the tune of fifty per cent.

Thus, whilst the tradition survives, the conditions go on changing. In the fluctuating fortunes of more than a score of shipyards from Glasgow Bridge to the Tail of the Bank there is the matter of an ode in the noblest classical tradition. The very names have the evocative force of such as Roland and Roncesvalles. But if one has recorded with appropriate regret the decline of individualism, that is all to the point for the time being. The tale is not yet told in full. The end is not yet in sight.

From George Blake's *Down to the Sea*, 1937.

WARTIME SHIPBUILDERS

At the gates of the yard the last cigarettes were thrown away, and then the men streamed on to the empty slipways and into the deserted shops. The yard began to live. Like a machine-gun burst, the first pneumatic riveter sent off its roar, a noise enough to knock your head off, and the first limelight flash of the welder's flame came from the rust-coloured plates lying on the skids. Up the ramp at the end of the yard, scores of men were trooping on to three or four destroyers lying in the water. And like an answer to this yard, the riveters from the yards across the river rapped out their fusillade.

It was like a battle. It was a battle. Who were the men? Pick them out at random, and it is astonishing how many of them were not lifelong shipbuilders. The slump left its mark on their lives. Here is a grimacing little man in his thirties, a droll with pop eyes and strong glasses, something of a comic turn. Nineteen years out of the industry. Packed up early in 1922, in a bad year; went on the dole for nine months; worked for six years as a gardener, which was changing one kind of open-air life for another. But gardening fell on bad times, so he went as a packer at a toffee works, then to a baker's; was a storekeeper and handyman. There was a large, grave man sitting on the automatic punch. This convulsive machine looks like a mixture of grand piano and dentist's chair. The chair jumps up and down, and at each jump a rivet hole is struck through the thick steel plate that will presently be part of a ship's hull. This man had been fourteen years out of the industry. Soft hands had been his trouble when he came back, as it is with all men who leave the heavy industries and then return.

There was the head of the frame-bending squad, waiting to draw the frame from the furnace. A lean, wild-looking, tight-breathing man, he had indigo specks on his face – an obvious pitman. He had been a trimmer, a builder and a crane driver. With him was a sad man who left the shipyards for the milk trade. He had been apprenticed to the shipyards and it had been waste of his time. He was thrown out. So he started a milk round, worked it up, until after years of pushing at it, he was selling his ten gallons of milk a day. He was called up. The end of that dream. He sold his business and came here. He thinks of one thing: getting the war over as quickly as possible and going back to the milk business. He was on his own. The slump in shipbuilding turned many energetic men into the builders of small businesses which hung together round the family.

There was a grocer who was now a foreman. He was a slight, middle-aged man

Marking rivet holes on a plate for the piano punch. This was one of the first mechanisation methods to be introduced into the shipyards. One operator and a helper could now do the job that had previously taken a squad of eight to ten men. Photograph by Cecil Beaton. (Imperial War Museum)

who wore a scarf and an overcoat, and was sheltering from the wind. The first thing he did was to apologise for his clothes; he'd just had 'flu. The northern shipyards are swept by bitter winds, but you don't go about in a coat and muffler. He had been in the shipyards before, but when they let him down he started, like so many others, one of those small mixed-grocery businesses. He ran this business with his son. His son was called up – that was the first blow. Then he was called up himself. So now his sister was trying to run the place.

'I made more money in the shop,' he said, 'and it was strange to me giving up everything and coming here. I want to get back. But, I will say this, shipbuilding is a man's job. You're one of thousands who are making something big.'

It is impossible to appreciate fully the work the shipyard workers were doing in this war, anywhere in Britain, unless one gets into one's mind that these people were scarred by the slump. They saw famous yards close. They saw places where they had spent years of their life put up to auction. A man's sense of right and wrong, the resources of his character, are bound up with his work and the place he lives in and, like the rest of us, the shipyard worker feels he was torn up and that his roots are raw. He sees, with bewilderment, that he is caught in some world process, larger than his town or his trade; the war was part of it. He could see the necessity of building ships to win the war; he was glad of the good money that helped him to make up the arrears of the slump – the impoverished home and the spoiled chances; but he glowered at the thought of being thrown on the scrap heap again.

From V. S. Pritchett's *Build the Ships* of 1946.

NEW CONSTRUCTION METHODS

After the war prefabrication was seen as the key to making Scottish yards more efficient. However, its introduction was far from easy and led to many problems.

If you had a major problem such as a tank top or a double bottom unit being made in the shop and developing a twist, now even if it's only got an inch of a twist you just don't get that out. There's no way you can get that out at the berth, and the only thing to do is remove the shell. It's got to be burned off again, and the unit's got to be kept perfectly flat, it's got to be secured down then the shell would have to be re-fitted as it should have been done in the first place. This was quite a common thing – that you had misalignment of butts and heights that obviously didn't match its next neighbour at the berth. And that used to give them quite a bit of trouble, and that was work the shipwright had to overcome at the berth and quite often entailed a wee bit of correction work, you know. But I don't think this was anything uncommon because when you bear in mind, taking a double bottom for example, which consists of a keel, a girder, the bottom shell of a ship and the tank top of a ship and you had roughly maybe four different butts. Now any one of these butts could be short in length, the calculation of the length could be a wee bit out so therefore it didn't quite match its neighbour at the berth so you had to correct something, and in correcting you sometimes lost a wee bit in length. And of course this began to show up – anything that was wrong with the bottom of the ship simply showed up higher up on the ship. Any trouble like that simply followed you right up the ship and it simply made your job a lot harder. At the very least it made the ship shorter in length.

Bobby Aitchison, foreman shipwright at Henry Robb's shipyard at Leith, speaking in 1984, on a tape held at the School of Scottish Studies.

Opposite: The platers' shop at Stephen's shipyard in 1950. The introduction of prefabrication led to huge demarcation disputes between platers and shipwrights. (Glasgow University Archives)

DEMARCATION TROUBLES

As well as bringing technical difficulties prefabrication also caused serious demarcation troubles. Prefabrication was carried out in the sheds by platers. This meant less work for the shipwrights on the berths. During one of the disputes at Stephen's Linthouse yard a journalist was shown around the yard by John Stephen.

From the din of the prefabrication sheds we went to the building berths – all six silent, crippled by the shipwrights' strike. Beside the berths lay massive sections of ships waiting to be lowered into place.

'We have about two-and-a-half ships in prefabricated pieces lying here,' said my guide. That position is largely the result of the 1957 strike of shipwrights. Many welders left the yard then because they were afraid the stoppage would be repeated. Only a month or so ago the firm were 100 welders short.

The amount of prefabrication being done at the yard has increased rapidly since 1948. Reconstruction work started about eight years ago, although the largest schemes were undertaken only in the last four years.

A new boiler shop and engine works and a new administrative block have been built. The firm still have their original six berths. At the moment they can build ships up to 50,000 tons. 'If we wanted to build larger ships we would have to consider building diagonally across two of the existing berths. That would make the launching easier, too, because the ship would be angled more down-river,' said Mr Stephen.

Outside the yard, the only sign of the dispute was a slogan chalked on the red-brick wall: 'Vive les shipwrights'. Underneath, in a different hand, was scrawled: 'Up the platers'.

From *The Scotsman* of 11 February 1959.

LET IT BE SHORT

The women of strike-hit Clydebank were praying last night. And as they totalled up the hire-purchase payments and grocery bills they had one question: How long will this last?

In aprons and slippers, they stood at their doorways waiting for their men to come home with what may be one of the last pay packets for many weeks. I talked to some of these women. They're frightened, confused and worried. Some of them don't know what it's all about. But they're going to stick by their men, whatever happens.

Yesterday, queues of worried women stood outside the local bakery factory hoping to be put on the payroll to gain a few extra shillings to keep the home going. The bakery factory at Clydebank is one of the few places where the women can get work. Said Mrs Alexandrina Frame, 30-year-old wife of a plater, of Glasgow Road: 'I've never had to work, but now I must. After this week there will be nothing except my pay.'

The young wives are the most confused. They gazed round their bright new homes – bought on the HP – and asked: 'How are we going to pay off the furniture?' Said Mrs Mary Durnin, 21, married a year, and with a young baby: 'I've heard awful tales from the older women about the 1926 depression. What's going to happen to us?'

And the women who are expecting babies are scared. Said 26-year-old Mrs Elsie Graham, of Glasgow Road: 'I have three young children and another on the way. We've just bought new furniture. I can't go out to work. What are we going to do?

'But whatever does happen, this strike is a good one. My father was out in the 1926 depression, so I know what I'm talking about. *If the lads don't fight now they'll be thrown on the scrapheap later on.*'

What will happen to the bright new furniture, the TV sets, the radios, if the strikers can't hand over the weekly payments? Said the manager of one of Clydebank's biggest HP stores: 'We'll give them a few weeks of course. But after that we'll just have to take everything back.'

And as an ominous footnote, a Clydebank pawnbroker commented: 'If this strike lasts long, I expect business will again be brisk for me.'

Margaret McGrath writing in *The Daily Herald*, 1 September 1958.

WHERE DO WE GO FROM HERE?

We've gone through a number of pretty tough years since the shipbuilding depression set in in 1958 and we've managed to survive, even though we've often wondered where the next job was coming from. We've all been helped in the British shipbuilding industry by the recent Government credit scheme (we got four ships under this scheme at Lithgow's) but that is finished now and we've got to stand fair and square on our own two feet from now on. I believe that the toughest time is still to come – that the real crunch will hit us in about a year's time, that more British shipyards will go to the wall or have to turn to making other things than ships.

We're probably now entering on the toughest period the shipbuilding industry of this country has ever known. The next few years will tell the tale and only the most modern, efficient and 'united' shipyards will survive. The competition is really tough at the moment and it is going to continue like this. The trouble is that we've still got too many shipyards in the world today for the number of ships which are needed and that's the whole crux of the problem. If we want to survive we're going to have to work, work and work like we've never worked before. I believe we can do it – in fact I know we can – we've got to!

I've no great fear of European competition. We're all in more or less the same boat together – we enjoy the same standards of living, the same democratic outlook towards things, we're more or less on a par with each other. The real

The bow section of *Wahine* being lifted into place at Fairfield's in 1965. The large crane in the background was installed as part of a modernisation programme at the yard in the early 1960s. (Scottish Maritime Museum)

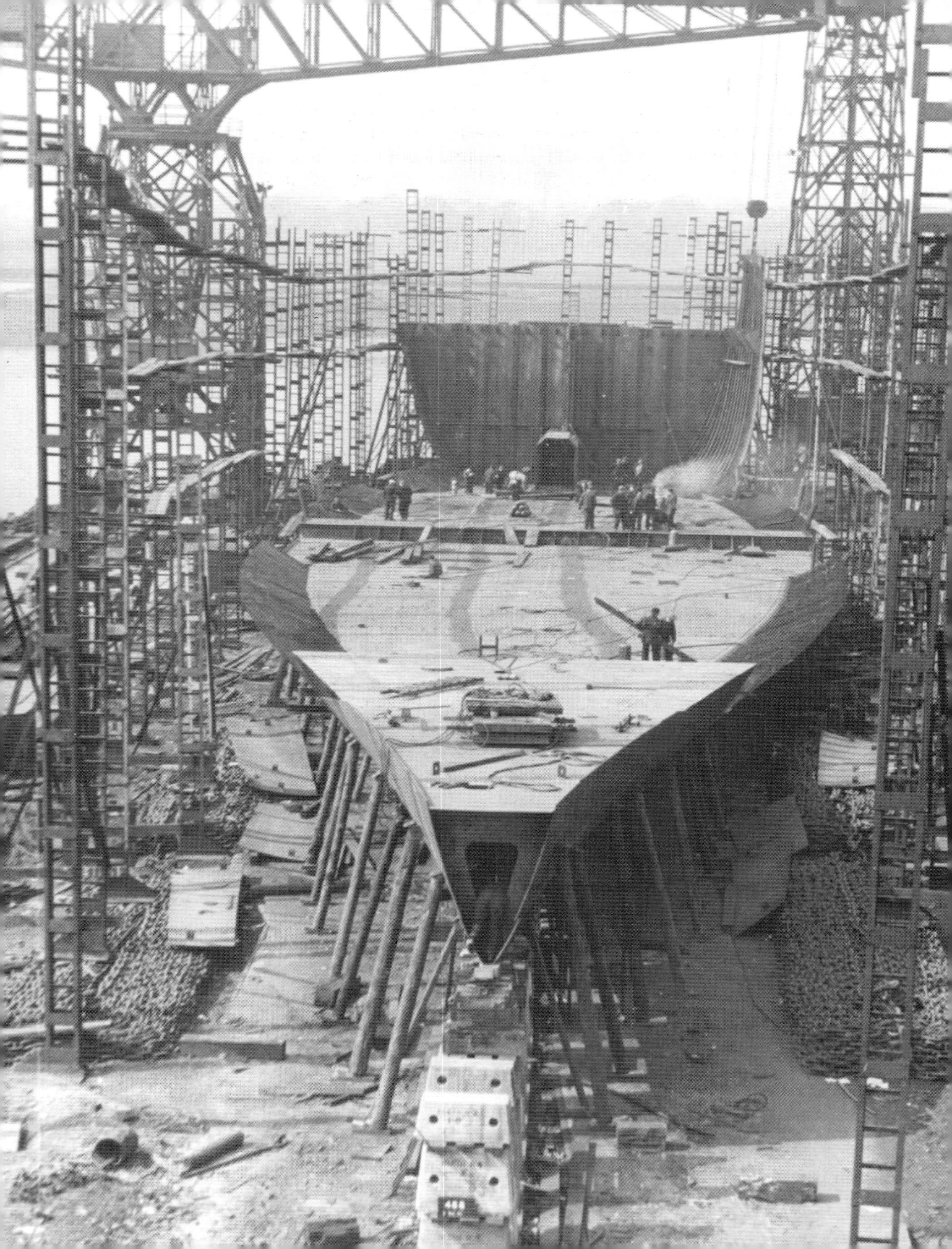

menace comes from the Far East, from Japan, where a nation of people different in outlook, different in their whole approach to life, has decided that they will be the premier shipbuilding country of the world. Make no mistake about it: apart from the smaller, more specialised type of craft, we can't hold a candle to the Japanese on price today, particularly for the really big tankers and bulk carriers.

There's a lot of talk about Japan enjoying a much higher standard of living than they used to, and this is perfectly true; but even if you take in all their fringe benefits and other 'perks' they still don't enjoy anything like our standard of living. They're probably 10% to 20% poorer off than we are, which accounts in great measure for the very much cheaper prices which they quote for their ships.

Mark you, they work hard and we can't ignore that. And in addition they've got an avowed policy, backed by their Government, to capture 80% of the world shipbuilding market. There's no doubt they're being helped by their Government to achieve this end and I believe it's costing them a packet.

We've got to have a strong shipbuilding industry in this country and in Western Europe for very many obvious reasons. It certainly would be to nobody's benefit if Japan cornered the world shipbuilding market. If only our own Government, together with the governments of the other European shipbuilding countries which are equally worried, could jointly declare their faith in their shipbuilding industries and state that they intend, by whatever means are necessary, to ensure that their shipbuilding industries are not wiped out, then I believe the Japanese threat would collapse like a pricked balloon and we would quickly get back to fair, reasonable and healthy competition again.

However, come what may, we believe that we're going to survive at Lithgow's. We've got to continue to muck in together, believing always in the future of shipbuilding, and Lithgow's, which is us. If we can do this – continue to believe in ourselves and our future – then I am certain that nothing can stand in our way.

Ross Belch, managing director of Lithgow's, writing in the *Lithgow Journal*, Autumn 1964.

INCONSISTENT ATTITUDES

The Geddes Report criticised the poor management, productivity, marketing, labour relations and virtually everything else to do with the shipbuilding industry. The report called for the creation of larger shipbuilding groups, and the government quickly forced the creation of Upper Clyde Shipbuilders and Scott Lithgow's on the Clyde and Robb Caledon on the East coast.

There seems to us to remain not far below the surface some conflict between shipbuilding as a craft and as an industry. Both inside and outside the industry there are many who feel that a ship has a value and romantic interest in itself. The pride in the craft displayed at all levels in the industry brings an economic as well as a social benefit. But it has slowed down adaptation to modern industrial conditions. The management functions have been widely assumed by

Opposite: A ship being built at Denny's yard in the 1950s, showing the introduction of prefabricated construction. (Scottish Maritime Museum)

A show of hands at the Clydebank yard of UCS during the work-in. (Scottish Media Group)

designers, whether naval architects or marine engineers. The early development of division of labour among shipyard workers has hardened into a rigid craft structure under which each man has been trained to keep to his own job. Many of the industry's attitudes and habits have been inconsistent with those of an industry whose object is to build and sell ships, as other industries make and sell their wares, as cheaply, quickly, aggressively and profitably as possible.

R. M. Geddes, *Shipbuilding Inquiry Committee Report*, 1965–66.

UCS IN LIQUIDATION

The shipyard mergers proposed by Geddes were poorly managed and grossly under funded. It was only a matter of time before more closures were threatened.

Fears that the Clydebank division of Upper Clyde Shipbuilders, where the Queen liners were built, would be closed with the loss of about 3000 jobs swept the town last night.

The decision will be made by a liquidator, to be appointed probably today, following yesterday's rescue operation by the Government which involves UCS going into liquidation.

It was confidently predicted last night that Mr Robert Courtney Smith, a chartered accountant who was the liquidator of the Fairfield Rowan Engineering Company, Govan, would be given the difficult task of re-organising UCS.

Indications are that up to 3500 of the 8500 staff and workers will lose their jobs in the drive to make UCS – which asked for nearly £6m in working capital to survive – into one of the country's most economic shipbuilders.

Shop stewards who met yesterday and will address meetings of workers at the yards this morning are pledged to fight the closure of any yard or the redundancy of one more man.

From the *Glasgow Herald* of Tuesday 15 June 1971.

THE WORK-IN BEGINS

The workers were not prepared to see the yards close without a fight. A young communist trade unionist by the name of Jimmy Reid launched the fight with perhaps the most famous speech in Scotland's industrial history.

This is the first campaign of its kind in trade unionism. We are not going on strike. We are not even having a sit-in. We do not recognise that there should be any redundancies and we are going to work-in.

We are taking over the yards because we refuse to accept that faceless men can take these decisions. We are responsible people and will conduct ourselves with dignity and discipline. There will be no hooliganism, there will be no vandalism, and there will be no bevvying.

We are not wildcats. We want to work. The real wildcats are in No. 10 Downing Street. They are the hardest-faced bunch of political gangsters I have ever met. They make Al Capone and his gunmen look like a troop of Boy Scouts. The biggest mistake we could make is to lie down, capitulate and grovel to them. We don't only build ships on the Clyde, we build men. They have taken on the wrong people and we will fight.

Jimmy Reid speaking to the massed workers of UCS at Clydebank on 30 July 1971.

FIGHTING FOR THE RIGHT TO WORK

A great memory for me was working in the yard at the time of the UCS crisis. I remember my shop steward, Adam, telling me I would be better leaving as I hadn't been there two years and would be made redundant. One of my colleagues, Tommy Bolam, and I went to see the head of our department, George Troup, and asked for his advice. He promised us that if we stayed our jobs would be secure as long as the yard remained open. The UCS had financial and moral support from workers all over the country. Our motto was, 'We'll fight for the right to work'.

We had lunchtime concerts in the canteen with folk artists like Matt McGinn, demonstrations and marches to the city centre from the yard. I went on one demonstration to lobby the Tory conference at Brighton. We travelled down by train overnight. Can you imagine a train full of shipyard workers with their carryouts of booze to help them get through the night? I wouldn't like to have been a cleaner on that one!

From Jim Collins' unpublished memoirs.

BALLAD OF THE TWO LEFT HANDS

When walking out one morning
Walking down Clydeside Street
I met a man with two left hands
Who said he was obsolete.

At noon the work horns sounded through
The shipyards on Clyde's shore
And told men that the day had come
When they'd work there no more.

Economy is hand and sweat
A welder in his mask
A new apprentice pouring tea
From his father's thermos flask.

And soon these men of several trades
Stood there on Clydeside Street
Stood staring at each new left hand
That made them obsolete.

'Beware of men in suits,' one said
'Take it from me, it's true
Their drivel economics'll
Put two left hands on you.'

All in the afternoon was shut
When I walked out again
The day had pulled on its black gloves
And turned its back on men.

I walked the dusk of darkened cranes
Clyde broke on Clyde's dark shore
And rivets fired where men still work
Though men work here no more.

High in the night's dark universe
I saw the promised star
That men I knew raise glasses to
In an illegal bar.

They toast that city still to come
Where truth and justice meet
And though they don't know where it is
It's not on Clydeside Street.

With thumbs stuck on the wrong way round
In two left-footed shoes
I saw a man search in his heart
And ask it, 'Are you true?'

That man who sat on Clydeside Street
Looked up at me and said
'I'll study this, then I'll pick clean
The insides of my head.'

And moonlight washed the shipyards then
Each crane was hung with stars
Rinsed in the moonlight we stared up
Like old astronomers.

Economy is hand and sweat
And foundrymen and fire
Revise your textbooks, multiply
Your guilt by your desire.

Such dignity, so many lives,
Even on Clydeside Street
When mind and heart together ask
'Why are we obsolete?'

From Douglas Dunn's *Barbarians*, 1979.

A DRAG ON OUR FORTUNES

Most of us felt that shipbuilding was becoming thoroughly uncompetitive in this county. Restrictive practices really killed British shipbuilding. Let me give you an example. A lot of pipework for the water supplied to the cabins and so on used to be done in ordinary zinc pipes – a plumber's job. But then it became more efficient to do them in copper pipes, which was the work of coppersmiths. The unions quarrelled over whose job it should be and the eventual compromise was that it had to be done by a coppersmith with a plumber standing by doing nothing. Thoroughly uneconomic, but the unions were very intransigent and short-sighted and that was that. There was little regret within the John Brown Group when we stopped building ships because the other parts of the group did not like their profits being whittled away to subsidise the losses of Clydebank. So the group as a whole was quite happy to get rid of that drag on our fortunes, even if many of us were devastated to lose our link with the romance of shipbuilding.

Lord Aberconway, company chairman of John Brown's speaking to Ian Johnston and Lewis Johnman in *Granta 61: The Sea*, 1998.

SHIPBUILDING HEADS FOR THE ROCKS

After the large groupings of shipyards failed to halt the decline nationalisation was seen as the only way to preserve the industry. However, the road to nationalisation was far from smooth and it was beset with problems from the very start.

Britain's shipyards were last night bracing themselves for a winter of crisis and uncertainty following yesterday's setback to the Government's nationalisation attempts. The earliest date that the yards can now be taken over by the state under a new Bill in the next Parliamentary session is June 1977 – a year behind the original time-table.

These 12 lost months, during which the industry is drifting in a sea of indecision, through the worst storms facing shipbuilding for decades, are likely to prove fatal for some yards.

All five Scottish yards on the nationalisation list are facing problems over the next two to three months. The Scott Lithgow Group on the Lower Clyde, who have been hard hit by a series of cancellations of important orders, are seeking Government help to maintain employment for their 8200 workforce.

On the East Coast Robb Caledon Shipbuilders' Leith yard must have an order before the end of the year to avert redundancies among its 800 workers, and Hall Russell at Aberdeen are in the same position.

Govan Shipbuilders and Yarrow Shipbuilders on the Upper Clyde are both urgently seeking large export contracts to avoid redundancies early in the new year.

Thus it seems inevitable that the Government, which had left the formulation of a national shipbuilding policy to its embryo British Shipbuilders Corporation, is going to be faced with a series of ad hoc decisions as local crises erupt around the coastline throughout the next six months.

Indeed, British Shipbuilders themselves – their initial planning work has been carried out by a full-time organising committee of seven – are now technically dissolved, with the failure of the enabling Bill.

In short, British shipbuilding is in a major mess – and this at a time when most shipbuilding nations are evolving policies of their own to protect the bulk of their industries during the three or four lean years ahead, when the world will have three times as many shipyards as there will be orders.

There are precious few bright spots in the situation. The political uncertainties of the next few months make it impossible to predict the future of the nationalisation bill once it is reintroduced after December 3.

If the Opposition agree to co-operate with the Bill it could receive Royal Assent next March. Then would follow about three months of work by British Shipbuilders in negotiating individual compensation with the yards' present owners, with vesting day probably in June.

But if the House of Lords maintains its present opposition – and it has open to it more areas of objection to the Bill than it used to destroy it this time – it could be October next year before it passes on to the Statute Book.

By that time the industry's overall order book would have shrunk to almost half the size needed to keep the present number of yards operating.

From *The Scotsman* of 23 November 1976.

IT DIDN'T SEEM TO WORK

British Shipbuilders, when they took over, it hopefully was to be a sort of blessing that was to end all kinds of worries about your future and your work, but somehow or other it didn't seem to work out that way at all.

The method of nationalisation was that yards still had their own autonomy to do what they liked. They still looked for their own orders. There was no direct involvement from British Shipbuilders. In the case of Robb's in Leith they only became involved in that last two or three years, rather than in the earlier stages. I mean they paid visits to the yards admittedly, they probably changed the financial aspect a little bit by having financial areas set out, of which Henry Robb's and Dundee was one. The two yards were obviously there to work and produce and make a profit, if possible, which was obviously the best way to do a job. But they gradually found that things just didn't go that way at all.

Bobby Aitchison, foreman shipwright at Henry Robb's shipyard at Leith, speaking in 1984, on a tape held at the School of Scottish Studies.

A BLOW TO THE COMMUNITY

The Thatcher government's passion for privatisation meant that British Shipbuilders' days were numbered. One by one the yards were either sold off or closed.

Sadness tinged with bitterness and resignation was the main reaction of business people and the public around Henry Robb yard today.

One publican reckoned 50 per cent of turnover came from the 'boys at the yard' while a former chargehand at Robb's described the closure as 'absolutely disgusting'.

The workforce at the yard have formed a close bond with the business community in Portland Place and North Junction Street, supplying a lot of the custom at newsagents, pubs and other shops.

Alex Marshal (43), of Leith, worked at Robb's until November when he took his redundancy. 'This closure is absolutely disgusting,' he said. 'It is just another example of the Government wielding the big axe.'

Another former Robb's worker Donald Rose (63) of Portland Place, said the closure was bound to come. 'I took my redundancy in December and it was

The QE2 under construction at John Brown's. There were so many problems in building the liner that it was delivered late and at a huge loss to her builders, leading ultimately to the demise of shipbuilding at Clydebank. (Scottish Maritime Museum)

Bottom:
In an attempt to compete with the big foreign yards Scott Lithgow's began building supertankers in two halves. The technique was quite successful but could never match the efficiencies of the purpose-built building docks in Japan. (Scottish Maritime Museum)

obvious then that British Shipbuilders wanted to close us down.'

Portland Place newsagent Mr Robert Johnson (60) said: 'Over the years we in this shop have got to know the boys there on first-name terms and they are a great bunch of lads.'

At the nearby ice cream shop, John Angelosanto (25) feared for the effect on the entire Leith community. 'This shop has been in our family since 1902. Our link with the yard goes back to when Robb's opened in 1918. Surely even at this late stage, something can be done to keep the yard in business.'

Publicans in the area have been dependent to a great extent on the shipyard workers for business over the years. At the Caley Inn, Mrs Isobel Carey (42) said 50 per cent of the turnover in her bar came from Robb's men. 'This decision is a real blow to this community.'

From the *Edinburgh Evening News* of 26 January 1984.

BIRDSONG

Nest-building was in full swing. The song of the birds rang out crisp and clear, echoing throughout the otherwise empty shed. I stood stock still. Rarely, I am sure, has so simple a sound caused so sudden and deep a depression. I was standing in what had been the main preparation bay of the now-closed shipyard where I had been chaplain. It had been a long time since any sound other than that of metal on metal had been heard there. Now the normally welcome sound of birds was a cruelly sharp and mocking reminder of all that had been. All the striving to build ships – all the human hopes and ambitions, achievements and sorrows involved in that striving – all was finished. A community was dispersed. It is taking a long time to get the chill of that moment out of my bones.

From Frank Kennedy's reflections in *God's Working World: Notes from a shipyard chaplain*, 1984.

TOUR OF A DERELICT YARD

After we had been through the formalities of security clearance, I was driven through one of the cavernous sheds at the rear of Cartsburn. This shed had been used for light-plate assembly but was now quite empty, as much of the plant and other machinery had already been disposed of. We sped along and I was informed that the immediate plan would involve the total demolition of all structures and buildings within the yards. When I somewhat optimistically inquired about the possibility of the preservation of just one crane for posterity, it was quickly affirmed that all structures would come down, although the dry dock, which could be traced back to 1810, would remain owing to its historic value. Crane demolition would be relatively straightforward and present no great problem; the main difficulty would be the uprooting of the slips' great concrete foundations. After basic demolition and site clearance, land engineering would be carried out to remove floor slabs and general foundations; levelling would then be undertaken.

I was dropped off at the east end of Cartsburn and left free to meander on my own. There was momentary gloom when passing through the empty vastness of a former welding shed before emerging into sunlight and the Cartsdyke sector. Cartsdyke had always appealed to me, although a reason could not be pinpointed. Perhaps because it had been known affectionately as the 'wee yerd'.

An assortment of redundant shipyard equipment, much of it hidden by shrubbery, littered the site. However, the two concrete slipways, which stretched 600 feet in length and declined slightly towards the water's edge, were relatively clear of vegetation. I glanced over to the west slip where the cargo liner *Mentor* was launched on 9th August 1979; she signalled the end of an era, being the last launch from Cartsdyke.

A few logs similar in size and appearance to telegraph poles lay amidst the small copse at the head of the berths. The larger ones had no doubt been used as side-shores to prop up the sides of the ship's uncompleted hull and the smaller, squatter ones used as bilge shores supporting the bottom of the hull. In the same location were also great blocks of timber, strewn about in a very haphazard fashion; the rectangular chunks probably had made up part of the 'standing' or 'fixed ways' upon which a ship slid down at her launch; the wedge-shaped pieces had been part of the 'sliding ways'. I noticed a discarded protective face-mask used by a welder, a large rusty spanner and numerous concrete keel blocks of varied size. I mused over the blocks and wondered how many bottoms they had supported.

From Michael Dick's book on the Greenock yards, *The 4.15 to Cartsdyke!* 1993.

THE EMBERS GLOW

JAMES: Come here, look. See that cran there? That's one of the few remaining heavy lifters on the Clyde. They knock them down. To make way for shopping centres, leisure complexes. It's as if they're ashamed of the past. Have you ever seen a cran demolished? They put explosives in the uprights about half way up and when it blows . . . one minute they're standing there majestic, contemptuous. The next they fall on their knees, arms outstretched in supplication. Praying, they seem to hang there for a second and then they fall, crashing their faces into the ground. Hardly any dust or rubble. So gracefully. So beautiful and dreadful their destruction. That's what we're good at now, demolition.

FLIPPER: This is not the boy that I knew. Fire in the belly, sparks in the eyes.

JAMES: It's out, Flip. They put it out. Not all at once. Just bit by bit. Drip, drip, drip. You don't notice until it's gone. They've won.

FLIPPER: Shite! They never win. They think they do. They only douse the flames. They throw a great wet blanket over it and leave it at that. A big puff of smoke and it's over. But underneath. Underneath the embers glow. As they threw the blanket a spark flew out to smoulder somewhere else.

From Frank Miller's play *Work-in*, 2001.

ENTHUSIASTIC OPTIMISM

The Govan yard was the last Scottish shipyard to remain in government ownership, and there was genuine optimism when a buyer was finally found who would continue to build ships there.

'I don't think anyone here has anything against our being in Norwegian ownership now,' says Mr Eric Mackie, president of Kvaerner Govan. 'In principle, true, many take the view that we should have remained in the public sector. But if we look at the realities and leave political attitudes aside, everyone has now seen that the recent takeover saved the yard from closure. You could say that Kvaerner has not eliminated 400 jobs, but rather rescued 1350.'

Mr Mackie feels that privatisation of the yard was the right thing to happen. 'It is not healthy for corporate culture and workforce morale to be a 'sheltered workshop'. We have to sharpen ourselves, feel the need to compete, and as a privately owned company know at all times that as long as we have work, it's because we're good and competitive.'

He notes that Kvaerner's top management has made this clear. 'It's not sound for anyone to live on gifts, whether from a government or from others. That's an attitude we welcome and accept.

'State ownership also poses purely practical problems. We cannot move freely

Helice ready to be launched. This was one of the first gas carriers to be built by Kvaerner after they took over the Govan yard in 1988. (Author's collection)

into other market areas. With the advantages associated with being in the public sector, this would create competitive distortions that would not be accepted by other industries. But now we can do it without problems.'

Mr Mackie agreed that Govan Shipbuilders was not as effective a company as it should have been, due to the way state ownership undermined work-force morale.

'Everybody performs best when they must strive to achieve their goals, and that's what we have to do now to a much greater extent than before. We must work without a safety net, and that in itself will enhance our performance.'

The first two orders were placed at the new Kvaerner yard to coincide with the signing of the acquisition documents during August. Govan is to build two LPG carriers, each of 56,000 m^3 and worth roughly £35 million. They are due to be ready in October 1990 and March 1991 respectively.

As Mr Mackie also emphasises, however, there is still a long way to go before Kvaerner Govan as a company lives up to the ambitions defined for it.

In order to maintain an acceptable profitability on the ships which have now been ordered, Kvaerner estimates that the Scots need to cut their indirect costs by around 24–30 per cent.

An investment of £10 million is under consideration, and a promise of support for 80 per cent of this sum was received in connection with the acquisition.

The most comprehensive element in this package is the conversion of two of today's three building berths into a single unit able to handle ships well beyond today's size ceiling. Estimated to cost £5.6 million – compared with a sales price of £6 million for the yard itself – this berth is due to be completed by early 1993.

Nevertheless, the limiting factor on the size of ship that can be constructed at the yard remains not so much the space available on land as the width of the river where the vessel is to be launched.

Mr Hans Jörgen Frank, the group executive vice-president who is also chairman of the Kvaerner Govan board, reports that he has detected no spirit of resignation over the prospect of fresh cuts at a company which has already been trimmed back a number of times in recent years.

'On the contrary, I see an enthusiastic optimism. Resignation was undoubtedly more apparent before we came on the scene. Now there is a positive "up-and-at-them" attitude which we find very encouraging, and which will boost Kvaerner Govan in the years to come.'

From *Kvaerner of Norway*, the house magazine of the Kvaerner Group, December 1988.

THE DUNNY MONEY

The new owners managed to carry on building ships but with a significantly smaller workforce. Many men were by now so disheartened by the uncertainty that they reluctantly took the offer of redundancy.

'Oh, it' s you, Joe.'

'Ay, I'm just back from the meeting up at Personnel. You didnae turn up.'

'No, well we're Joint Conveners, so I thought one of us would be enough.'

'Well, they want another 450 for redundancy.'

'Ay, and they'll get them.'

Joe felt the defeatism in Cammy's voice. Wee Cammy, who had fought redundancy all the way to the point where his line had become repetitious and boring. He could hear him now. 'If you take the redundancy money, you're selling your job. It's no yours tae sell and nobody will ever be able to buy it back. No that anybody should ever have to buy a job. Jobs canny be bought and sold like cans of beans. Jobs are your birthright.' That was Cammy's line as month after month hundreds took what they called the dunny money.

Cammy asked, 'So what's the next move?'

'I've called a mass meeting for three o'clock to put it to the men.'

Cammy sighed deeply. 'Ay, and they'll accept it.'

'Well, what option do they have? There's no more boats tae build. The game's ended. Will you take the meeting, Cammy?'

'No, I couldnae face the men. You take it as Joint Convener.'

Joe reached over a bracket and squeezed Cammy's wrist. 'Cammy, you've put up a helluva fight. The men have great respect for you.'

'Ay, they won't when I take my dunny money.'

Joe pursed his lips. 'Look, Cammy, nobody will blame you. At your age you're probably on the maximum. What other chance would you ever have of gathering a pot of money after a lifetime of service?'

'Ay, but I'm selling a job,' Cammy said, 'a job that won't exist after next week.'

Cammy stroked his chin. 'This lot that'll be going, they're steelworkers; my boys. Can you think what the dunny money will do to some of them? For a start there's Alky McKellar, they'll get him behind the door some Sunday morning. Then there's the betting shop crowd who'll shovel it into Ladbroke's satchel. Sure, some will be sensible and get a decent holiday and maybe a motor, but after about 18 months or so they'll wonder what's hit them and what won't be hitting them is a pay packet every Friday.'

From Jimmy Miller's short story *The Dunny Money*, 1989.

FIGHTING FOR THEIR FUTURE

In 1999 the Kvaerner Group decided to withdraw from shipbuilding world-wide and left the future of the Govan yard hanging in the balance once more.

Shipyard workers last night defiantly vowed to fight for their future – despite their plant being put up for sale.

They reckon a buyer can be found for the giant Kvaerner works at Govan on the Clyde – saving 1,200 jobs.

The firm's Norwegian bosses told the stunned workforce yesterday the yard was to close after days of speculation.

The company also revealed it is pulling out of its engineering works in Clydebank – threatening more than 600 jobs.

Albert Midwinter, 50 – who has been at the Govan yard for 34 years – said:

The fall of a Goliath. The massive crane at Scott Lithgow's was demolished in 1998. (Author's collection)

'We are not about to give up the ghost. Our workers have the resolve and the fight to survive.'

Dad-of-three Albert, from Blantyre, Lanarkshire, added: 'We all take pride in our work. We are the best in Britain. Our workers will do a job for anyone. In fact, our guys are so flexible they should be nick-named the rubber men. We don't want a hand-out from anyone – just a hand.'

His son George Midwinter, 26, has been at Kvaerner's for the past nine years. He said: 'This yard has been threatened with closure even before my dad began working here. But the place is still open.'

'We are all extremely positive and optimistic. We know we can do the job better than anyone else. Nobody wants to consider the worst.' Dad-of-two John Hearn called for famous ex-shipyard workers to back their campaign.

John, 42, of Govan, said: 'Morale among the guys is unbelievable. What we need now is all the former shipyard workers like Billy Connolly and Alex Ferguson to come forward and throw their weight behind us.'

Gutted Stephen Joyce, 29, told how he has been forced to postpone wedding plans while the jobs axe looms.

Stephen of Erskine, said: 'My fiancée and I bought a house seven months ago. We were also planning to get married this year but have decided to put it back and wait and see what happens.'

Stephen – whose grandad, dad and brother all worked at the yard – added: 'There is still a big family atmosphere here and we will stick together and fight.'

Plater Eugene McCabe, 22, from Govan, feared he could be on the scrapheap by the summer.

But the dad-of-one said: 'The guys are feeling optimistic. We are confident we can find a buyer.'

Yard convenor Jamie Webster told how workers were committed to finding a buyer. Jamie added: 'There is no despondency among the workforce. Kvaerner may leave, but the yard and its workers will continue to be a success.'

Alan Carson and Larissa Kemmet writing in the Scottish *Sun*, 14 April 1999.

PRIDE OF THE CLYDE

Growing up on the lower Clyde
Argyll was greener on the other side
We watched the last Cunarder glide
Down to the sea

I wrote that song for my father, who lasted just a few years longer than the yards he worked in. Kincaid's where he was an apprentice is a McDonald's now. Local lads used to serve their time. Kids the age he was in 1930 now serve burgers. Times and towns move on. Fast food; slow decline. The symbolism couldn't be starker. And now it's Govan's turn.

I'm not nostalgic for other men's sweat
There's a lot about the old days we should forget
But Clydebuilt boats could be sailing yet
Down to the sea

Most of what the east coasters and others know about the yards is what they heard from people who couldn't wait to get out. Billy Connolly, Alex Ferguson, Jimmy Reid and Gus Macdonald have spoken and written movingly, funnily and loyally about that nearly vanished world. Though not as able maybe as those local heroes, there were plenty more where they came from, clever boys who should have answered a call more compelling than the knocking-off-time klaxon.

Listen to the voices of skilled tradesmen
Sold down their own river for thirty yen
But you don't need ships to sail again
Down to the sea

There was pride, craft, solidarity and camaraderie, ability and indomitability. OK, so Stanley Spencer was a war artist engaged in propaganda but he captured in his paintings (and letters) what was special about the yards; what was world class.

Every apprentice that learned a trade
Every ship they ever made
Those are ghosts that won't be laid
(They sail) Down to the sea

Opposite top: One of the last launches at Ailsa Troon. When the *Atlantic Challenge* was launched in 1998 the future of the yard did not seem to be in doubt. Just two years later it was shut. (Author's collection)

Opposite bottom: A sign of the times. Although Buckie Shipyard has recently begun building new ships once more, they buy in the bare hulls cheaply from Russia and then merely fit them out. (Author's collection)

Shipyard patter wasn't watter. Clydeside humour comes in two varieties; black and gallows, a chesty chuckle in the face of adversity, not jokes, or schticks or routines, but comedy improvised out of, to sustain, and enrich, life. Haw Jimmy; the urge for naming for instant intimacy and rapport. Awright Big Man; the need to scale existence up from the drawing board. Clydeside's love of the larger than life.

Many of the tallest, funniest tales gloried in the murkier side of the myth – the malingering, the petty theft, the phoney compensation claims, the bullying and victimisation, the jobs for the boys, the chancers and cowboys and no-users who were far from skilled; and always, always, the bigotry, a sickening sectarianism, no industry in Scotland did more to foster.

This town's reason was its river and that's still so
Though all it does these days is flow
In welder's dreams tugs still go
Down to the sea

In 1990, Bill Bryden built and launched right there in Govan a kind of ark Cunarder. What happened, unforgettably, in the Harland and Wolff, was as near as most of the huge audience will get to the atmosphere of a launch. The memorial he and his team constructed moved us, deeply and literally.

Dad and I were sitting behind the bowler hatted 'foreman', Jimmy Logan, when we set sail. Grown men wept, making an exhibition of themselves for once, instead of exuding inhibition in best, west of Scotland style. Watching Bill Bryden's earlier (and still unsurpassed) homage to the Clyde, *Willie Rough*, my father shed a rare and secret tear, tears of recognition, grateful tears. Bill Bryden didn't come to the Lyceum from Scott Lithgow but he read and listened, adding his own tragi-comic voice and vision to the evolving folktale, to the myth, the true and necessary myth.

My father's eyes were boiler-suit blue
He took pride in what he'd learned to do
Now no one needs the craft he knew
(To go) Down to the sea

There is an exhibition of R. B. Kitaj's prints in Edinburgh just now. 'Revolt on the Clyde', the first one proclaims above an image of MacDiarmid. The Gallery of Modern Art owns a copy; and so it should. The nation should be grateful for all that agitation and steadfastness. In the *Willie Rough* years of the First World War and its aftermath 'Clydegrad' was genuinely and alarmingly revolutionary. Revisionist historians have debunked some of posterity's wilder claims. Yet important truths persist at the nub of the Myth of Red Clydeside.

The Jimmies, Airlie and Reid, the strategist and the orator, could tap into that in Clydeside's last stand. Today, across the river in Govan, the socialist game is up and the talk is calm, pragmatic and resigned. Only dignity remains. And dignity has no negotiating power.

Growing up on the Lower Clyde
Argyll was greener on the other side
We watched the last Cunarder glide
Down to the sea

I feel for the Kvaerner workforce and wish I had more to offer than a threnody. From Greenock to Govan, we've been great at building ships. We're even better at reinventing ourselves. Fishing, tobacco, sugar, timber, rope had all been staples before the heyday of the yards.

Until the Industrial Revolution, Govan was a beauty spot. Local poets bemoaned the despoilation of Glasgow, a greener place then. With the closing of the century, that era has finally ended. The river goes on and so must we.

The real pride of the Clyde is its people who, with the help of the new parliament, must seek a fate beyond the shipyard gate. Who knows, perhaps a more fulfilling destiny, even than the trade for which they are world renowned. They have our thanks. The whole country is proud of them. Govan's achievement will never be forgotten. Today a robust and resilient community has to face up to the challenge of change. We owe them more than burgers.

Donny O'Rourke writing in the *Sunday Herald*, 18 April 1999.

NO SURRENDER

Against all the odds the Govan yard did manage to survive.

The men of Govan took control of their lives. And they took control of the political agenda in a way that people like them hadn't managed to do for decades. They did it without strikes or sit-ins. They kept doing their jobs, they showed potential buyers that this was a workforce committed to making the yard a viable enterprise again. They pressurised politicians relentlessly, they used the media as a weapon to shame, embarrass and flatter. They took a simple proposition – that people had a right to the dignity of work – and they never let go of it. Certainly they were lucky that the fight was being waged at a time when the political parties were trying to maximize their support in the new Scottish Assembly. And they had good friends in men like their old workmate Gus Macdonald. But the victory belonged to the workers in the end. Everybody knew that. They had looked long enough at the world beyond the gates, and promised themselves they wouldn't easily submit to the slow death of joblessness.

From Fergal Keane's *A Stranger's Eye: A foreign correspondent's view of Britain*, 2000.

ONE MORE TRAGEDY

After many years of uncertainty the Ailsa Troon yard also looked to have bounced back with a number of big orders for fishing vessels and a Cal Mac ferry. In the summer of 2000, however, its parent company decided to cut its losses and close the yard.

Troon was a town in despair last night following news that its biggest employer, the Ailsa shipbuilding and repair yard, is to close.

Management was accused of betrayal during a series of stormy meetings with workers.

A barmaid in the town's Lonsdale Bar said the workforce had always bounced back from previous crises but seemed resigned to the fact that, on this occasion, the axe had swung for the last time.

'The men have only just heard about it and it still hasn't sunk in for some of them,' she said. 'Closure will affect almost every business in the area.'

For shipwright Willie Hunter, 64, a former Ailsa apprentice like his father and grandfather before him, redundancy is a more attractive prospect than for the younger family men among a workforce facing an uncertain future.

'The mood today is very despondent,' he said. 'It has been hanging over us for so long. We kept hoping the gap between contracts would be filled, but it was no use.

'The men more or less blame the management, but I think they did their best. If a place is not viable, you can understand it. They haven't been making money for a good few years.

'I'm in a fortunate position because I'm 64. When I started in 1952, there were 50 or 60 shipwrights, but now there are only two of us. There's nothing left for the younger ones, unless they're prepared to travel.'

Mr Hunter added: 'I would hate to see those docks filled in. It's a tragedy all round.'

A younger colleague added:

'I'm 36 and even that is considered old these days. What alternative is there to the yard around here? There's not a lot, and I've got a wife and kid to support.'

Union leaders and politicians had been bracing themselves for the bad news. Local union representative David Fitzpatrick accused management of not doing enough to save the facility.

'They took it over four years ago from receivership and kept the same management that got us into it in the first place. They obviously knew how the company was doing, but seemed to think that the shipyard would run itself,' Mr Fitzpatrick said.

'We feel betrayed by bad management and bad pricing. In the last two years, the management team has not won one substantial order.'

From *The Herald* of Saturday 19 August 2000.

Macduff Shipyard specialises in building fishing boats and is one of the few continuing success stories in Scottish shipbuilding. Its repair business sees it through the lean times but recently it has been so busy that it has had to subcontract the building of hulls to other yards. (Author's collection)

ACKNOWLEDGEMENTS

I would like to thank all those ex-shipbuilders who have given me so much advice, support and encouragement in preparing this book. I would also like to thank Susan for her patience and understanding through many a long night and lost weekend whilst I have been writing this book.

The editor and the publishers acknowledge their gratitude to those copyright-holders or agents who have given permission for extracts to be reproduced in this anthology. Whilst every effort has been made to identify copyright owners, in some cases we have not been able to do so. We will be pleased to hear from copyright owners in such cases.

Extracts from *Down to the Sea, Scottish Enterprise: Shipbuilding* and *The Shipbuilders* by George Blake reproduced by permission of David Higham Associates.

Extract from *Landfall at Sunset* by David Bone reproduced by permission of Gavin Sprott.

Extracts from Jim Collins' unpublished autobiography reproduced by permission of Jim Collins.

Extracts from *Gullibles Travels* by Billy Connolly reproduced by permission of Billy Connolly and Sleepy Dumpling Music Ltd.

Extracts from *Made in Govan: An oral history of shipbuilding on the Upper Clyde 1930–1950* by David Crooks (Ed.), reproduced by permission of Glasgow Museums.

Extract from *The 4.15 to Cartsdyke!* by Michael Dick reproduced by permission of Michael Dick and the Pentland Press.

Barbarians by Douglas Dunn reprinted by permission of PFD on behalf of Douglas Dunn.

Extracts from *Apprentice* by Tom Gallacher reproduced by permission of Tom Gallacher.

Extracts from *Shipbuilding Inquiry Committee Report* by R. M. Geddes (Crown copyright) reproduced by permission of Her Majesty's Stationery Office.

Extract from 'The Oral History of Upper Clyde Shipbuilders' by Roy Hay and John McLauchlan reproduced by permission of The Oral History Society.

Extracts from *The Holy City* by Meg Henderson reproduced by permission of HarperCollins Publishers Ltd.

Extract from *The Dark Horizon* by Alexander Highlands published by Jarrolds. Used by permission of the Random House Group Limited.

Extracts from 'Scotland's Last Great Artefact' in *Granta 61: The Sea* by Ian Johnston and Lewis Johnman reproduced by permission of Ian Jack and Granta.

Extracts from *A Stranger's Eye: A foreign correspondent's view of Britain* by Fergal Keane reproduced by permission of David Godwin Associates.

Extract from *God's Working World: Notes from a shipyard chaplain* by Frank Kennedy reproduced by permission of the Scottish Churches Industrial Mission.

Extract from the *Kirkintilloch Herald* reproduced by permission of the *Kirkintilloch Herald*.

Extracts from *The Winter Sparrows: A Glasgow childhood* by Mary Rose Liverani reproduced by permission of Mary Rose Liverani.

Extract from *Scotland's Record* by J. J. McCall reproduced by permission of Caversham Communications Ltd.

Extract from John McCash, tape T0084, reproduced by permission of East Dunbartonshire Museums.

Text from *Over The Wall* exhibition by Kevin McDermott reproduced by permission of Kevin McDermott.

Extract from Matt McGinn's autobiography reproduced by permission of Janette McGinn.

The Champagne Flows (Can o' Tea) by Matt McGinn © Copyright 1964 (renewed) by Appleseed Music, Inc. All rights reserved. Used by Permission.

Extracts from *Iron* reproduced by permission of the Collins Gallery, Strathclyde University and Tom McKendrick.

Extracts from *Making Ships, Making Men: Working for John Brown's between the wars* by Alan McKinlay reproduced by permission of West Dunbartonshire Libraries.

Extracts from *Work-in* by Frank Miller reproduced by permission of Frank Miller.

Extracts from *Tenements as Tall as Ships* by Jimmy Miller reproduced by permission of Jimmy Miller's family and Govan Workspace Ltd.

Extracts from *Scottish Journey* by Edwin Muir reproduced by permission of Mainstream Publishing.

Extracts from *Who Told Clutha?* and *The Clydesiders* by Hugh Munro reproduced by permission of Hugh Munro's family.

'Pride of the Clyde' by Donny O'Rourke reproduced by permission of Donny O'Rourke.

Extracts from *At the Sharp End!: A shipbuilding autobiography* by George H. Parker reproduced by permission of Brown, Son & Ferguson Ltd.

Extracts from *The Straight Man: My life in comedy* reproduced by permission of Weidenfeld & Nicholson and Nicholas Parsons.

Extract from the UCS work-in speech by Jimmy Reid reproduced by permission of Jimmy Reid.

Extract from *Sappy Sooracks and Burnt Sugar* by Ellen Robertson reproduced by permission of Ellen Robertson and the Pentland Press.

Extract from *A Govan Childhood: The 1930s* by George Rountree reproduced by permission of George Rountree and John Donald Publishers.

Extract from the Diaries and Papers of Joseph Russell 1834–1917, Shipbuilder, Port Glasgow, reproduced by permission of Glasgow City Archives.

Extracts from the *Glasgow Herald, The Herald, Evening Times* and *The Bowler and the Bunnet* reproduced by permission of the Scottish Media Group.

Extracts from *The Scotsman* and *Edinburgh Evening News* reproduced by permission of The Scotsman Publications Ltd.

Extracts from *I Belong to Glasgow* and *A Parochial View of Glasgow* reproduced by permission of Alfred Forbes Smith.

Extract from *Work, Welfare and the Price of Fish: Life in Aberdeen 1925–1955* reproduced by permission of Aberdeen City Council and Walter Watt.

Extracts from *Industrial Deafness* and *Ergonomic Workstations and Spinning Teacans* by Brian Whittingham reproduced by permission of Brian Whittingham.

BIBLIOGRAPHY

MEMOIRS AND BIOGRAPHY

Wilfred Ayre, *A Shipbuilder's Yesterdays*, Aberdour, 1968.

David Bone, *Landfall at Sunset*, London, 1955.

Jim Collins, unpublished autobiography.

Billy Connolly, *Gullibles Travels*, London, 1982.

John G. Inglis, *Inglis, Glasgow: The story of a shipbuilding family*, 1977.

Frank Kennedy, *God's Working World: Notes from a shipyard chaplain*, Edinburgh, 1984.

David Kirkwood, *My Life of Revolt*, London, 1935.

Catriona Levy, *Ardrossan Shipyards: Struggle for survival 1825–1983*, Ardrossan, 1984.

Mary Rose Liverani, *The Winter Sparrows: A Glasgow childhood*, London, 1976.

Matt McGinn, *McGinn of the Calton: The life and works of Matt McGinn, 1928–1977*, Glasgow, 1987.

George H. Parker, *At the Sharp End!: A shipbuilding autobiography*, Glasgow, 1992.

Nicholas Parsons, *The Straight Man: My life in comedy*, London, 1994.

W. G. Riddell, *Adventures of an Obscure Victorian*, London, 1932.

W. G. Riddell, *The Thankless Years*, London, 1948.

Ellen Robertson, *Sappy Sooracks and Burnt Sugar*, Bishop Auckland, 1996.

George Rountree, *A Govan Childhood: The 1930s*, Edinburgh, 1993.

The Diaries and Papers of Joseph Russell 1834–1917, Shipbuilder, Port Glasgow, held at Glasgow City Archives (AGN1427).

Alfred Forbes Smith, *I Belong to Glasgow*, Glasgow, 2000.

George Strachan, *From Ticket Boy to Director*, Glasgow, 1921.

REPORTAGE

George Blake, *Down to the Sea*, London, 1937.

George Blake, *Scottish Enterprise: Shipbuilding*, Edinburgh, 1947.

Michael Dick, *The 4.15 to Cartsdyke!*, Bishop Auckland, 1993.

Fergal Keane, *A Stranger's Eye: A foreign correspondent's view of Britain*, London, 2000.

J. J. McCall, 'The World's Best Shipbuilder', in W. M. Ballantine (Ed.), *Scotland's Record*, Edinburgh, 1946.

C. E. Montague's introduction to Muirhead Bone's, *The Western Front*, London, 1917.

Edwin Muir, *Scottish Journey*, London, 1935.

James Hamilton Muir, *Glasgow in 1901*, Glasgow, 1901.

V. S. Pritchett, *Build the Ships: The official story of the shipyards in wartime*, London, 1946.

David Rose, 'Three Vital Members of the Body of a Firm called John Brown's' in *Scotland*, February, 1967.

BIBLIOGRAPHY

ORAL HISTORY

Clyde Shipbuilding: A collection of source material, Glasgow, 1995.

Work, Welfare and the Price of Fish: Life in Aberdeen 1925–1955, Aberdeen, 1997.

Bobby Aitchison, School of Scottish Studies, Tapes Aitchison B1 & B2.

David Crooks (Ed.), *Made in Govan: An oral history of shipbuilding on the Upper Clyde 1930–1950*, Glasgow, 1991.

Roy Hay and John McLauchlan, 'The Oral History of Upper Clyde Shipbuilders', *Oral History*, Spring, 1974.

Ian Johnston and Lewis Johnman 'Scotland's Last Great Artefact', in *Granta 61: The Sea* (edited by Ian Jack), Oxford, 1998.

John McCash, Oral history archive, Auld Kirk Museum, Kirkintilloch, Tape T0084.

Alan McKinlay, *Making Ships, Making Men: Working for John Brown's between the wars*, Clydebank, 1991.

NEWSPAPERS AND HOUSE MAGAZINES

Beardmore News

The Clyde Apprentice Strikers' Bulletin, 1937

Daily Chronicle

Daily Herald

Daily Record

Edinburgh Evening News

Evening Times

Glasgow Herald

The Herald

Keel, the newspaper of the Govan Shipbuilding Group

Kirkintilloch Herald

Kvaerner of Norway, the house magazine of the Kvaerner Group

Linthouse News

Linthouse Works Magazine

Lithgow House Magazine

Lithgow Journal

Scott Lithgow Journal

The Scotsman

Scottish *Sun*

Shipyard Spotlight

Shipyard and Engineering Spotlight

Sunday Herald

Sunday Times Magazine

BROADCAST MEDIA

The Bowler and the Bunnet, Scottish Television, 1967.

Clydebuilt, BBC Radio Scotland, 1990.

Iron, a video to accompany Tom McKendrick's exhibition at the Collins Gallery, 1997.

Iron, BBC Scotland EX:S, 1997.

GOVERNMENT REPORTS

R. M. Geddes, *Shipbuilding Inquiry Committee Report*, 1965–66.

FICTION

Dot Allan, *Deepening River*, London, 1932.
James Barke, *The Land of the Leal*, London & Glasgow, 1939.
James Barke, *Major Operation*, London, 1936.
George Blake, *The Shipbuilders*, London, 1935.
Edward Gaitens, *Dance of the Apprentices*, 1948.
Edward Gaitens, *Growing Up and Other Stories*, London, 1942.
Tom Gallacher, *Apprentice*, London, 1983.
Margaret Hamilton, 'Bung', in Fred Urquhart and Giles Gordon (eds.), *Modern Scottish Short Stories*, London, 1978.
Meg Henderson, *The Holy City*, London, 1997.
Alexander Highlands, *The Dark Horizon*, London, 1971.
Jimmy Miller, *Tenements as Tall as Ships*, Glasgow, 1992.
Hugh Munro, *Who Told Clutha?*, London, 1958.
Hugh Munro, *The Clydesiders*, London, 1961.
Edward Shiels, *Gael over Glasgow*, London, 1937.

DRAMA

Frank Miller, *Work-in*, unpublished, performed at The Citizens' Theatre 2001.
T. M. Watson, *Diplomacy and the Draughtsman*, Glasgow, 1929.

POETRY

Douglas Dunn, *Barbarians*, London, 1979.
John F. Fergus, 'The Yairds', in Hamish Whyte (Ed.), *Noise and Smoky Breath, Glasgow*, 1983.
Matt McGinn, *McGinn of the Calton: The life and works of Matt McGinn, 1928–1977*, Glasgow, 1987.
Alfred Forbes Smith, *A Parochial View of Glasgow*, Coldingham, 1997.
Bill Sutherland, *A Clydeside Lad*, Glasgow, 1990.
Brian Whittingham, *Industrial Deafness: Images of a Clydeside shipyard 1965– 1974*, Glasgow, 1990.
Brian Whittingham, *Ergonomic Workstations and Spinning Teacans*, Glasgow, 1992.